HISTORY OF LINCOLNSHIRE

Edited by
MAURICE BARLEY

VOLUME XI

LINCOLNSHIRE TOWNS
AND INDUSTRY
1700–1914

by

NEIL R. WRIGHT

THE HISTORY OF LINCOLNSHIRE COMMITTEE

THIS project for a History of Lincolnshire was begun in 1965 under the chairmanship of Dr Alan Rogers, then of the University of Nottingham and now Professor in Continuing Education in the New University of Ulster. The first volume appeared in 1970. The Committee planned a total of twelve volumes, of which seven have already appeared. The present volume is the eighth and the remaining four are in advanced stages of preparation.

Lincolnshire is not one of the favoured counties of England. It has never had its own history produced by an industrious eighteenth- or nineteenth-century antiquary. It is not that there have been few students of Lincolnshire history; rather the size of the county, among other factors, presented problems in bringing together all the material. The Victoria County History proceeded no further than one volume.

The first steps were taken by the Lincolnshire Local History Society, now the Society for Lincolnshire History and Archaeology, with which the Committee still works in close collaboration. The aim was to publish volumes by specialists already engaged in work on particular periods and subjects, aimed at the general reader as well as the scholar. The series will provide a more or less comprehensive account from prehistoric times down to the second half of the present century.

The series was fortunate in having as its first general editor Dr Joan Thirsk of St Hilda's College, Oxford, but commitments obliged her to relinquish this task. Maurice Barley, Professor Emeritus of Archaeology in the University of Nottingham, has taken her place and the Committee is deeply indebted to him for all his work.

An initial financial basis was provided by the Pilgrim Trust, the Seven Pillars of Wisdom Trust, the Marc Fitch Fund, the Lincolnshire Association and the Willoughby Memorial Trust. Help in other ways has been given by the Lincolnshire Association, the Lincoln City and County Library and Museum Services, the Society for Lincolnshire History and Archaeology, the Community Council of Lincolnshire and the Departments of Adult Education and Geography of the University of Nottingham.

This volume and volumes VII and X could not have been published without a financial guarantee generously offered by the Lincolnshire County Council; and we are most grateful to them for this help. Robey of Lincoln Ltd have given a special donation towards the costs of the coloured dust jacket: other gifts towards production costs from Fisher Clark of Boston (Norprint International Ltd), the Lincoln, Rutland and Stamford Mercury (EMAP Provincial Newspapers Ltd), the Lincolnshire Standard Group and Ruston-Bucyrus Ltd are gratefully acknowledged.

Paul Everson has been production editor for this volume and has been greatly aided by the sympathetic co-operation of Graham Maney of W. S. Maney and Son Ltd. The Committee also wishes to thank Elizabeth Everson, who does so much work on the distribution of the books, and is grateful to many others who have assisted in so many ways.

DENNIS MILLS
Chairman

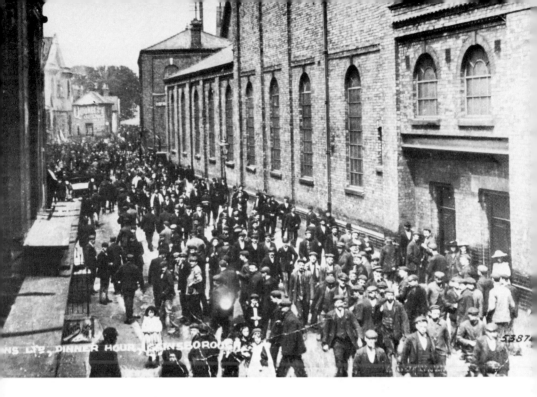

The Britannia iron works of Wm Marshall and Sons, Gainsborough employed 3,600 men and boys in 1904 and covered 28 acres. The nineteenth-century industrialization of Lincolnshire reached its peak with great engineering firms like this in the years before 1914.

HISTORY OF LINCOLNSHIRE

XI

Lincolnshire Towns and Industry 1700–1914

by

NEIL R. WRIGHT, D.M.A.

LINCOLN

HISTORY OF LINCOLNSHIRE COMMITTEE

for the Society for Lincolnshire History and Archaeology

1982

PUBLISHED BY

THE HISTORY OF LINCOLNSHIRE COMMITTEE

47 NEWLAND, LINCOLN

© THE HISTORY OF LINCOLNSHIRE COMMITTEE

ISBN 0 902668 10 2

PRINTED IN ENGLAND BY

W. S. MANEY & SON LIMITED HUDSON ROAD LEEDS LS9 7DL

TO ANNIE

CONTENTS

PART I   THE RURAL SETTING 1700–60

CHAPTER I   THE RURAL SETTING

Manorial courts; parish government; municipal corporations; political patrons; the appearance of towns; town amenities; medicine; leisure pursuits; transport improvements and commerce; highways; industry

PART II   THE INDUSTRIAL REVOLUTION 1760–1845

CHAPTER 2   BY LAND AND WATER

Fossdyke; turnpike roads; waterways — the Grundy period; later turnpike roads; waterways — the Jessop period; waterways — the Rennie period; new bridges; the coaching age

CHAPTER 3   GEORGIAN COMMERCE AND INDUSTRY

Commerce; merchants and bankers; boat building; textile industries; other industries; craftsmen; engineering

CHAPTER 4   GEORGIAN TOWNS

Growth of population; new housing; architecture; urban problems; town improvements; education; the old poor law; health care; recreation; religion and morality; reform

PART III   THE RAILWAY AGE 1845–1914

CHAPTER 5   THE ARRIVAL OF RAILWAYS

Early schemes; railway mania; New Holland ferries; a plethora of schemes; construction; openings; consequences for travel

LIST OF PLATES

LIST OF TEXT FIGURES

Acknowledgements

The plates and figures are published by permission of the following: Lincolnshire Museums, Museum of Lincolnshire Life (dustjacket and plate IX); Lincolnshire Libraries, Gainsborough Library (frontispiece); Dr M. J. T. Lewis (plate I); *Lincolnshire Life* magazine (plate II); Mrs J. C. B. Thompson (plate IV); Shuttleworth Agricultural College (plates V and VI); Boston Borough Council, Guildhall Museum (plate VII); Lincolnshire Libraries, Lincoln Central Library Local Collection (plates VIII and XIII, figures 5, 7, 8, 12 and 26); Scunthorpe Borough Council, Museum (plate X); Bass Museum of Brewing History (plate XI);Mr R. E. Hooley and Ruston Gas Turbines Ltd (plates XII and XIV, figures 29 and 33); Mr P. Chowne (plate XV); Mr J. Sass (figures 11 and 14); Mrs W. J. Hughes (figure 13) and Mr M. Pointer (figure 34). Figures 9, 28, 30, 31 and 32 were taken from copies of the *Stamford Mercury* and *Illustrated London News* kindly lent for the purpose by the Lincolnshire Library Service; plate III and figures 36, 37 and 38 were taken from books in the possession of the author.

ACKNOWLEDGEMENTS

THIS work includes material collected over a period of ten years or more and during this time I have received help from a great many people. Neville Birch, Michael Lewis, Chris Page, Catherine Wilson, Chris Johnson, Michael Lloyd and others have given me the benefit of their kowledge of Lincolnshire's history and industrial archaeology; I also owe a debt to other local historians past and present who have published material in this area and many of them are named in the bibliography.

I should also like to thank the staffs of Lincoln Central Library, Boston Library, Gainsborough Library, the Lincolnshire Archives Office, the Map Room of the British Library and the Museum of Lincolnshire Life, for their help with my research. Jayne Knight provided an invaluable service by helping with the final typing of the manuscript.

I am grateful to Mick Clark, who very professionally redrew the maps (figures 1, 2, 3, 19 to 25, and 27) and figures 4, 6, 10 and 15 to 18 from material supplied by the author. Help with finding and photographing other illustrations has been given by Elizabeth Melrose and the reference library staff of Lincoln Central Library, Geoff Young, Catherine Wilson, Ken Benton, J. E. Scott, Stephanie Meads, Ray Hooley, John Goldsmith, P. M. B. Slater, Stan Mitchell, Gus Smalley, G. W. Skevington and Peter Chowne.

The History of Lincolnshire Committee through their Chairmen, Alan Rogers and Dennis Mills, have been helpful and very patient. Their editor and sub-editor, Maurice Barley and Paul Everson, have brought the work through from manuscript to finished book; they and Michael Lewis have read the manuscript and suggested improvements, and any remaining inadequacies and imperfections are my own.

Finally I must thank my understanding wife who has lived with this project since our marriage and to whom I have dedicated the volume.

Yarborough Lodge   N.R.W.
Lincoln

July 1982

LIST OF ABBREVIATIONS

ABBREVIATION   FULL TITLE

Ambler, ed., *Workers and Community*   *Workers and Community: The People of Scunthorpe in the 1870s*, ed. R. W. Ambler, Scunthorpe, 1980

Boyes and Russell, *Canals*   J. Boyes and R. Russell, *The Canals of Eastern England*, Newton Abbot, 1977

Brears   C. Brears, *Lincolnshire in the Seventeenth and Eighteenth Centuries*, London, 1940

Defoe, *Tour*   D. Defoe, *A Tour through the whole island of Great Britain*, London, 1724–26, republished 1971

Dow, *Great Central*   G. Dow, *Great Central*, London, 1959

Dudley, *Scunthorpe and Frodingham*   H. E. Dudley, *The History and Antiquities of the Scunthorpe and Frodingham District*, Scunthorpe, 1931

Gillett, *Grimsby*   E. Gillett, *A History of Grimsby*, London, 1970

Grinling, *Great Northern*   C. H. Grinling, *The History of the Great Northern Railway*, London, new edn 1966

Henthorn, ed., *Trent, Ancholme and Grimsby Railway*   *Letters and papers concerning the establishment of the Trent, Ancholme and Grimsby Railway, 1860–62*, ed. F. Henthorn, LRS, vol. 70, Lincoln, 1975

Hill, *Georgian Lincoln*   J. W. F. Hill, *Georgian Lincoln*, Cambridge, 1966

Hill, *Victorian Lincoln*   J. W. F. Hill, *Victorian Lincoln*, Cambridge, 1974

Holm   S. A. Holm, *The Heavens Reflect our Labours*, Scunthorpe, 1974

Honeybone, *Grantham*   M. Honeybone, *The Book of Grantham*, Buckingham, 1980

Ind. Arch.   *Industrial Archaeology*

Kelly's Directory   *Kelly's Directory of Lincolnshire*, London, 1st edn 1885, 2nd edn 1889, 3rd edn 1892, 4th edn 1896, 5th edn 1900, 6th edn 1905, 7th edn 1909, 8th edn 1913

LAOR   *Lincolnshire Archives Office Archivists' Reports*

Leleux, *East Midlands Railways*   R. Leleux, *The East Midlands*, A Regional History of the Railways of Great Britain: 9, Newton Abbot, 1976

LHA   *Lincolnshire History and Archaeology*

LIA   *Lincolnshire Industrial Archaeology*

Lincolnshire Library   MSS in Lincoln Central Library

Lincs. Mag.   *Lincolnshire Magazine*

Loc. Hist.   *Local Historian* formerly *Amateur Historian*

LRS   Lincoln Record Society's publications

RCHM, *Stamford*   Royal Commission on Historical Monuments, *The Town of Stamford — An Inventory of Historical Monuments*, London, 1977

Robinson, *Louth*   D. N. Robinson, *The Book of Louth*, Buckingham, 1979

Rogers, ed., *Stamford*   *The Making of Stamford*, ed. A. Rogers, Leicester, 1965

Ruddock and Pearson   J. G. Ruddock and R. E. Pearson, *The Railway History of Lincoln*, Lincoln, 1974
SM   *Lincolnshire, Rutland and Stamford Mercury*
Stark, *Gainsborough*   A. Stark, *History and Antiquities of Gainsborough*, Gainsborough, 1817, 2nd edn 1843
Thompson, *Boston*   P. Thompson, *History and Antiquities of Boston*, Boston, 1855
Trans. Newcomen Soc.   *Transactions of the Newcomen Society*
VCH, *Lincs.*   *Victoria History of the County of Lincoln*, II, ed. W. Page, London, 1906
Walshaw and Behrendt, *Appleby-Frodingham*   G. R. Walshaw and C. A. J. Behrendt, *The History of Appleby-Frodingham*, Scunthorpe, 1950
White and Tye, *Grimsby and Cleethorpes*   P. White and A. Tye, *An Industrial History of Grimsby and Cleethorpes*, Grimsby, 1970
White, *Directory*   W. White, *Directory of Lincolnshire*, Sheffield, 1826, 1st edn 1842, 2nd edn 1856 (reprinted 1969), 3rd edn 1872, 4th edn 1882, 5th edn 1892
Young, *General View*   A. Young, *General View of the Agriculture of Lincoln*, London, 2nd edn 1813, reprinted Newton Abbot, 1970

CURRENCY

This volume contains references to units of the old sterling currency which was replaced on 15 February 1971 by the new decimal currency. The following table is included for the benefit of anyone unfamiliar with the old currency.

	STERLING	DECIMAL
One penny	1*d.*	0.416p
Six pence	6*d.*	2.5p
One shilling (12 pence)	1*s.* 0*d.*	5p
One pound (20 shillings)	£1 0*s.* 0*d.*	£1.00
One guinea (21 shillings)	£1 1*s.* 0*d.*	£1.05

FOREWORD

NEIL WRIGHT's volume will evoke both personal memories and a lively interest in a recent but vanished age. It deals with aspects of the history of modern Lincolnshire essential to its understanding and of more than local importance; the decision to separate urban and industrial history from agrarian and political has more than justified itself. Neil Wright describes the coming of the railways, the emergence of two new towns — the largest in the county (Grimsby and Scunthorpe) — and the achievements of the engineering industries of Gainsborough, Grantham and Lincoln, and all this with a wealth of factual and statistical information, enlivened by social detail and perceptive comment. Everyone has heard of the railway mania of the 1840s; it becomes more than a textbook phrase when one learns of a temporary stock exchange opened in Lincoln to deal in railway shares. Equally, the rise of the Grimsby fishing industry is a familiar fact, but not that the smacks were crewed by London apprentices who when they absconded were sent to the new prison in Lincoln. It is a matter of more than local pride to read of entrepreneurs who sent agricultural machinery all over the world, developed the first packing machinery (for pipe tobacco) at Gainsborough and the first tracked vehicles at Grantham.

For older readers, this book will recall personal memories or family traditions: of Gainsborough when it was still a thriving company town; of Lincoln when the daily timetable of working-class life was determined by the works' buzzer; of driving a car or a flock of sheep onto the New Holland ferry by means of the floating pontoon first installed in 1849; of seeing the brown sail of a keel on the Fossdyke. Young readers, especially those interested in industrial archaeology, will enjoy the informed treatment of industrial and technological innovations of the age of steam and the early stages in the age of oil.

MAURICE BARLEY
General Editor

INTRODUCTION

FOR three-quarters of the period covered by this volume most
Lincolnshire people lived outside towns and during the first
century the most common industrial buildings were rural
windmills and watermills. At the same time the unincorporated
towns were subject to the administrative and judicial authority of
the county justices meeting in quarter sessions. By 1914, in contrast, most Lincolnshire people were living in towns, which also
contained most industrial premises and the offices of elected bodies
whose jurisdiction extended over the surrounding rural areas.

This volume considers the effects of revolutionary changes in
transport and industry on a somewhat remote agricultural county.
It concentrates on changes in the towns, including small towns and
urban districts as well as the six boroughs, and touches only where
necessary on agricultural, administrative and other aspects of Lincolnshire life which have been the subject of other volumes in this
series. It brings together elements from the great range of local
material published in recent years, along with the author's own
researches, to present a broad picture of urban and industrial
developments in Lincolnshire from the eve of the Industrial Revolution to the Edwardian summer preceding the First World War.
These developments are also related to the rest of the kingdom.

The volume has been divided into three parts reflecting the major
changes brought about by the first stages of the Industrial Revolution and then by the arrival of railways. The first break is indicated
by the date 1760, an arbitrary choice to represent changes spread
over several decades, but the date 1845 represents the succeeding
five years during which the basic network of the county's railways
was laid down.

PART I
THE RURAL SETTING
1700–60

CHAPTER 1

THE RURAL SETTING

I N eighteenth-century eyes, Lincolnshire was remote, little
known and unfashionable. Of its few towns of note, Lincoln,
Boston and Stamford had fallen sadly from their medieval
glory. Although they and the numerous smaller towns served as the
usual centres of administration and commerce, industry was
minimal, communication by land and water restricted and uncer-
tain, and the seaports much decayed. Yet Lincolnshire prospered,
for its real wealth, as well as much of its life, sprang from the land.
Its deficiencies, whether in minerals, overseas trade, lordly man-
sions or romantic scenery, were redeemed by the produce of its
pasture and arable. Like England at large, it was still in 1700 quite
thinly populated, and its people lived close to the soil. Many, even
in the towns, would spend their lives not far from their place of
birth; skilled craftsmen might cross into adjacent counties in
pursuit of their calling and the marketing of agricultural produce —
wool, corn and livestock — might involve journeys as far as the
West Riding and London, but only the clergy and gentry would
have much experience of the wider world. Lincolnshire moreover
was, as it always had been, isolated from the rest of the kingdom.

Lincolnshire was effectively a peninsula connected to the rest of
England by a wide isthmus lying between Stamford and Newark.
Between the outfalls of the Welland and the Trent the county was
bounded by the Wash, the North Sea and the Humber. North of
Newark the Trent was unbridged and passage across that river or
the Humber was dependent on several ferries. In the early eighteenth century Daniel Defoe took the ferry over from Barton to
Hull, sharing an open boat with horses and cattle for the four-hour
crossing, and found it 'ill-favoured and dangerous'. The ferry
across the Trent at Gainsborough overturned in 1760 and six people
lost their lives, but for local people the rivers were important traffic
routes. In the south of the county the estuaries of the rivers entering
the Wash were wide and dangerous owing to shifting sands and

travellers had either to cross with a guide or take a longer route into East Anglia through Spalding and Wisbech.[1]

Lincolnshire was the second largest county in England and Wales, and its population was spread fairly evenly over the varied landscape of the county with the main towns located on or near the edges. The geology of Lincolnshire is a series of hills and valleys rolling from east to west. Inland from the sand dunes of the North Sea coast is the Marsh, extending up to the foot of the chalk and sandstone of the Wolds, which rise to over 450 feet. West of the Wolds are the Ancholme valley and the extensive fens which stretch from Lincoln down to the Wash and Cambridgeshire: some parts of this great flat area are below sea level and 'hills' of sixteen feet or so were of local significance in times of flood. Westward the country gradually rises to the limestone uplands of the Lincolnshire Edge and Lincoln Heath, broken by the Witham gap at Lincoln; the uplands widen at the southern end and extend into Leicestershire, Rutland and Northamptonshire. In the north there is a third escarpment of Lower Lias, lying between the Cliff and the Trent, but this only extends about twenty miles south of the Humber. West of the limestone uplands are the wide valleys of the Trent and the upper Witham, and in the north Lincolnshire also included the Isle of Axholme on the west bank of the Trent.

Distances across the county are considerable; Stamford is eighty miles from Barton-on-Humber and Gainsborough is fifty miles north-west of Wainfleet. For some administrative and judicial purposes the county was divided into the three parts of Lindsey, Kesteven and Holland, each of which had its own commission of the peace. The five boroughs were excluded from county juris-diction and to Lincoln and Grantham were attached some rural parishes. Louth was not a parliamentary borough but was recog-nized as a municipal borough by an act of 1832. Kingston-upon-Hull is a Yorkshire town on the north bank of the Humber but by 1700 its influence extended over a considerable part of north Lincolnshire from Gainsborough in the west to Grimsby in the east, linked by the busy waterways of the Trent and Humber.

Each of the towns served one or more of four functions: as an administrative centre of government, the home of an industry or industries, a market for the communities around, and as a con-venient halting place for travellers on one or more busy routes. Towns were also the habitations of professional men, such as attorneys and physicians, who could serve the surrounding area as

[1] Defoe, *Tour*, p. 413; White, *Directory*, 1856, p. 167.

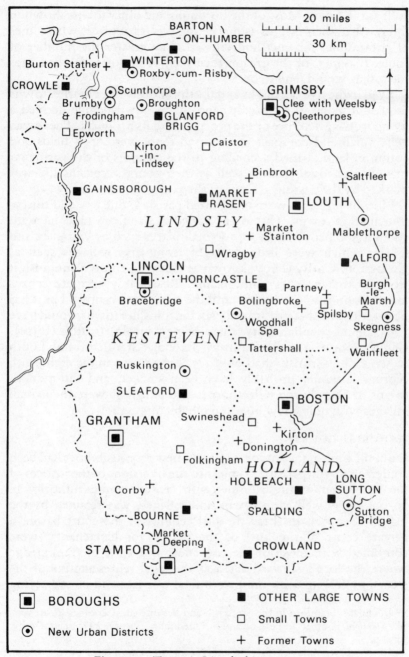

Figure 1 *Towns in Lincolnshire 1700–1914*

well as the town. Most of the boroughs and other towns shown in figure 1 had their origins as marketing centres at places where lines of communication met and crossed. The greater the number of routes that met, or the greater their relative importance, the larger the towns would tend to be.[2]

Even in the five boroughs and the thirty or so other market towns the countryside was close at hand; many townspeople derived a living from agriculture or the processing of its products. The towns were small and compact and around them were open fields and common land farmed according to the customs of the particular manor. For townsmen as well as their country cousins life was marked by the passing seasons of the year.

Lincolnshire had over six hundred parishes, one city and thirty-four market towns. The towns varied in size from Lincoln, with about 4,500 people in 1750, to small places such as Wainfleet and Corby which were little different from large villages such as Gosberton. Corby is now known as Corby Glen, to distinguish it from Corby in Northamptonshire. Reasonably accurate census information is not available until the nineteenth century but it has been estimated that in 1750 only six Lincolnshire towns would have 2,500 or more inhabitants, these being Lincoln, Boston (3,300), Gainsborough (3,000), Stamford (2,600), Grantham and Louth (2,500 each). Grimsby had only 1,524 in 1801 so in the eighteenth century it would probably have been smaller, and the modern towns of Scunthorpe, Cleethorpes and Skegness were then small villages with only a few hundred inhabitants each.[3]

MANORIAL COURTS

From the time of the Tudor monarchs new responsibilities had been conferred on the parishes, subject to the oversight of the justices of the peace, but until the nineteenth century some authority in boroughs, as well as in towns and villages, was retained by the manorial courts. In these the proceedings of the court baron, a private court of the lord of the manor for his tenants, were combined with those of the court leet and view of frankpledge where the lord's steward acted as the legal representative of the crown in dealing with minor criminal offences and in overseeing

[2] J. Thirsk, 'Stamford in the Sixteenth and Seventeenth Centuries' in Rogers, ed., *Stamford*, p. 61; R. E. Pearson and R. O. Knibbs, *Towns and Transport*, Derby, 1974, p. 7.
[3] C. M. Law, 'Sources for Urban History 4. Some Notes on the Urban Population of England and Wales in the Eighteenth Century', *Loc. Hist.*, 10 no. 1 (1972), p. 24.

the now moribund frankpledge system, by which every man had to be enrolled in a group of pledges to act as sureties for his good behaviour.[4]

In Lincoln, Boston and Grimsby the corporations had by 1700 acquired the lordship of the manor in order to exercise these powers, although parts of Lincoln were in the separate manorial liberties of the Bail and Beaumont Fee. In these towns the corporation and the parish vestries assumed many of the functions of the courts leet in appointing public officers and seeing to the running of the towns.[5]

Gainsborough lacked a municipal corporation, so the great court baron, court leet and view of frankpledge of the Hickman family retained considerable importance in the government of the town until the nineteenth century. The owners of certain tofts in the town formed the jury which met twice a year. They heard presentments of nuisances, made orders about the fields and streets of the town and regulated the markets. Each year the court elected its officers: the burgess constable, foreign constable, burgess bailiff, borgrave, searchers of the market, frankpledges, searchers and sealers of leather, ale tasters and scavengers. Before 1660 the churchwardens and overseers also reported to the court but after the Restoration there was a stricter distinction between manorial and parochial duties. Until improvement commissioners were appointed in Gainsborough late in the eighteenth century the jury continued to order the repair of streets and lanes, to build staithes and remove encroachments.[6]

The manorial court also had a persistent and important role in the supervision of weights and measures, the checking of ale, beer, meat and coal, and the suppression of local nuisances such as unscoured drains, unmended highways, trees overhanging the road, refusal to pave frontages, emission of smoke, allowing pigs to roam in streets, insanitary privies and cesspools. It made byelaws to control these matters and also to control the open field system of agriculture, which was in the charge of officers appointed by the court. Throughout the eighteenth century and into the nineteenth the manorial courts were under siege from the growing powers of municipal corporations, parish vestries, quarter sessions, petty sessions, small debts courts and urban improvement commissioners. By the era of municipal reform their functions, except

[4] Stark, *Gainsborough*, p. 154.
[5] White, *Directory*, 1856, pp. 108, 109; *LAOR* 8, p. 33.
[6] Stark, *Gainsborough*, p. 179.

perhaps in a very few cases, had dwindled to the conveyancing of copyhold property; the rest was ceremonial.[7]

PARISH GOVERNMENT

Parish government was based on the vestry meeting, usually held in the vestry room of the parish church and open to all ratepayers. The main vestry meeting in each parish was in Easter week to audit the accounts and elect new officers. The people were summoned to meet in the church but almost invariably adjourned to the public house. Parishes varied in size and population and there were also variations in the efficiency of their administration. The parishes were under the supervision and control of the justices of the peace, who were appointed from the corporations in the boroughs and from the squires in the small towns. During the eighteenth and nineteenth centuries justices had extensive and varied powers. There were only three thousand in the whole country in 1689, but their numbers increased during the eighteenth century. Many new justices came from the clergy, who were rising in social status.[8]

Town parishes had the same responsibilities as rural parishes, even in Stamford with six parishes and Lincoln with fifteen. The vestry appointed a churchwarden, a surveyor of highways (usually a man of property), an overseer of the poor and a parish constable, who each managed a part of the parish's responsibilities for a year. The churchwarden was the highest official; his original duty was to look after the parish church but as time went on he also became responsible for many civil duties. Since the Highways Act of 1555 each parish had been responsible for the upkeep of its roads and their unpaid surveyor had power to commandeer almost any able-bodied male parishioner for four (later six) days' unpaid labour each year — 'statute labour', 'menwork' or 'boonwork' as it was often called. Some manorial officials such as the constables in Gainsborough might have a traditional involvement in street repairs dating from before the 1555 act. Except for the old Roman highways, the roads were not made with hardcore and the maintenance was simply to level the ruts by harrowing the earthen surface and to throw more earth and stones on to it from the fields and roadsides. For this work the horses and ploughs of the parish were also at the command of the surveyor. In the parts of Holland

[7] Barton-on-Humber Local History Class, *Barton-on-Humber in the 1850s. Part Three. Parish and Government*, Barton-on-Humber, 1979, p. 4; Brears, p. 53.

[8] *Barton-on-Humber in the 1850s. Part Three*, p. 4; Brears, p. 54; K. B. Smellie, *A History of Local Government*, London, 1963, pp. 11, 15; J. H. Plumb, *England in the Eighteenth Century*, London, 1950, p. 34.

stone was not readily available and the roads were said to be generally made with 'silt, or old sea-sand'. Large parts of the fens were subject to intercommoning and no single parish had responsibility.[9]

In Lincoln the parish vestries could keep up the minor streets and lanes and bear the cost by a parish highway rate but the main roads were more of a problem, particularly in the parishes with a small population on the edge of the city. Even by the start of the eighteenth century the common council were sharing the cost of High Street south of Gowts bridges and some of the roads on Lincoln hillside and Cross O'Cliff Hill. In 1738 the common council started a long-term programme to improve the highway from the Old Packhorse inn in St Mark's parish to Great Bargate in St Botolph's parish, raising it up to form a rampart or ramper. But in spite of this activity it was still the parishes which were officially responsible for maintaining the standard of the road.[10]

Each parish also had a statutory responsibility for the poor, but in each town there were several charities for the distribution of coals and cloth to the poor and in some towns there were also charitable almshouses for the aged and infirm. In several villages almshouses for the aged poor were established by charitable benefactors and called 'hospitals'. They provided accommodation for a small number of old people and gave some assistance in their dotage, sometimes including a distinctive charity uniform. The main towns were not so well provided for; although there were at least four hospitals in Stamford by 1701 and almshouses in Louth, Sleaford, Bourne and Holbeach, there were none in the other boroughs. From 1723 onwards out-door relief was cut down and there was an increase in the number of workhouses. In 1749 the overseers of Barton-on-Humber took over as the parish workhouse a house which had been bequeathed in 1701 for 'the use and habitation of the poor'.[11]

MUNICIPAL CORPORATIONS

Lincoln city and the towns of Boston, Grantham, Stamford and Grimsby were boroughs, where charters had established a municipal corporation with powers and privileges, including the right to return two members to parliament. The number and titles of

[9] P. Dover, 'Turnpike Roads in the Algarkirk-Fosdyke-Sutterton Area', *Industrial Archaeology Newsletter*, 1 no. 3 (1966), p. 2; I. S. Beckwith, *The Industrial Archaeology of Gainsborough*, Gainsborough, 1968, p. 5; G. Hindley, *A History of Roads*, London, 1971, p. 59; Young, *General View*, p. 453.
[10] Hill, *Georgian Lincoln*, p. 145.
[11] White, *Directory*, 1826, p. 66.

members of the corporation varied from town to town, though in all except Grantham the chief magistrate was by 1700 called the mayor and the other members usually included aldermen and common councilmen.

In each borough, justices of the peace were drawn from the members of the corporation, and in Lincoln and Grantham their jurisdiction extended beyond the borough. The liberty of Lincoln included four parishes south of the city and the soke of Grantham comprised certain parishes near that town.

Only in Boston and Grimsby were the boundaries of borough and parish matched. In Lincoln there were fifteen parishes and the hill-top areas of the city around the castle and the cathedral, known as the Bail and the Close, were outside the jurisdiction of the corporation and constituted a detached part of the wapentake of Lawress. Similarly in Stamford there were six parishes in the town but St Martin's on the south bank of the river Welland was outside the borough. The borough of Grantham (fig. 2) occupied only a small area at the heart of the parish which also included the townships of Spittlegate, Harrowby and Manthorpe with Little Gonerby. Spittlegate township was also excluded from the soke of Grantham and lay instead in the wapentake of Winnibriggs and Threo.[12]

Each corporation employed a town clerk, coroner and other officials and also conferred the post of recorder or high steward on a powerful patron who could exercise influence on their behalf in London. In other towns such as Spalding charity trustees such as the town husbands became centres of unofficial authority.[13] Louth did not have a municipal corporation but the warden and six assistants, established in 1551 to manage the grammar school and almshouses, had subsequently been given extensive responsibilities for the government of the town. The warden and one of the assistants were also justices of the peace.

The municipal corporations were privileged political bodies, close and self-perpetuating, charged with maintaining law and order. They had a general responsibility for the well-being of their town and the management of corporate property, but their responsibility was a moral one, not enforceable by law, and they rendered no public account. Their specific powers were small, and as they levied no rates they made little direct impact, save ceremonially, on the lives of the citizens. People's contacts with the parish

[12] Ibid., p. 127.
[13] C. Holmes, *Seventeenth-Century Lincolnshire*, Lincoln, 1980, p. 30.

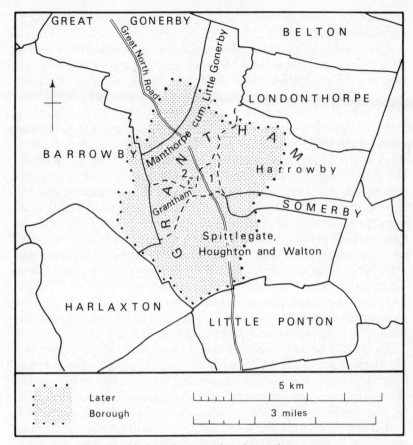

Figure 2   *Grantham parish and townships c. 1850*
1. Grantham borough   2. The Grange

were closer, for it collected poor rates and organized the upkeep of
the roads.

Each of the corporations owned considerable property and managed the town's charities, spending the rents and other traditional
income, such as market tolls, as they saw fit. The sources of income
of Boston corporation included tolls on horses, carts, wagons,
cattle, sheep and wool passing over the town bridge into or through
the town, or unloading therein. It was as likely to be spent on their
own entertainment as on works for the public good and the action
of Mayor John Lobsey in 1736 was noteworthy as an exception.
The sum of £100 usually spent on city feasts instead paid for the

erection of a neat Butter Market, with a room over, next to St
Peter-at-Arches church.[14]

The freemen of a municipal borough formed a constituent part of
the corporation and as such enjoyed special rights and privileges
which were gradually eroded during the eighteenth century. Each
borough admitted freemen according to its own peculiar customs
and byelaws. Their rights and privileges, though varying, generally included a right to vote at parliamentary elections and
exemptions from tolls and dues. One of the most cherished privileges of the Lincoln freemen had been the monopoly of the crafts
and trades, which had been protected by the craft guilds or companies, but by 1739 only two remained — the tailors and the
cordwainers (i.e. shoemakers). The common council still tried
sometimes to maintain their monopoly but in 1772 the cordwainers
gave up and let their hall. The freemen resident in Lincoln also had
exclusive rights to put cattle on the Holmes and the Monks Leas and
a privileged position with regard to grazing the West and South
Commons. The number of non-freemen living in Lincoln
increased and other people outside tried to claim the freedom by
right of patrimony in order to get a vote. The council resisted this
until 1775 when the courts decided against them.[15]

There was great variety in the franchises of all parliamentary
boroughs during the eighteenth century; in some places it was
based on the payment of local taxes and in others on the ownership
of specific pieces of property. In all five boroughs it was exercised
by the freemen, but great power lay in the corporation, which
might try to control the admission of new freemen. At Boston
restrictions were made on the number of freemen by the imposition
of a heavy fine for admission.[16]

POLITICAL PATRONS

There was great variety, too, in the parliamentary aspects of the
Lincolnshire boroughs. Lincoln was one of the most independent
and popular boroughs, in contrast to Grimsby, whose small elect-
orate of about eighty made it among the most corrupt boroughs in
England. The election of MPs was often more profitable than
commerce in the decayed port.[17]

[14] H. Porter, *Boston 1800 to 1835*, I, Lincoln, 1941, p. 5; White, *Directory*, 1826,
p. 44.
[15] Hill, *Georgian Lincoln*, p. 244; White, *Directory*, 1826, p. 46.
[16] A. Weston, 'Lincolnshire Politics in the Reign of Queen Anne 1702–14; Part II
The Boroughs', *LHA*, 6 (1971), p. 84.
[17] Ibid., pp. 89, 92; Gillett, *Grimsby*, p. 138.

In the other three boroughs noble families had a persistent influence. The earl of Rutland had a seat at Belvoir Castle near Grantham and the earl of Lindsey had Grimsthorpe Castle and an elegant mansion at Eresby near Spilsby. After 1714 they increased their influence in Grantham and Boston respectively.

In all eleven members of the Bertie family represented Boston in parliament at different times but the duke of Ancaster (as Lord Lindsey became in 1715) lived many miles from the town and the noble influence was not so pervasive as in Stamford or Grantham.

Other prominent whigs included the marquess of Granby, son of the duke of Rutland, and Sir John Brownlow (c. 1690–1754) of Belton, near Grantham, who sat in the Commons from 1713 to 1741 and was created Viscount Tyrconnel in the Irish peerage in 1718. In eighteenth-century Lincolnshire the dominant families were Lords Rutland, Ancaster and Tyrconnel and the rich Heathcote baronets, who occupied fine country houses built or enlarged in the late seventeenth century.[18]

Aristocratic representation gave the boroughs a powerful political patron with an interest in the borough's welfare, and this paternalistic relationship became greatest in Stamford, where the Cecil family, earls of Exeter, came to have control over all the jobs which were vacant, including the elections of MPs. In the seventeenth century, Stamford had been dominated by the Bertie family of Uffington, cousins of the earl of Lindsey, but the Cecil family and many on Stamford corporation disliked the speed with which the Berties had abandoned James II in 1688 and the Cecils gained increasing influence on the corporation and took control in 1734. After that date no parliamentary candidate opposed to Lord Exeter was elected until 1831; from 1734 to 1809 there was not even a contest. In 1747 Lord Exeter purchased the manor of Stamford from Harry Grey, fourth earl of Stamford. Once the Cecil family of Burghley House had gained control Lord Exeter's agent dominated the counsels of the corporation; he nominated who should receive charity or places in the grammar school. Burghley also acquired the right to nominate the town's incumbent clergy.[19]

Excluding Grimsby and Stamford, which were outside party battles, there was a consistent and forceful strain of toryism in Lincolnshire in Queen Anne's reign but after the accession of George I the whig ascendancy spread over Lincolnshire, eclipsing the tory squires who were the traditional leaders of the county.

[18] Weston, 'Lincolnshire politics', p. 96.
[19] Rogers, ed., *Stamford*, pp. 95, 97, 108.

New families who had prospered in the professions and the East India Company settled on landed estates in Lincolnshire during Queen Anne's reign and later took control with the deliberate building up of great estates. These included Sir Gilbert Heathcote (1652–1733) who was a founder of the Bank of England, a director of the East India Company and reputed to be the richest commoner in England, worth £700,000. His son John, of Normanton (Rutland), became MP for Grantham in 1715. The sons of Sir Francis Chaplin, lord mayor of London in 1678, established themselves at Tathwell near Louth. Other families were the Claytons who held great influence in Grimsby from the late seventeenth century until the early nineteenth century, and the Banks family who were set up on an estate at Revesby near Horncastle in 1714 by Joseph Banks I (1665–1727), a Sheffield attorney, and leased the lordship of Horncastle from the bishop of Carlisle.[20]

THE APPEARANCE OF TOWNS

Lincoln, Boston and Stamford had all declined since the Middle Ages. In 1724 Daniel Defoe described Lincoln as 'an ancient, ragged, decayed and still decaying city', full of the ruins of monasteries and religious houses. The houses and churches of Lincoln had suffered much during the Civil War and in 1700 many of the scars still remained. Only two churches below hill had services every Sunday; one of these was St Peter-at-Arches, which the corporation had rebuilt in the modern style in 1724. The bishop of Lincoln lived at Buckden Palace near Huntingdon, in the centre of his extensive diocese, and the ruins of his old medieval palace in Lincoln were used as a quarry. South of the Stonebow, cottages and churches were strung out along High Street for over a mile (see fig. 20). Above hill, around the cathedral and the castle, were the town houses of some of the county gentry, used when they were visiting Lincoln for the assizes, quarter sessions, races, elections or musters, and Defoe considered this the only area worthy of being called a city. In the cathedral close were the residences of the clergy, encircled by a wall whose gates were locked every night.[21]

Stamford had shrunk within its old walls as shown in figure 25, but the recent rise in its population led to derelict sites being used

[20] Weston, 'Lincolnshire politics', pp. 89, 94; G. Jackson, *Grimsby and the Haven Company*, Grimsby, 1971, p. 2; *The Letters and Papers of the Banks Family of Revesby Abbey 1704–60*, ed. J. W. F. Hill, LRS, vol. 45, Lincoln, 1952, p. xv.
[21] Defoe, *Tour*, p. 410; Hill, *Georgian Lincoln*, pp. 5, 62.

again.[22] At Boston (fig. 19) the south end of the medieval town was abandoned and the old mart yard ceased to be used as a market-place and gradually became the private yard of the grammar school. The town of Grantham lay on the west side of the narrow Witham valley, and was centred around the market-place where the main road to the south-west joined the Great North Road (fig. 23). Louth, the principal town in north-east Lincolnshire, was located on the eastern edge of the Wolds, looking across the marsh to the old port of Saltfleet. Figure 24 shows it was a compact town like Stamford, its main streets parallel to the little river Lud, and still following their medieval pattern. Eighteenth-century Grimsby (fig. 21) was smaller than Louth, extending from St James's church to the old haven. Also larger than Grimsby was the rising port of Gainsborough (fig. 22) alongside the Trent, and another rising town was Glanford Brigg, where a main road crossed the river Ancholme in the corner of Wrawby parish. After 1669 a grammar school was established there and in 1699 a small chapel of ease was built.

In each town different parts of the streets or market-place were set aside for the sale of different produce, in one place corn, another meat, here fish and there butter, eggs, poultry and cheese. The latter were usually sold by country women and several towns provided covered butter markets for them, often with a public room above: Boston in 1732, Lincoln in 1738. Some towns also provided other market buildings, such as the butchery, corn cross and fish stones in Boston market-place.

In 1700 most houses in Lincolnshire towns would be made from mud and stud, which required only the skill of the village carpenter and the knowledge of the villagers who could dig earth and puddle it, or the fine Lincolnshire limestone in appropriate areas. Most mud-and-stud cottages had a thatched roof, usually of straw rather than reed even in the fens and the marsh, and in many homes the floor was bare earth.[23]

Timber framing began to go out of use about this time; the rich refaced their houses in stone or brick. Few buildings were of brick with pantiled roofs except grand new houses such as those of Sir Cecil Wray and John Disney above hill in Lincoln. The Tudor manor house at Alford was cased in brick and several new cottages were built at about this time.

[22] RCHM, *Stamford*, p. xliii.
[23] M. W. Barley, *Lincolnshire and the Fens*, Wakefield, 2nd edn 1972, pp. 100, 106; E. M. Sympson, *Cambridge County Geographies — Lincolnshire*. Cambridge, 1913, p. 86.

Towns with houses of wood and thatch were particularly susceptible to serious fires. In 1681 more than half of Caistor was burnt and forty-five families were reduced to poverty, and in 1707 a disastrous fire at Grantham burnt down seventeen houses and caused damage estimated at £3,000. A great fire at Spalding in 1715 caused damage worth £20,560. Other fires occurred at Louth (1721), Stamford (1727), and Barton-on-Humber (1732). At Stamford in 1675 and Boston in 1677 the corporations had ordered that tiles or slates must be used for all new buildings; brick then came into common use in Boston. Bricks were traditionally made on site for any building, but from the late seventeenth century onward it must have been possible to buy bricks in any quantity in or near a town.[24]

The eighteenth century saw a complete change in the physical appearance of Stamford. Affluence, fashion and the presence of good building stone nearby resulted in the wholesale refronting or rebuilding of houses in the current style. In almost every case both workmanship and design were by men living and working in Stamford, and these same craftsmen also worked in the surrounding area. This local style developed in Stamford was based on the pattern books which were published in the 1720s and 1730s. Although some towns started to revive during the first half of the eighteenth century and some new buildings were erected, few new streets were laid out and the old pattern persisted.[25]

TOWN AMENITIES

As larger numbers of people came together in towns, matters such as the supply of water became a problem, but the growth of the towns also gave scope for other amenities to be developed. The main sources of water were from rivers or private wells, though old conduits existed in Lincoln and Grantham, and in 1697 William Yarnold of St Albans was given a contract to carry water by engines and other instruments from the Welland to the market cross in Stamford, and then by pipes through the streets to houses whose owners were prepared to pay. Between 1704 and 1707 Boston corporation erected a lead-lined stone cistern in the market-place to be supplied with water from the West Fen and an act of 1711 allowed a 'water house or mill' to be erected at Cowbridge to supply the main cistern, from which other reservoirs were supplied. The system was evidently unsatisfactory since in 1746 the

[24] Brears, pp. 101, 102; Honeybone, *Grantham*; Barley, op. cit., p. 103.
[25] RCHM, *Stamford*, p. xliii; J. Harris, 'The Architecture of Stamford' in Rogers, ed., *Stamford*, pp. 83, 84.

corporation employed Thomas Partridge to bore for water in the market-place.[26]

Nearly every Lincolnshire town had a free grammar school by 1700, those in the five boroughs and Louth having been founded between 1540 and 1567 and others during the seventeenth century. The founders had endowed them with property to pay for the salary of the master and usher (assistant master) but time had devalued the endowments and charges were made for the teaching of additional subjects. In some cases the 'free' scholars received a second-class education as more attention was given to those who paid fees. Some schools lacked even buildings and were taught in part of the parish church. A few more grammar schools were established in the early eighteenth century and several other charity schools were founded at the same time to provide elementary education for greater numbers. The establishment of many charity schools during the early eighteenth century arose from a new spirit of piety. In Boston Laughton's endowed school was established in 1707 and the Blue Coat charity school in 1713. The Blue Coat scholars had to wear a distinctive uniform, as did those of the schools established at Stamford in 1704, Spalding in 1710 and Spilsby in 1716. These four schools, together with five in Lincoln and others in Epworth, Wyberton and Denton were directly influenced by the Society for the Promotion of Christian Knowledge formed in London in 1699. The charity schools were based on a subscription system, paid by their supporters, and were the first institution to provide education on a large scale for both sexes. The Boston Blue Coat school had fifty boys and fifty girls in 1713, and as well as reading and writing the girls were also taught 'plainwork, knitting and marking'. After the first quarter of the eighteenth century there were virtually no new schools established in Lincolnshire towns until the nineteenth century.[27]

MEDICINE

In 1700 there were few surgeons in the county and most illness was dealt with by traditional remedies and herbal cures. Physicians and surgeons could provide medical attention for those who could afford to pay or to paupers paid for by the parish, but most of the population between these extremes found it difficult to obtain

[26] Ibid., p. 72; Thompson, *Boston*, p. 96.
[27] D. H. Webster, 'A Charity School Movement? The Lincolnshire Evidence', *LHA*, 15 (1980), pp. 39, 43; S. J. Curtis and M. E. A. Boultwood, *An Introductory History of English Education since 1800*, London, 4th edn 1966; Thompson, *Boston*, p. 292.

professional medical assistance. In some places men in the class of society above paupers joined friendly societies, paying a monthly subscription for sickness and funeral benefits, but they met in public houses and were expected to spend part of their subscriptions there. In Lincoln one was formed at the Royal Oak in 1734, another at the Peacock in 1737, and others later in the century.[28]

LEISURE PURSUITS

Only the rich had much time for leisure but on occasions the masses could also watch or participate in traditional sports, as when a bull or a bear was baited by dogs for the pleasure of the crowd. There was a ring embedded in the market-place at Boston to which a bull could be tethered and there were similar bull rings in Lincoln, Horncastle and Grimsby. In Stamford the 600-year-old custom of bull running took place every year on 13 November. The butchers of the town provided a bull to run through the streets chased by men and dogs, who tormented it with sticks and stones, with the object of driving it to the town bridge and ditching it, with great damage to persons and property. There were cock-pits in the yards of many prominent inns and the sport had noble support, as did horse-racing and hare-coursing; outside most towns were commons or marshes which offered suitable open country for horse races.[29]

In 1700 there were no theatres in Lincolnshire but strolling companies of players visited the county and played where they could, particularly where the gentry were gathered for a race meeting or similar event. Sometime after 1718 a theatre was built in Stamford and about 1731 Erasmus Audley erected a small playhouse in Lincoln, underneath the castle walls in Drury Lane. Elsewhere players used a granary or, in Spalding, the courtroom of the town hall.[30]

Societies were also formed for more intellectual pursuits in Lincoln, Stamford and elsewhere. The Gentlemen's Society at Spalding was launched by Maurice Johnson in 1710 for members to read the London periodicals and discuss literary topics; in the late 1720s its interests became much wider and included antiquarian matters. The London papers could be read in Lincolnshire, and

---

[28] Hill, *Georgian Lincoln*, p. 59.
[29] White, *Directory*, 1826, p. 183; Hill, *Georgian Lincoln*, pp. 6, 17; Honeybone, *Grantham*, p. 125.
[30] F. Hance, *Stamford Theatre and Stamford Racecourse*, The History of Stamford vol. 3, Stamford, *c.* 1975; Thompson, *Boston*, p. 211; N. R. Wright, *Spalding — An Industrial History*, Lincoln, 1973, p. 69.

about 1712 the *Stamford Mercury* was commenced as the first county newspaper. Attempts to start other newspapers in Lincoln in 1728 and 1744 were unsuccessful. Neither were there any libraries except in private houses, the cathedral or some of the larger parish churches, such as Grantham or Boston.[31]

TRANSPORT IMPROVEMENTS AND COMMERCE

From about 1650 a marked increase can be discerned in movement along the county's roads: movement of farmers and merchants dealing in agricultural produce, and hawkers, migratory journeymen and craftsmen, seasonal labourers as well as strolling players and fairground folk. As early as 1685 a stage-coach service was advertised from London to Stamford and other places but the journey to Stamford took two days and cost 20s. Amongst the leisured class the attractions of the coast were already becoming known. In 1725 the Wastney family visited Alford 'to bath in the sea' nearby and in 1741 the road to Freiston seaside was marked on a published map of Boston. New inns for travellers were built in Stamford and Grantham, and on the road round the Wash at Bicker (Red Lion 1665), Kirton (King's Head 1699) and Holbeach (Old Saracen's Head). The Half-way House between Lincoln and Newark on the Fosse Way belongs to this period, and these purpose-built inns on country roads are a testimony to the increase in traffic.[32]

Stamford was the nearest Lincolnshire town to London and was often the first to pick up new London fashions. As well as the first newspaper in the county it also had the earliest assembly rooms, theatre and race ground. The population of Stamford started to expand in the late seventeenth century as the increasing number of travellers used it as a halting place on the road to the north. In 1724 Daniel Defoe said that both Stamford and Grantham were famous for 'the abundance of very good inns, some of them fit to entertain persons of the greatest quality'.[33]

The Trent was one of the busiest rivers in England, carrying pottery, cheese and beer from Staffordshire, iron, lead and mill-stones from Derbyshire, timber from Sherwood Forest and wool and grain from Lincolnshire down to the Humber for Yorkshire or for forwarding by coastal or foreign shipping. In return iron, tin,

[31] Hill, *Georgian Lincoln*, p. 61; *The Minute Books of The Spalding Gentlemen's Society 1712–1755*, ed. D. M. Owen, LRS, vol. 73, Lincoln, 1981, p. xii.
[32] N. C. Birch, *Stamford — An Industrial History*, Lincoln, 1972, p. 26; *LAOR* 9, p. 35.
[33] Rogers, ed., *Stamford*, pp. 61, 71; Defoe, *Tour*, p. 419.

salt, hops, groceries, dyers' wares, oil, tar, hemp, flax, wines and spirits, and luxury goods from London and overseas were carried inland for distribution by the tradesmen of the market towns. Lincoln had traded with the midlands since the Middle Ages and it also developed connections with Yorkshire after the Aire and Calder navigation was opened in 1704. Gainsborough and West Stockwith in Nottinghamshire flourished as goods were transferred between sea-going and river vessels. In 1724 Defoe stated that ships of two hundred tons' burthen could get up as far as Stockwith but that larger ships had to load and unload at Burton Stather a few miles down river.[34]

Commercial activity in the rest of the county was largely confined to the movement of agricultural produce and to supplying items the community could not produce for itself, although the work of some craftsmen might also have a wide sale. In 1697 a Brigg bridle-maker had sold his manufactures in Lincoln, Howden and Grantham and a Skirbeck fellmonger dying in 1671 had at his death goods in coasters bound for Lynn and Scarborough.[35]

Lincolnshire was on the wrong side of the kingdom to participate in the lucrative trades of the eighteenth century, with Asia and America, and all around the coast from the Wash to the Humber its decayed ports such as Boston, Grimsby, Wainfleet, Barton-on-Humber, Spalding and Saltfleet served only a local hinterland; their foreign traffic was very small. Boston had been the principal medieval port but in 1683 only eleven vessels sailed from there to London. In contrast twenty-one vessels sailed from Gainsborough to the capital in 1704–5. The great majority of ships leaving Gainsborough and Stockwith were bound for London, with others going to Lynn, Yarmouth, Chatham, Newcastle and Sunderland. Boston's traffic had declined since the Middle Ages and its channel had become silted and shallow like the haven at Grimsby. The bulk of the midland traffic went out through the Thames or the Humber, to the advantage of the new port of Kingston-upon-Hull. Hull developed the largest coastal trade on the east coast apart from the coal ports, and Lincolnshire ports, even as far south as Boston, looked to transhipping goods via Hull. By 1700 the development of Hull had largely deprived the Lincolnshire ports on the Humber of their share of Trent trade, and keels carried traffic between Hull and much of north Lincolnshire. Saltfleet on the coast near Louth had also been an ancient port, and although much of the town had

[34] I. S. Beckwith, *The History of Transport and Travel in Gainsborough*, Gainsborough, 1971, pp. 14, 22; Defoe, *Tour*, p. 454; Boyes and Russell, *Canals*, p. 264.
[35] *LAOR* 9, p. 51; *LAOR* 6, p. 60.

gradually been washed away it retained a weekly market until about 1790 and cargoes were still landed on the sands in the nineteenth century.[36]

By 1700 Kings Lynn had replaced Boston as the principal port on the Wash and in 1709 Boston was the nineteenth port in England for tonnage of registered shipping, with 1,010 tons including fishing boats. Despite its decline relative to other English ports, Boston was still the main port in Lincolnshire and the second largest town in the county. Cargoes from Boston included wool, wheat, rye, barley, and smaller amounts of peas, beans, butter, tallow, woad and hemp. Only a small amount of coal came into Boston in the early eighteenth century, in 1730 amounting to just 0.12% of the coal leaving Newcastle. Foreign trade was also limited, but in 1735–36 imports included some timber from Norway, bricks from Rotterdam and wine from Spain and Portugal; that year only three foreign shipments left Boston. The condition of Boston haven continued to decline. In 1751 Nathaniel Kinderley reported that 'Boston haven is worse than it was ever known to be: for, whereas thirty years ago, a ship of 250 tons could get up to Boston town, now, even a small sloop of but forty or fifty tons, and which draws but six feet of water, cannot sail to or from the town but at a spring tide'.[37]

Some of Lincolnshire's rivers had been navigable for centuries, the river Witham and the ancient Fossdyke as well as the tidal Trent, but keeping them open was a continuous problem, particularly where there was a conflict with the needs of drainage for farmland. By 1700 a nine-and-a-half-mile navigation had been made beside the river Welland from Stamford to Deeping St James, where it rejoined the river to flow to Spalding and so on to the Wash. This navigation was completed sometime between 1664 and 1673 under an act obtained by Stamford corporation in 1620, confirming an act of 1570 which had not been implemented. Cargoes carried on the canal included coal and groceries inwards and agricultural produce, malt, timber, stone and slates from Ketton and Collyweston outwards. Traffic on the canal from Stamford had to be transferred to lighters at Spalding and from them to sea-going vessels anchored in the Wash.[38]

---

[36] M. J. T. Lewis and N. R. Wright, *Boston as a Port*, Lincoln, 1974, p. 8; Beckwith, *Transport and Travel in Gainsborough*, p. 22; White, *Directory*, 1826, p. 235.
[37] Lewis and Wright, op. cit., p. 9.
[38] Birch, *Stamford — An Industrial History*, p. 25; Boyes and Russell, *Canals*, pp. 240, 244.

Lincoln corporation used the powers of an act obtained in 1671 to improve the ancient Fossdyke from their city to the Trent at Torksey, and also to improve a hundred-yard stretch of the Witham from Brayford Head to the High Bridge. Brayford Pool was the harbour of Lincoln where the Fossdyke joined the Witham. Under the 1671 act a sluice was built at Torksey for the first time but even so the largest boats to Lincoln could carry only eighteen tons. Merchants were encouraged to erect warehouses on the waterside in Lincoln but the income from tolls was insufficient to maintain it and the Fossdyke deteriorated during the early years of the eighteenth century. In 1735 wagons loaded with hay were seen to pass over the navigation near Torksey. The situation was similar in other parts of the county, particularly the Ancholme valley and the fens, where seventeenth-century drainage works involving river improvements had been 'sporadic in character, small in achievement and temporary in result'. Despite this it was still possible in 1730 for the newly appointed rector of Coningsby to take boat at Donington for the final part of his journey to Coningsby and in 1740 a mob, mainly of women, prevented a boat laden with wheat sailing from Bourne to Spalding.[39]

HIGHWAYS

The roads of the county were also in a bad state in 1700, and there were only a few causeways or bridges across the fens. During the first half of the eighteenth century the only good road between Kesteven and Holland was the Bridgend causeway between Horbling and Donington and the Wolds were virtually an island surrounded by fens and marshes. Parts of the fens were liable to floods for much of the year and roads then disappeared. In the summer of 1709 Bishop Wake was travelling from Horncastle to Boston when his coach overturned in the middle of a slough and he had difficulty in getting it out. When he found the waters were out and the banks dangerous he took to his horse.[40]

Parishioners were responsible for their own roads but as the eighteenth century advanced the long distance exchange of goods increased. The parish system of highway maintenance felt the strain as it was unjust to expect farmers and labourers to work unrewarded for the benefit of strangers. The resentment of the forced

[39] N. C. Birch, *Waterways and Railways of Lincoln and the Lower Witham*, Lincoln, 1968, p. 1; H. C. Darby, *The Draining of the Fens*, Cambridge, 2nd edn 1956, p. 48; A. Rogers, *A History of Lincolnshire*, Henley-on-Thames, 1970, p. 79; D. Neave, 'Anti-Militia Riots in Lincolnshire, 1757 and 1796', *LHA*, 11 (1976), p. 21.
[40] Hill, *Georgian Lincoln*, p. 122.

labourers was matched by the reluctance and lack of knowledge of the parishioners selected as surveyors for a year. The situation was made worse by changes in the use of roads. More wheeled wagons appeared from the end of the seventeenth century and large droves of cattle moved about the country, many going directly to Smithfield market or to pastures nearer London for fattening. An ordinance issued in the late seventeenth century authorizing the levying of rates for supplementary servicing of the roads was not widely adopted; in 1796 the highways of Spilsby were still maintained by statute labour without a rate. Sir Francis Dashwood (1708–81) had an estate at Nocton and in 1751 he erected a unique land lighthouse on Dunston Heath to guide travellers across the unenclosed heath between Sleaford and Lincoln. Dunston Pillar had a light at the top, replaced in 1810 by a statue of George III cast in Coade stone. The base of the pillar still stands and the top third of the statue is now in the grounds of Lincoln Castle.

The ineffectiveness of the parish system led to the development of a parallel system. The improvement of stretches of main roads was entrusted to *ad hoc* statutory bodies known as turnpike trusts, but this system was only adopted on a small scale before 1750. Turnpike trusts took over existing stretches of road and improved them or constructed new roads. To recover their costs they erected 'bars' or 'turnpikes' across their road at intervals and charged tolls on road users. The trusts' initial expenditure of obtaining their act and carrying it out was often covered by a loan, and much of the trusts' income in the following years would be used to repay the loan with interest.

The first turnpikes in Lincolnshire were on sections of the Great North Road, one of the busiest roads in Britain. It was turnpiked from Spittlegate (Grantham) to Little Drayton near Retford in 1726 and from Stamford to Grantham in 1739. The creation of a trust did not necessarily bring great improvements and in 1739 the road north of Grantham was described as 'a narrow paved causeway for horses, with an unmade road on each side of it. The paved part of the road was traversed by strings of packhorses thirty or forty in number'. In 1749 the short stretch of road from Stamford to Wansford Bridge was also turnpiked, as the section south of Wansford had been in 1711.[41]

After the Great North Road was turnpiked many droves of cattle from Scotland bound for Smithfield market in London still used the ancient Sewstern Lane from Newark to Stamford, which for many

41 Birch, *Stamford — An Industrial History*, p. 26.

miles formed the boundary between Lincolnshire and Leicestershire. Some cattle were driven east across Lincolnshire to Norfolk
and Suffolk to be fattened and sent off during the winter in weekly
droves to London. In the middle of the eighteenth century forty
thousand highland cattle were said to go to Norfolk yearly.[42]

Some Lincolnshire woldsmen buying Scottish cattle for the same
purpose launched the first initiative for a turnpike to serve the needs
of the county. The main road between Lincoln and the Wolds at
Wragby crossed clay lands with little gravel close by. Repairs with
wood and mud reduced it to such a state that travellers would rather
detour through the fens and a turnpike act was obtained in 1739,
taking over the whole road from Lincoln via Wragby to Baumber,
just north of Horncastle. For some years this was an isolated stretch
of turnpike road and it was not until 1756 that trusts took over other
main roads in the county.[43]

On Lincolnshire roads at the start of the eighteenth century
people were far outnumbered by animals. As well as cattle bound
for Smithfield, Lincolnshire-bred sheep also went south every
week to provide the capital with large quantities of cheap mutton.
Geese were bred in Lincolnshire, being plucked five times a year to
provide quills for pens and feathers for beds, and some sent to
London for meat travelled on their own feet after first being driven
through wet tar. The production of mutton was a secondary
consideration in Lincolnshire, whose sheep were bred mainly for
their wool, on which the rural economy of Lincolnshire was very
dependent. In 1700 the county supplied short or carding wool to the
English woollen or clothing industry but its reputation came
increasingly to rest on the production of long or combing wool for
the worsted industries of East Anglia and the West Riding, of which
it was the main supplier until the nineteenth century.[44]

The long wool came from the large sheep which grazed on the
Outer Marsh, the drained fens and other lowlands. The poor soil on
top of the Wolds and the heath supported only small sheep which
produced the short or carding wool. As Perkins says, most of the
clip of both long wool and carding wool was sold to the staplers of

[42] W. G. Hoskins, *The Making of the English Landscape*, London, 1955, p. 243;
Hill, *Georgian Lincoln*, pp. 124–26; S. and B. Webb, *The Story of the King's
Highway*, London, 1913, p. 67.
[43] Beckwith, *Transport and Travel in Gainsborough*, p. 7; Hill, *Georgian Lincoln*,
pp. 124–26; *LAOR* 8, p. 56.
[44] J. A. Perkins, *Sheep Farming in Eighteenth and Nineteenth Century Lincolnshire*,
Lincoln, 1977, pp. 6, 7; Sympson, *Lincolnshire*, p. 77; Wright, *Spalding — An
Industrial History*, p. 30.

East Anglia and, increasingly as the eighteenth century progressed, to those of the West Riding. Large numbers of staplers visited Lincolnshire each year. Most came from the manufacturing areas although some were based in the county, like a Gainsborough woolman of 1667 who had six packhorses and a shop in Wakefield.[45]

Lincolnshire also supplied London with vast numbers of duck, mallard, teal and widgeon that were caught in decoys in various low-lying parts of the county. Both Fuller and Camden wrote enthusiastically of the wealth of wild fowl in Lincolnshire, and Pennant in 1768 refers to this county as 'the great magazine of wild fowl in this kingdom'. Some of the decoys were rented for as much as £500 per annum. In 1724 Defoe reported a trade in live fish to London, chiefly tench and pike, carried in great water-filled butts on wagons. However, wheeled traffic was still unusual and goods which could not be moved on the hoof would be carried on pack animals.[46]

During the eighteenth century another commercial crop was cranberries, introduced at the start of the century by a native of Westmorland. By the time of enclosure just after 1800 there were up to three hundred acres of the East Fen dedicated to their cultivation to supply markets in Cambridgeshire, Lancashire and Yorkshire where cranberry tarts were much in vogue.[47]

Lincolnshire bred more horses than were needed locally and the excess was sold to dealers of Nottinghamshire and Derbyshire for use in coal and lead mines or to Yorkshire buyers for breeding. Most of the fairs in Lincolnshire were for horses, cattle or sheep and at many general merchandise was also for sale. The horse fair at Horncastle was famous beyond the county and one of the largest fairs in England for cattle and merchandise was held at Stow Green north of Folkingham, away from any settlement. Other goods sold at Lincolnshire fairs included flax and hemp at Belton, Crowle and Epworth on the Isle of Axholme and at Folkingham, Donington and Spalding in the fens. However there was no fair for the sale of wool, which was purchased by staplers visiting producers individually.[48]

Smith's Bank had been founded at Nottingham before 1688 but there were no banks in Lincolnshire until the second half of the

[45] Perkins, op. cit., pp. 9, 11; *LAOR* 6, p. 60.
[46] Defoe, *Tour*, p. 416; Sympson, *Lincolnshire*, p. 76.
[47] W. O. Massingberd, 'Industries', in VCH, *Lincs.*, p. 387.
[48] T. W. Beastall, *Agricultural Revolution in Lincolnshire*, Lincoln, 1979, p. 4; Rogers, *A History of Lincolnshire*, p. 67, White, *Directory*, 1856, p. 723.

eighteenth century. Until then the customers of Smith's included merchants and businessmen from Grantham, Lincoln and Gainsborough as well as Nottinghamshire and Derbyshire.

INDUSTRY

Industry in the early eighteenth century was on a small scale and did not need the same large concentrations of workers as later factories. Most people in Lincolnshire worked on the land, and in the towns the main industries were milling, malting and tanning. Commerce employed some people as porters, warehousemen, carriers and the crews of inland vessels. Entries in the parish registers also indicate that there was shipbuilding in Gainsborough in the seventeenth century, and in 1749 a sail-making manufactory was set up in Spalding. The main sources of power were wind and water, and mills were as common in the country as in the towns. Lincoln had a row of hilltop windmills beside the Burton Road and Louth and Grantham each had several watermills, but there were other concentrations of watermills on the river Welland between Stamford and Market Deeping and on the Rase between Tealby and West Rasen. Most mills were grinding corn for flour but a few also made paper, fulled cloth or ground seeds for oil. Windmills were mainly wooden post-mills with perhaps a few smock mills; brick tower mills were not common until the nineteenth century.[49]

Most industrial concerns were processing the agricultural products of the surrounding area and only a few were producing specialized products for the local markets. Lincolnshire was a major producer of wool, flax and hemp but was hardly involved in the manufacture of textiles. The spinning of jersey and worsted had been encouraged as an occupation for the poor during the seventeenth century. A 'jersey school' set up in Boston in 1595 soon became a house of correction, but one established in Lincoln in 1661 lasted long into the eighteenth century. The weaving of linen, introduced to Appleby in north Lincolnshire by the Winn family in the seventeenth century, was also seen as a means of relieving poverty. They planted acres with flax, dug forty-two steeping pits at Carr Side and built weaving sheds. During the eighteenth century the linen industry flourished not only in Appleby and adjacent villages but also across the Trent on the Isle of Axholme. John Wesley himself later described Epworth as a little town of about nine hundred people with three or four factories for spinning.

---

[49] Hill, *Georgian Lincoln*, p. 100; Beckwith, *Industrial Archaeology of Gainsborough*, p. 4.

Hemp was also grown for the weaving of rope, and in the early eighteenth century the occupations of people in the Isle included weavers, sackweavers, flaxdressers and ropers, and close to their houses were hemp yards, hemp crofts and hemp lands. Even before 1700 Gainsborough sackcloth was to be found in Boston. The area between Spalding and Crowland also grew hemp and flax and about 1700 there were weavers in Stamford and Bourne. Fullers earth was occasionally brought in via Grimsby for some of the few water-driven fulling mills in the county, such as the Bridge Street mill in Louth, but an attempt by Arthur Moore to set up woollen manufacture in Grimsby was unsuccessful.[50]

Large areas of the sandy uplands around Brigg and elsewhere were farmed as warrens and the processing of rabbit or 'coney' skins was an extensive industry at Brigg until the nineteenth century. The crushing of rape seeds to produce oil was well established in the Isle of Axholme and the Spalding and Crowland area, where rape was grown. By 1657 there were at least four windmills used for crushing rapeseed on the Isle and one in Gainsborough. The oil served as an alternative to Mediterranean olive oil in uses such as the preparation of wool. The by-product of crushing was called cake; in England in 1700 it was used only for fuel, although as early as 1667 it had been tried for cattle in Lincolnshire and was already widely used as such on the continent. In 1700 rape was still the main seed used, but in 1709 a mill for crushing linseed, said to be the first mill built specifically for that purpose, was leased at Gainsborough. It stood on the hill above the town and was destroyed by fire in 1754. In 1741 there was also a wind-powered 'oil engine' near the Black Sluice just outside Boston.[51]

The extensive grazing of cattle and sheep in the East Midlands led to the development of leather industries. By 1700 tanning was starting to become localized in a few centres, although it was still to be found on a smaller scale in many other places. About 1700 leatherworkers were the largest occupation group in Stamford and tanning was also important at Grantham, Horncastle and Lincoln,

[50] Thompson, Boston, p. 230; H. E. Dudley, 'Linen Weaving at Appleby', Lincs. Mag., 1 (1932–34), p. 246; L. G. H. Lee, 'Wesley's Travels in his Own County', ibid., p. 90; LAOR 6, p. 60; Rogers, ed., Stamford, pp. 63, 64; H. W. Brace, History of Seed Crushing in Great Britain, London, 1960, p. 16; J. D. Birkbeck, A History of Bourne, Bourne, 2nd edn 1976, p. 55; Gillett, Grimsby, p. 139.
[51] Brace, History of Seed Crushing, pp. 11, 20, 21, 27; F. H. Molyneux and N. R. Wright, An Atlas of Boston, History of Boston vol. 10, Boston, 1974, p. 14.

but in the nineteenth century it declined in comparison with Leicester and Northampton.[52]

Until the nineteenth century malt liquor was the normal beverage of most people — strong beer and ale for adult men in normal times, table beer and small beer for family and servants. Brewing was a domestic craft in many households and inns made their own, but most people bought from common brewers. There were brewers throughout the county for beer was a bulky product to transport and the market for any brewery in 1700, by land carriage, was only four to six miles. The main ingredients of beer are malt and yeast and there were many maltings in the county. In 1683 there were so many in Lincoln that the justices sought to reduce the number. After the Welland was made navigable to Stamford a flourishing malt trade developed in the town, and by 1700 malting and the malt trade were two of Stamford's most thriving activities. Several maltings were established along Water Street near the riverside wharf and elsewhere in St Martin's, some of which still stand.[53]

As well as brewing their own beer some people kept pigs, but other household needs were met by imports into the county or by the work of local craftsmen. Joiners also made furniture; when a Gainsborough joiner died in 1697 he had among his stock furniture ready made up, French beds, tester beds and livery cupboards. During the seventeenth century the potters of Burslem and Ticknall had come to supply most of the needs of the midlands, but eastern Lincolnshire was an inaccessible area and although the potters at Old Bolingbroke fell on hard times they continued in production for most of the eighteenth century as successors to the medieval potters of nearby Toynton. Theirs was a cottage industry, the craftsman and his family with perhaps a few labourers and apprentices producing useful earthenware vessels for the surrounding community.[54]

In several Lincolnshire towns, particularly Gainsborough and Lincoln, there were makers of clay tobacco pipes. It was a humble trade and the makers tended to live in the poorest parts of towns, with a small kiln behind public houses or in the corner of their house

[52] Rogers, ed., *Stamford*, pp. 63, 64, 92; *LAOR* 6, p. 60.

[53] P. Mathias, *The Brewing Industry in England 1700–1830*, Cambridge, 1959, pp. xxii, xxv; *LAOR* 2, p. 6; *LAOR* 7, p. 15; Rogers, ed., *Stamford*, p. 71; Boyes and Russell, *Canals*, p. 240; RCHM, *Stamford*, p. 156.

[54] *LAOR* 9, p. 51; R. H. Healey and E. H. Rudkin, 'Lincolnshire', in *The English Country Pottery. Its History and Techniques*, ed. P. C. D. Brears, Newton Abbot, 1971, pp. 193–95.

or yard. It was a craft handed on from father to son, and declined in the late eighteenth century when snuff became the popular way to take tobacco.[55]

There were a few bell-founders in the county, such as Alexander Rigby who was master of the long-established Stamford foundry until his death in 1708, when the foundry closed, and Humphrey Wilkinson of Lincoln who supplied bells to various churches in the county between 1695 and 1718, having cast a new bell for the Cutlers' Company of Sheffield in 1689. John and James Harrison were clock-makers in north Lincolnshire, who constructed the large and unique turret clock at Brocklesby Park about 1727. In 1736 the brothers moved to London and John eventually obtained the prize for perfecting the first successful chronometer for use at sea, but James returned to Barrow-on-Humber in 1739 and set up as a miller and bell-founder. The Harrison family were bell-founders until 1835, moving to Barton towards the end of the eighteenth century. Another small-scale industry was the making of paper. One paper mill at Caistor apparently ceased sometime after 1703 but others were started at Tealby by 1721 and at Houghton near Grantham about 1731 and continued in each place for over a century. By 1700 soap making was no longer a domestic occupation and many towns had a soapmaker: there were several in Gainsborough by the end of the seventeenth century and in the early 1700s Ann Wade had a soapworks in Corby Glen. It was an objectionable process producing a foul smell, lots of steam and large quantities of waste from the production of the alkali.[56]

---

[55] P. Wells, 'The Clay Pipe Makers of Boston', *Aspects of Nineteenth Century Boston and District*, History of Boston, vol. 8, Boston, 1972, pp. 13, 14; J. E. Mann, *Clay Tobacco Pipes from Excavations in Lincoln 1970–74*, Lincoln Archaeological Trust Monograph Series xv–1, London, 1977, p. 2.

[56] Birch, *Stamford — An Industrial History*, p. 1; T. North, *The Church Bells of the County and City of Lincoln*, Leicester, 1882; L. Gittins, 'Soapmaking and the Excise Laws, 1711–1853', *Industrial Archaeology Review*, 1 no. 3 (1977), pp. 265, 274; *LAOR* 8, p. 33; D. I. A. Steel, *A Lincolnshire Village. The parish of Corby Glen in its historical context*, London, 1979, p. 9.

PART II
THE INDUSTRIAL REVOLUTION
1760–1845

CHAPTER 2

BY LAND AND WATER

U NDER the four Georges, the isolation of Lincolnshire was much reduced by improvements to roads, waterways and ports (fig. 3). The existing but neglected system of navigable rivers was restored and supplemented by new tributary waterways, while massive reclamation works in the fens generated wide and deep drains which often doubled as navigations. In a parallel development, and frequently with the same promoters as the waterways, turnpike trusts were created to improve the main roads. Main roads were, however, relatively few, and the resulting network of turnpikes was thinly spread in comparison with an industrialized county like Nottinghamshire. Major road bridges thrown across the large rivers around the boundary linked the county more effectively to the outside world. Finally, the ports of Gainsborough, Boston and Grimsby all enjoyed expansion. By 1830, movement of people, livestock and goods both in and out of Lincolnshire and within it had been made markedly easier and cheaper than in 1700.

Lincolnshire's waterways were essentially local, in contrast to those of other midland counties which became part of a regional and then national system, and their purpose was to secure an outlet for the surplus goods of the countryside and to import coal, mostly for domestic use. Most Lincolnshire waterways had only the Fossdyke to connect them to the midlands and Yorkshire, and many locks in the county were designed for the Lincolnshire ketch, a version of the Humber keel, rather than for midland narrow boats. There was little need for substantial engineering except in the sea-locks built at Boston, Tetney, Grimsby, South Ferriby, Keadby and Torksey.[1]

FOSSDYKE

One of the first steps in eighteenth-century improvements was the restoration of the Fossdyke to a fully navigable condition. In

[1] A. Rogers, *A History of Lincolnshire*, Henley-on-Thames, 1970, p. 79.

33

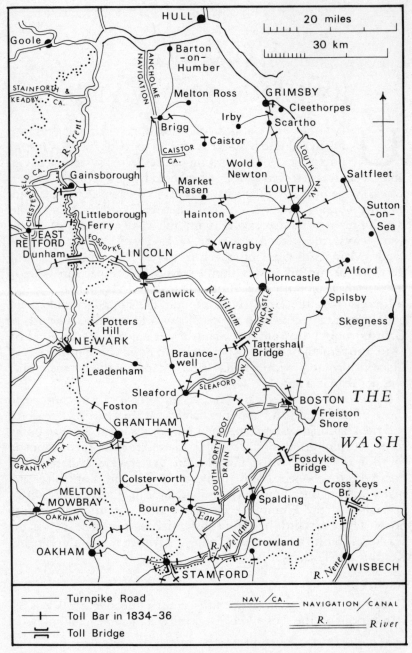

Figure 3   *Turnpike roads, toll-bridges and navigable waterways: navigable drains around Boston are not shown*

September 1740 Lincoln corporation leased the waterway for 999 years to Richard Ellison (1686–1743) of Thorne in the West Riding of Yorkshire, a merchant actively involved in various Yorkshire waterways. In 1737 he had joined with two others to lease the tolls of the Dun navigation downstream from Sheffield. Ellison paid £75 p.a. for the Fossdyke but retained all the tolls and had to provide and maintain a depth of three feet six inches throughout the waterway. He died in 1743 and his son Richard Ellison II (1717–92) was mainly responsible for the restoration of the waterway, which was completed early in 1744 at a cost of over £3,000. The first coal it carried into Lincoln was sold at 13s. per chaldron, the former price being 21s. Annual income from the tolls rose from £75 in 1740 to £500 in 1750 and £2,367 in 1789, and the common council of Lincoln were accused of lack of foresight, and even corruption, in leasing them away. The Ellisons made a fortune and acquired a country house at Sudbrooke but the rising tolls reflected increasing trade from which others also profited. The improvement of the Fossdyke was an isolated event and it was twenty years before similar works took place on the Witham and the Ancholme.[2]

TURNPIKE ROADS

Although the failure to reconcile the needs of drainage and navigation left the rivers in a state of neglect, the main roads of the county received considerable attention. In 1751 a general act made turnpike acts easier to obtain; between 1756 and 1765 thirteen new turnpike trusts were established and two others enlarged. A few other roads were turnpiked in the following sixty years but most minor roads were left to the old parish system. Figure 4 indicates the great increase in the length of road affected.

The passing of a turnpike act indicates the need for improvement and the presence of a local group able and willing to obtain the necessary powers; it does not indicate that such powers were fully used or effective. Arthur Young declared that 'without a very general public spirit, and proprietors being of ample fortune, or great spirit of exertion, such schemes rarely succeed'. One act obtained in 1765 authorized several roads in north-west Lincolnshire but only the main road from Bawtry to Louth was improved. In 1756 several roads in Kesteven were turnpiked but in 1770 Young said of one of the roads, between Bourne and Colsterworth, 'we were every moment either buried in quagmires of mud or

---

[2] Hill, *Georgian Lincoln*, pp. 128, 129, 130; Boyes and Russell, *Canals*, p. 258.

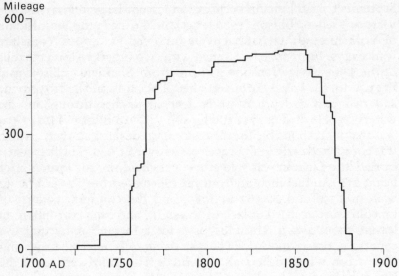

Figure 4   *Total mileage of turnpike roads in Lincolnshire*

racked to dislocation over pieces of rock which they term mending'.[3]

Despite deficiences in the system, turnpike roads had, on average, more spent on them than did other roads and they were often
notably better. Each turnpike trust was initially set up for
twenty-one years but when their term neared its end the trustees
invariably had it extended. So they ceased to be temporary organ-
izations to supplement parish repair and became semi-permanent
self-elected highway authorities for those roads. Parishes retained
their highway responsibility in respect of turnpikes but could
commute it to a monetary payment. In the early nineteenth century
pauper labour was used on road maintenance, as in the Isle of
Axholme where roads were paved with Yorkshire flags for a width
of one horse in the period 1810–12, and in 1824 James McAdam said
that pauper labour was also being used by turnpike trusts in this
county.[4]

Lincolnshire was later than some counties in having turnpikes
and the trusts never controlled as large a proportion of its roads as in
a county such as Derbyshire, perhaps because Lincolnshire had less

---

[3] W. Albert, *The Turnpike Road System in England 1663–1840*, Cambridge, 1972,
p. 29; Young, *General View*, p. 453; Rogers, *Lincolnshire*, p. 76.
[4] G. Hindley, *A History of Roads*, London, 1971, p. 67; Albert, op. cit., pp. 29,
158; S. and B. Webb, *The Story of the King's Highway*, London, 1913, p. 77.

traffic and easier terrain. In 1837 there were twenty-nine trusts in the county controlling 550 miles of roads. Most trusts controlled between ten and twenty miles of road; a few had less and eight had more, some including side roads. Large trusts like the one for the Lincoln Heath to Peterborough road were divided into districts, each with its own trustees, officers and accounts. In several cases the county boundary marked the limit of a trust's authority or divided it into districts. Trusts raised loans for their initial establishment, and the tolls were mortgaged from the start. Further works needed further loans and the trusts were continually in debt, sometimes even being unable to pay interest. The Sleaford–Tattershall trust paid interest in 1825 for the first time since it was formed in 1793, because since 1816 the road had been supported and kept in repair by the parishes through which it passed. Only a small part of a trust's income might actually be used for the upkeep of the road and even that might disappear if creditors took over the tolls completely, as happened on the Lincolnshire section of the Great North Road in 1847.[5]

The establishment of the Lincoln–Wragby–Baumber trust in 1739 was an isolated occurrence and the real growth of Lincolnshire turnpikes started in 1756. Then the Wansford–Stamford trust took over the road from Stamford to Bourne and thereafter turnpikes spread northwards and eastwards over the county. Most trusts established in the 1750s were for roads in Kesteven and across the fens to the Holland towns. The Lincoln–Baumber trust took over the road from Wragby to Hainton in 1759 and was extended to the edge of Louth in 1780, but most of the main trusts in Lindsey were established in the single year 1765.

In 1756 two acts were obtained for the road between Lincoln and Peterborough, one creating the Lincoln trust and the other establishing the Lincoln Heath to Peterborough trust, divided at a point in Brauncewell parish north of Sleaford. The Lincoln trust also controlled a few short roads on the edge of the city and the road west to the ferries across the Trent at Dunham and Littleborough. As the act affected the road through the Close, the dean and chapter gave up their ancient right to shut the gates.[6] In 1777 the trust also took over the Newark road from Lincoln to Potter Hill on the Nottinghamshire boundary. The trust controlled all the roads converging on Lincoln from the south and the toll bar at Great South Bar Gate became one of the most profitable in the county.

[5] Rogers, *Lincolnshire*, pp. 73, 76; Albert, *Turnpike Road System*, p. 238.
[6] Hill, *Georgian Lincoln*, p. 123.

South of Brauncewell the Lincoln Heath–Peterborough trust took over not only the main road but also three important side roads, from Sleaford to Great Hale on the Holland boundary, from Hacconby to Bridge End near Donington, and from Bourne to Colsterworth. In 1822 it also took over the road from Bourne to Spalding.

In 1757 and 1758 further acts created new trusts to connect the main Holland towns to the roads of the Lincoln Heath–Peterborough trust, the first from Spalding across the Stone Bridge at Deeping St James to the main road at Maxey Outgang, the second from Boston to Swineshead North End where the turnpike divided into two branches which joined two side roads of the Lincoln Heath trust. The original scheme had been to join Boston and Donington via Gosberton, but that road was only turnpiked as far as the east bank of Bicker haven. This trust also built a branch road to Langrett ferry (now Langrick bridge), to gain access to the gravel bed at Amber Hill in the middle of the Holland Fen, which they used for road maintenance.

Between 1758 and 1764 other acts were obtained for turnpiking three roads crossing the western boundary of Kesteven and two other main roads in south Holland. The two roads turnpiked in 1764 ran from Spalding north to Donington and east to Tydd Gote near Wisbech, with a side branch to Cross Keys Wash. This was the wide estuary of the river Nene on the county boundary and despite the danger of shifting sands travellers and droves of cattle were regularly guided across between the inns on each bank. In 1765 the road between Wisbech and Kings Lynn was turnpiked and this included a side branch to the Norfolk bank of Cross Keys Wash.

The mileage of turnpike roads in Lindsey was trebled by four acts passed in 1765. The first act related to the road from Bawtry to Louth and then southward along the edge of the Wolds to Dexthorpe, joining the new Alford–Boston turnpike at Ulceby Cross. Their main road ran from Bawtry to Hainton, crossing the Trent by the Walkerith ferry just north of Gainsborough, and from North Willingham to Dexthorpe was the so-called 'second district'. The road from Dunham ferry to the Great North Road at Great Markham was turnpiked at the same time but most traffic out of Lincolnshire went south towards London.

The other major trust formed in 1765 took over the road north from Lincoln via Brigg to the ferry at Barton-on-Humber and so the whole ninety miles from the Humber bank to the Great North Road at Norman Cross was turnpiked. The Brigg trust acted quickly and twelve months after obtaining their act they had completed improvements on all their roads at a cost of between £80 and £120 per mile. In 1786 this trust took over a branch from Brigg to Caistor. The other trusts created this year were for the roads from Alford to Boston and from Grimsby to Wold Newton, the latter being an isolated stretch of turnpike. The initiative for a turnpike to Grimsby had come from Caistor, then a more import-ant local centre, but the improvement of the Irby road on the way to Caistor was deferred. In 1766 meetings were held to consider turnpiking the road from Boston to Wainfleet and funds were raised but in the event no act was obtained. By that year most of the turnpike trusts in Lincolnshire had been set up and the few new trusts established after that date were mainly for shorter roads, such as those from Scartho to Louth and Spittlegate to Bridge End.[7]

Nearly all the roads into Lincoln, Louth and Stamford were turnpiked and most roads at Lincoln came under a single trust. Around Stamford eight roads were nominally controlled by six different trusts but in such small provincial trusts a small group of active trustees might control several connected trusts; in 1833 Sir James McAdam told a parliamentary committee that five or six trusts near Stamford were run by the same trustees.[8]

WATERWAYS — THE GRUNDY PERIOD

At the same time as the main roads were taken in hand there was activity to improve rivers and to create a navigation from Louth to the Humber. Two engineers involved in many of the works were John Smeaton (1724–92) and John Grundy Jnr (1719–83). Smeaton established a national reputation with the construction of the Eddystone lighthouse in 1756–59 and thereafter he was consulted on engineering projects throughout the kingdom. Grundy of Spalding (see plate IV) was well known in Lincolnshire and adjacent counties as a surveyor and drainage engineer, like his father before him, and was a friend of Smeaton, who had a high regard for his abilities. Professor Skempton considers that Grundy was perhaps the first civil engineer in this country to have been trained for the profession and to work as a consultant, purely on civil engineering, throughout the greater part of his career. He enjoyed the patronage of the duke of Ancaster and in 1748 constructed the Great Water

---

[7] P. R. White, 'The Brigg Turnpike Trust in Early Years', *LIA*, 5 no. 1 (1970), pp. 2–7; Rogers, *Lincolnshire*, p. 73; Gillett, *Grimsby*, pp. 160–61; Albert, *Turnpike Road System*, p. 102.
[8] Albert, op. cit., p. 63.

Dam to create the ornamental lake at Grimsthorpe Castle, one of the earliest examples of modern principles in dam construction.[9]

In 1756 Grundy made a preliminary feasibility survey of a line for a navigation from Tetney haven on the Humber to Louth, using the river Lud for part of the route into the town. This was at the time of some of the first canal schemes in England, coming three years before the duke of Bridgewater obtained the act for his famous canal, but events moved slowly. In 1760 Smeaton confirmed Grundy's proposals but the act was not obtained until 1763. Construction started in 1765, the first five miles were opened on 18 May 1767, and it was opened right through to Louth in May 1770.[10]

Charles Chaplin (1730–92 or 94) of Tathwell leased the tolls for a seven-year term and in 1777 he gave £7,000 for necessary improvements in return for a ninety-nine-year lease of the waterway. Until 1828 the Chaplins virtually ran the concern, paying an annual rent of £1,375 plus the cost of repairs but retaining the tolls, which rose from about £2,000 p.a. at the start to about £5,000 p.a. in the late 1820s. The legality of the lease was challenged in the 1820s but the position was regularized by an act of 1828, which confirmed the lease for its original term.[11]

Grundy and Smeaton also worked with Langley Edwards (d. 1774) on a scheme for the improvement of the Witham. They produced a joint report in 1761 to which was attached a map made by Grundy in 1762, and this became the basis of a project advanced by a committee headed by Lord Vere Bertie (d. 1768). It largely followed one drawn up by Grundy in 1757, except that the proposed sluice at Boston was now to be located above the town instead of at the town bridge. The scheme had several opponents, some fearing that the water level in the Fossdyke might fall and others that land in Holland Fen would be flooded, but Boston corporation supported it and the act was passed on 2 June 1762. It divided the Witham between Lincoln and Boston into six drainage districts, each managed by a separate committee, and also set up a separate commission for the navigation. Edwards was in charge of the works, which were virtually complete by 1770. Between

[9] A. W. Skempton and E. C. Wright, 'Early Members of the Smeatonian Society of Civil Engineers', *Trans. Newcomen Soc.*, 44 (1971–72), pp. 23, 25, 27, 28; *LAOR* 25, p. 92; Thompson, *Boston*, p. 265; G. Binnie, 'The Evolution of British Dams', *Trans. Newcomen Soc.*, 47 (1974–76), p. 210.

[10] Boyes and Russell, *Canals*, pp. 304, 305, 307.

[11] R. Russell, *Lost Canals of England and Wales*, Newton Abbot, 1971, p. 241; N. J. L. Lyons, 'Some Comments on the Louth Navigation Act of 1828', *LIA*, 4 no. 1 (1969), p. 2; Boyes and Russell, *Canals*, pp. 307, 308.

Chapel Hill and Boston the river was diverted into a completely new channel, as Grundy had suggested in 1753, shortening the distance from thirteen and a half to eleven miles. At Boston was the Grand Sluice, with three pairs of pointing sea-doors and a navigable lock, which at that date was probably the largest structure of its kind built in England. About 1770 other locks were built at Kirkstead, Barlings and Stamp End on the edge of Lincoln.[12]

The improved drainage by the Witham paved the way for the enclosure of fens all along the west side of the river between Lincoln and Boston, and at the southern end the enclosure of the 22,000 acres of Holland Fen led to the only open opposition to enclosure in eighteenth-century Lincolnshire. The act for Holland Fen was obtained in 1765 and the award made in 1769 but at once fences were destroyed, corn stacks burnt, cattled maimed and at least one man killed. In all probability Boston would have been fired had it not been protected by four troops of the Scots Greys. The 1769 award divided the fen between the ten parishes that shared common rights over it, and most of the parishes quickly obtained acts to divide their portions between the individual commoners. By 1774 eight of the ten parishes had enclosed their fen and abolished common rights. Holland Fen was immediately adjoining Boston; the town itself received 1,514 acres, and the port prospered as it started to move the grain which came off the new enclosed fields. Traffic on the Witham increased and the tolls at Boston and Lincoln rose from £263 in 1763–64 to £316 in 1771, £498 in 1782 and £898 by 1790. Income from the Fossdyke traffic similarly increased, though until after 1798 the shallowness of the Witham at Brayford Head and under High Bridge prevented vessels sailing right through and the porterage of goods provided dues for Lincoln corporation and employment for the citizens. Soon after the Witham act was obtained the Ancholme was surveyed for the local landowners by Thomas Yeoman and a similar act received the royal assent in 1767. This set up a five-man body of commissioners of the Ancholme drainage and navigation, who undertook the improvement of the river between Brigg and the Humber, erecting a new sluice and lock at South Ferriby.[13]

Between the river improvements of the 1760s and the canal mania of the 1790s there were four or five schemes mooted for

[12] Hill, *Georgian Lincoln*, p. 131; J. H. Hopper, 'Lincolnshire Worthies No. 6 — The Two John Grundys', *Lincolnshire Life*, 20 no. 3 (1980), pp. 24–27.
[13] Brears, p. 136; F. H. Molyneux and N. R. Wright, *An Atlas of Boston*, Boston, 1974, p. 36; Hill, *Georgian Lincoln*, p. 134; C. J. Page, *History of the Ancholme Navigation*, Lincoln, 1969, p. 1; Boyes and Russell, *Canals*, p. 291.

waterways in Lincolnshire but only the improvement of the Trent and the modest Bourne Eau were carried out. The Eau was a natural stream which linked Bourne to the river Glen at Tongue End, three and a half miles away, and so to the Welland at Surfleet. It had long been navigable but in 1781 an act vested it in trustees who were to make it five feet deep and thirty feet wide where the existing banks would allow. The act allowed 2s. 6d. per ton to be charged on all 'goods, wares, merchandise or commodities whatsoever'. In 1772 Grundy surveyed a route along the upper Witham for a canal from Grantham to Newark and in 1774 there were abortive plans for a canal from Sleaford to the Witham at Chapel Hill, the latter being revived in 1783 and 1791.[14]

LATER TURNPIKE ROADS

Between 1765 and 1826 only six new turnpike trusts were set up in Lincolnshire but a similar number in adjacent counties extended up to or just over the boundary, particularly on the west. Since 1665 the road along the east bank of the Welland between Spalding and Brotherhouse had been subject to tolls levied by the Deeping Fen adventurers. They had erected the bank to protect South Holland Fen but in 1675 it was part of the main route from London into south Lincolnshire, along the Welland bank from Peakirk to Spalding, and in 1772 that route was the subject of a turnpike act. However the act was allowed to lapse after twenty-one years and other drainage authorities took over the maintenance of the banks, continuing to levy tolls at Cowbit Bar and Gilbert's Bar, the latter being midway between Crowland and Peakirk. Use of the Crowland–Peakirk section evidently declined after the Crowland–Eye road was turnpiked in 1817, although tolls were still being collected in 1849, and it was omitted from an act of 1838 which made Barrier Bank a turnpike again, and so subject to the general legislation affecting such roads, for the next thirty-one years.[15]

In general turnpike trusts did not improve roads within towns, since they were mainly used by local traffic, but there were exceptions in Stamford, Lincoln and Boston. Under an act of 1776 the Wansford–Stamford–Bourne trust widened the Great North Road through Stamford from the town bridge to Scotgate. This involved

[14] J. Priestley, *Navigable Rivers and Canals*, London, 1831, reprinted Newton Abbot, 1969, p. 83; Honeybone, *Grantham*, p. 57; Hill, *Georgian Lincoln*, p. 134; C. J. Page, *Sleaford — An Industrial History*, Lincoln, 1974, p. 28; Boyes and Russell, *Canals*, pp. 259, 283.

[15] W. H. Wheeler, *A History of the Fens of South Lincolnshire*, Boston, 2nd edn 1896, p. 107; Brears, p. 148; *SM*, 16 February 1849.

the removal of the old Bridge Gate and town hall, and the present town hall was erected at the cost of the turnpike. Renewal of the act in 1798 gave the trustees similar powers to replace the old town hall in Bourne but they did not do this and in 1820 were given power to demolish the 'very ruinous and decayed' building without being obliged to replace it. The new town hall in Bourne was paid for by public subscription. With the aid of public subscriptions the Lincoln trust improved the road up the eastern side of the hill from Clasket Gate to Potter Gate. The New Road, now called Lindum Road, was opened in 1786. This involved the removal of what remained of the medieval Clasket Gate, one of several gateways which were to disappear in Lincoln and Stamford during the reign of George III. In the 1840s the Lincoln trust opened a new area of development in the city by building a new road from the foot of Canwick Hill to Thorn Bridge on the Witham. In Boston trusts were liable to repair parts of West Street and Wide Bargate; a plaque still remaining in the latter street indicated the end of the Alford–Boston trust's liability.[16]

WATERWAYS — THE JESSOP PERIOD

For long the Trent had been navigable for river craft as far up stream as Wilden ferry near Long Eaton but in the 1770s several new canals debouched into the Trent and the increased traffic on the river led to demands for its improvement. William Jessop (1745–1814), a pupil of John Smeaton, surveyed the river for a group of promoters in 1781–82 and by an act of 1783 they improved the river between Gainsborough and Wilden ferry. Jessop remained as the Trent Navigation Company's resident engineer and settled at Newark. During the 1790s there was a mania of canal promotion in England and he was closely involved with those in Lincolnshire and the rest of the kingdom. As early as 1784 he had shared with John Hudson of Kenwick Thorpe near Louth in an abortive survey for a canal from Alford. The following year a canal was proposed through Leicestershire to Oakham and in December meetings in Stamford considered its extension to their town, but their hopes were fruitless and canal boats never did enter Stamford from the west.[17]

The low price of wheat and the declining yield on consols in the late 1780s and the successful example of earlier canals turned

---

[16] Hill, *Georgian Lincoln*, p. 146.
[17] P. Riden, *The Butterley Company 1790–1830*, Chesterfield, 1973, p. 4; P. S. Bagwell, *The Transport Revolution from 1770*, London, 1974, p. 16; Hill, *Georgian Lincoln*, p. 134; Boyes and Russell, *Canals*, p. 303; C. Hadfield, *The Canals of the East Midlands*, Newton Abbot, 2nd edn 1970, p. 94.

speculators away from enclosures to investment in canals. In the four years 1791 to 1794 forty-two new canals were successfully launched in Britain, including four local ones promoted by Lincolnshire people. Canals and navigations would improve communication between this agricultural county and the coal mining and industrial areas to the west. In 1787 John Dyson and John Gibson opened a short canal across flat country between Tattershall and the nearby river Witham, and Sir Joseph Banks (1744–1820) was perhaps the prime mover in a scheme to extend the waterway up the river Bain to Horncastle in his territory. Sir Joseph also encouraged a Sleaford group led by Benjamin Handley (1754–1828) to revive the idea of making the Slea navigable from their town to the Witham. Joseph Banks (fig. 5) was not only a dominant personality in Lincolnshire but also operated on the national and international scene. He was a naturalist, explorer, friend of George III, president of the Royal Society and supporter of any Lincolnshire works which he anticipated were for the public good. It might well be said that no major undertaking in south Lincolnshire at that time was successful without his support, such was his influence within the county and in London. [18]

The promoters of the Slea and the Bain were in close contact with each other; in 1791 Jessop surveyed both rivers and also investigated the impediment to navigation through Lincoln caused by the narrow and shallow passage under High Bridge and the staunch at Brayford Head, with John Hudson participating in the survey of the Slea. Acts for the Horncastle and Slea navigations passed on 11 June 1792, and the Horncastle act included provisions for the two companies and the Witham Navigation commissioners to finance works at Lincoln to connect the Witham and Fossdyke. The Slea navigation was opened in 1794, the cost being covered by £16,000 raised from shareholders and £2,500 raised on security of the tolls. Later it was extended a mile upstream to quarries at Boiling Wells. The public wharf was built on the site of gardens behind the Bedehouses and a piece of land on the opposite bank of the river was made into an island, the new cut forming a turn-round for the boats. The navigation office on the wharf was erected in 1838. [19]

[18] Bagwell, op. cit., p. 17; Boyes and Russell, *Canals*, pp. 259, 283; Hill, *Georgian Lincoln*, pp. 134–35; W. M. Hunt, 'The Horncastle Navigation Engineers 1792–94', *Journal of the Railway and Canal Historical Society*, 25 no. 1 (1979), p. 2.
[19] Hunt, loc. cit.; Page, *Sleaford — An Industrial History*, p. 28; Priestley, *Navigable Rivers and Canals*, pp. 338, 576; Hill, *Georgian Lincoln*, p. 135; Boyes and Russell, *Canals*, p. 284; W. M. Hunt, 'The Sleaford Navigation Office', *LHA*, 10 (1975), p. 26.

Figure 5   *Sir Joseph Banks (1744–1820)*

While the Slea works went ahead the Horncastle navigation was
held up for lack of a resident engineer and Banks wrote to Jessop for
help in finding one. William Cawley, recommended by Jessop, was
employed from April to October 1793 and proved a disaster; his
efforts culminated in the blowing up of Tattershall lower lock.
Banks tried to get a new engineer through John Rennie, a
Scottish-born engineer of considerable energy and talents who until
this time had done no work in Lincolnshire, but in fact the solution
was found locally. John Dyson had been one of the partners who

built the Tattershall canal, which the Horncastle navigation purchased, and subsequently Dyson was a member of a separate firm which erected the locks on the Slea navigation. By February 1794 he was available and became resident engineer to the Horncastle, handing over a year later to Thomas Hudson. Construction of the Horncastle navigation was slow and ate up the funds, even though parts were opened early to provide some toll income. Early in 1797 it reached Dalderby ford but no further progress was made for two years and the severe winter of 1799–1800 even destroyed work already done. A second act of 1800 allowed them to raise further capital, the extra eventually being supplied by the two local landowners, Banks and Lord Fortescue. The final section of the Horncastle navigation was formally opened on 17 September 1802. The tolls on the Slea were fixed at a maximum of 2s. per ton for the whole distance; from £490 in 1795 the income rose to £562 in 1806, £1,010 in 1824 and almost £2,000 in 1856. For the first years the tolls paid off the debt but after 1811 the company started paying a dividend. The Horncastle took twenty years to clear its initial debts.[20]

In 1791 Jessop was also surveying canals from Nottingham to the Erewash valley and from Radcliffe-on-Trent to Grantham. Opposition by Lincoln and Newark corporations, Radcliffe landowners, Sir Joseph Banks, the Ellisons and others defeated a Grantham bill promoted in 1792 but Jessop re-surveyed the western end, moving it from Radcliffe to Trent Bridge opposite Nottingham and making other changes to suit the objectors, and a new bill received the royal assent on 30 April 1793. The thirty-three mile long Grantham canal was a more expensive undertaking than the navigations to Sleaford and Horncastle. From Grantham it cut through a ridge at Harlaxton (shown in plate II) and then followed the contours around the vale of Belvoir, dropping 140 feet by eighteen broad locks. The canal cost about £118,500 and a second act was obtained in 1797 to enable the full sum to be raised.[21]

The resident engineers were James Green of Wollaton for the Nottinghamshire section and William King for the eastern section. Green had worked under Jessop on the Nottingham canal and King was agent to the duke of Rutland over whose land much of the eastern section was built. Unusually, since he was an employee,

[20] Hunt, 'Horncastle Navigation Engineers', pp. 3, 6, 8, 10; Boyes and Russell, *Canals*, pp. 270, 271, 274; Priestley, op. cit., pp. 339, 577; Page, op. cit., p. 29; N. C. Birch, *Waterways and Railways of Lincoln and the Lower Witham*, Lincoln, 1968, p. 14.
[21] Hadfield, *Canals of the East Midlands*, pp. 61, 62; Hill, *Georgian Lincoln*, p. 136.

King was also given a seat on the board. The eastern section was reported to be navigable in February 1797 and the first load of coal from Hickling to Grantham was carried in April. It was met by the alderman and corporation and nearly a thousand spectators, and was given to the poor. The western section was probably opened during that summer and the three-bay canal warehouse at the basin in Grantham was built in 1798. The company kept its tolls high, and at the end of the century they brought in just under £5,000 per annum, but this encouraged competition from land transport and other waterways such as the Melton and Sleaford.[22]

Two other canals authorized in 1793 were the Caistor on 3 June and the Stainforth and Keadby on 7 June. The former was only four miles long with five locks, extending from the Ancholme half-way towards Caistor, and its tolls were not even sufficient to pay the interest on the loans. The latter was really a Yorkshire canal which strayed into Lincolnshire. It extended for fifteen miles across the Isle of Axholme from Keadby on the Trent to Stainforth on the Dun navigation and was built to avoid the shoals in the lower part of the Dun river, thereby improving the outlet from Sheffield and the waterways of south Yorkshire. It passed through flat country and apart from the tide-lock at Keadby it had only one other lock, with a five feet fall, at Thorne. Despite this it was an expensive canal; by 1809 the company had raised nearly £44,200 but needed authority to raise a further £10,000 from its shareholders.[23]

WATERWAYS — THE RENNIE PERIOD

Proposals for further improvements to the waterway system continued to be made until the 1830s and from 1798 John Rennie became involved in several Lincolnshire schemes, including drainage works and harbour improvements as well as bridges. The difficulties over the Horncastle navigation and the effect of this on Banks's opinion may have been the reason Jessop was never made a fellow of the Royal Society, and why new schemes in Lincolnshire were given to Rennie. One of John Grundy's last projects had been to produce plans for a dock at Hull, which was opened in 1778 and at fifteen acres was the largest completed in the eighteenth century. The increase in traffic soon made this inadequate and thought was given in Grimsby to creating a dock or improving the haven so that

[22] Hadfield, op. cit., p. 62; Hill, *Georgian Lincoln*, p. 136; Honeybone, *Grantham*, p. 87; M. Pointer and M. G. Knapp, *Bygone Grantham*, Grantham, 1977, p. 17; Rogers, *Lincolnshire*, p. 80.

[23] Russell, *Lost Canals of England and Wales*, p. 247; Boyes and Russell, *Canals*, p. 302; Priestley, *Navigable Rivers and Canals*, pp. 224, 587.

the town might benefit from some of this surplus trade. In 1787 Jonathan Pickerrell of Whitby was commissioned to draw plans for a dock and later John Hudson also proposed improvements to the haven.[24]

An act of 1796 formed the Grimsby Haven Company with power to improve the port, essentially by erecting a lock across the haven about 150 yards in from the high water mark and dredging the basin so formed. In February 1798 Rennie was appointed engineer to the company, but the earlier estimates had been grossly inadequate and economies had to be made as the work progressed. Eventually the six-acre dock was officially opened on 30 December 1800 and consisted of a channel one hundred feet wide and fourteen feet deep extending three hundred feet upstream from the lock, with beyond it the narrower haven extending up to the town. By 1800–1 the company had spent £58,000, of which the greater part was on the substantial sea-lock.[25]

The commissioners of the Ancholme, concerned to improve the drainage of the land on each side of their river, asked Rennie to submit a report. This was considered in January 1802, but in view of the expense he presented a revised report which was the basis of two acts obtained that year, the second extending the navigation up to Bishopbridge with two new locks.[26]

In 1799 Rennie was asked to report on the possibility of draining the East, West and Wildmore fens, a tract of 40,000 acres north of Boston. It was a tremendous undertaking because even in dry summers large parts of the East Fen were often under two feet of water. Despite disagreement among the people with interests in the fens, acts were obtained in 1801 and the massive undertaking began. Rennie designed two distinct networks of drains: catchwater drains round the edge to prevent the area being flooded by water flowing off the Wolds and internal drains to carry water from the fens themselves. The internal drains converged on a new fourteen mile long drain to enter Boston haven at Hob Hole sluice, opened in 1806, while the catchwater drains flowed into the haven through the new Maud Foster sluice, opened in 1807. Three new cast-iron footbridges including Hospital bridge (fig. 6) were erected across the Maud Foster drain in Skirbeck. The cost of the

[24] Hunt, 'Horncastle Navigation Engineers', p. 10; Skempton and Wright, 'Early Members of the Smeatonian Society', p. 27; G. Jackson, *The Trade and Shipping of Eighteenth-Century Hull*, York, 1975, pp. 52–53; idem, *Grimsby and the Haven Company*, Grimsby, 1971, p. 8.

[25] Jackson, *Grimsby and the Haven Company*, pp. 17, 22.

[26] Page, *History of the Ancholme Navigation*, pp. 2, 6.

Figure 6   *Hospital bridge across the Maud Foster drain at Skirbeck, Boston; cast at Butterley iron works, Derbyshire, 1811. In the background can be seen the Maud Foster windmill built in 1819.* (Drawn by M. Clark for this volume, from a photograph)

Figure 7   *An 1817 view of Gainsborough bridge (built 1790); sails of oil mills visible in the background*

E

drainage and enclosure was borne by selling nearly one third of the area, totalling 13,956 acres, for £596,060 between 1802 and 1810. Boston bankers, merchants and solicitors such as Edward Wilford and Thomas Fydell purchased nearly five square miles of fenland but other areas were purchased by Samuel Thornton (767 acres), Lord Carrington and Thomas Thompson of Smith's Bank (604 acres) and John Rennie himself (376 acres). New townships such as Carrington and Thornton-le-Fen were created on the sold lands and the rest was divided among adjoining parishes whose people had common rights over the fens, Boston receiving 1,330 acres. The final drainage works were completed in November 1813 and great areas were converted to the growing of cereals, which could be moved by boat along the drains to Boston and Hob Hole sluice.[27]

The construction of the Slea and Horncastle navigations and other improvements put more traffic on the Witham and the Fossdyke. In January 1810 it was reported that the tolls on the Witham had risen to £3,000 and in 1811 those on the Fossdyke were £5,159. By an act of 1808 a new company took over the Witham navigation and carried out improvements recommended by Rennie in 1807, including new locks at Stamp End and Bardney and the removal of old ones. Between March and September 1819 tolls on the Witham exceeded £4,100 and in 1825 those on the Fossdyke were over £8,000.[28]

The waterway and drainage works from 1790 onwards brought increasing commerce to Boston and the town embarked on a vigorous period of growth. In 1806–8 a new cast-iron town bridge was erected in the centre of Boston, the first cast-iron bridge designed by Rennie. The corporation did not carry out Rennie's 1802 proposal to straighten the haven between Boston and the Wash but a survey of the harbour in 1811 by Netlam and Francis Giles on his behalf led to an act of 1812 and the works were carried out in 1814–15. This involved the removal of projecting jetties and the construction of brick wharfs following the curved line of the river to give a clear flow for the silt-laden water. Packhouse quay and Doughty quay were improved, many warehouses were built up to the water's edge and in 1817 the corporation built the London warehouse (shown in plate III) on Packhouse quay, incorporating new offices for pilots and wharfingers. After the canals of the 1790s had been completed no others were built in Lincolnshire although several were proposed. In the first decade of the century these

[27] H. C. Darby, *The Draining of the Fens*, Cambridge, 2nd edn 1956, pp. 233, 235.
[28] *SM*, 19 January 1810; Boyes and Russell, *Canals*, pp. 258, 265.

included schemes affecting Market Rasen, Alford and Stamford, and in the 1820s other schemes were proposed for Alford, Market Rasen, Wragby, Holbeach and Stamford, followed in 1833 by a proposed trunk route between Grantham and Sleaford to connect Boston to the midlands. The 1820s also saw efforts to complete Rennie's proposed improvements to the Ancholme and Boston haven, acts being obtained in 1825 and 1827 respectively on the advice of his son Sir John Rennie. The works on the Ancholme included the new bridge at Brigg (1827) and the fine suspension bridge at Horkstow (1834), one of the oldest surviving bridges of this type.[29]

NEW BRIDGES

The road improvements of the reign of George III included the construction of several bridges funded, like the turnpikes, by levying tolls to pay off the initial cost of construction and subsequent maintenance expenses. In 1793 a new turnpike trust was created to make a new road from Sleaford to Tattershall ferry and erect a bridge there, which was completed in 1795, but the other important bridges were near the edge of the county. Access to the north of England was greatly improved by the opening of a bridge across the Trent at Gainsborough in 1790 (fig. 7), the first bridge to be built below Newark. Lincoln corporation had opposed proposals for a Gainsborough bridge in 1786, fearing that the piers would impede navigation, but an act was passed the following year. At the same time roads were turnpiked from the west end of the bridge to East Retford and to the Bawtry–Hainton road at Gringley-on-the-Hill. The bridge designed by William Weston still remains, although widened; the tolls were let for £815 in 1814, £1,055 in 1827 and between £700 and £900 in subsequent years. In the 1780s it had also been proposed to bridge the river at Dunham, the nearest Trent ferry to Lincoln, and this scheme was revived in 1827 after the turnpike road between Lincoln and Dunham had been improved. An act was obtained in 1830 and the bridge opened in 1832; it was designed by George Leather (1787–1870) of Leeds and stood until 1978.[30]

[29] M. J. T. Lewis and N. R. Wright, *Boston as a Port*, Lincoln, 1974, p. 42; *SM*, 17 May 1805; Boyes and Russell, *Canals*, pp. 240, 296, 303; Hadfield, *Canals of the East Midlands*, p. 97; Page, *History of the Ancholme Navigation*, p. 7; Thompson, *Boston*, pp. 365–66.

[30] M. J. T. Lewis, *Dunham Bridge — A Memorial History*, Lincoln, 1978, pp. 10–12, 14, 16, 49; Hill, *Georgian Lincoln*, pp. 136, 196, 210; N. Pevsner and J. Harris, *The Buildings of England — Lincolnshire*, London, 1964, p. 245.

Travel in south-east Lincolnshire was improved by the construction of roads and bridges across the wide estuaries of the Welland and the Nene. The provisions of the Welland Improvement Act of 1794 for 'making a public way over Fosdyke Wash' were not exercised but in 1811 a new act formed a company to build a bridge over the river at Fosdyke and erect an embankment across the rest of the half-mile wide estuary, with a road along the top. John Rennie had designed a wooden bridge with two leaves in the centre which could be raised for the passage of ships sailing up to Spalding, but a public house and warehouses were erected at Fosdyke bridge for vessels stopping there. Work on the bridge and embankment started in 1812 and was completed in 1815 at a cost of about £20,000.[31]

In 1826 a new turnpike trust was formed for the road from Fosdyke bridge north to the Boston–Donington turnpike at Swineshead and an act of the following year authorized improvement of the Nene outfall through Cross Keys Wash. This scheme was a larger version of the Fosdyke Wash project, including diversion of the river into a new channel, erection of a bridge designed by Thomas Telford and casting up an embankment across the rest of the estuary, also known as Sutton Wash, allowing the land behind to be reclaimed for agriculture. The bridge and new river channel were opened in June 1830 and the embankment was completed a year later. On 4 July 1831 the *Union* from Norwich to Newark was the first stage-coach to cross the embankment, and was met by a great crowd at the Lincolnshire end; the opening of the Cross Keys bridge also led to a considerable improvement in the use of the Fosdyke bridge since both were on the old route known as Washway Road.[32]

In the opening years of the nineteenth century a few short roads were added to the turnpike network in Lincolnshire, that from Louth to Grimsby in 1803 (despite opposition from Grimsby) and from Grantham to Bridge End in 1804, but a proposal to turnpike the busy Grantham–Lincoln road in 1815 was unsuccessful.[33]

From the mid 1820s traffic on the turnpike roads grew and trusts sought additional sources of income to pay for further improvements. In a few cases, as at Gainsborough and Louth, the

[31] Wheeler, *A History of the Fens*, pp. 437, 449; M. Searle, *Turnpikes and Toll-Bars*, London, 1930, p. 331; Boyes and Russell, *Canals*, p. 250.
[32] Boyes and Russell, *Canals*, pp. 213, 215; *SM*, 9 July 1830, 8 July 1831, 12 September 1834.
[33] Gillett, *Grimsby*, p. 206; Honeybone, *Grantham*, p. 56.

funds of local charities were used. J. L. McAdam, surveyor of the Bristol trust, developed a superior type of road surface, well-drained and flat. Following complaints by the Post Office and carriage owners the Brigg trust dismissed their surveyor in 1822 and appointed 'one who was familiar with McAdam's principles' and the trust for the Rutland section of the Great North Road employed McAdam himself until 1827 when they sought someone who was less in demand and could give more attention to their road. Several trusts made efforts to reduce the gradients on hills such as Casterton near Stamford and Canwick near Lincoln. During the 1820s Thomas Telford's assistants spent eight years surveying the Great North Road from London to Edinburgh with a view to its comprehensive improvement, following the example of the Holyhead road. The plans of the parliamentary committee as revealed in April 1830 would have omitted Stamford, Colsterworth and Grantham from the new route but the government would not grant the necessary funds and the scheme was not carried out.[34]

THE COACHING AGE

The improvements in roads produced by the turnpike trusts made it possible for horse-drawn coaches to be used more extensively, and by 1769 a coach could travel from Stamford to London via Royston in a day, the fare being 16s. for travelling inside the coach; by 1776 the journey from London to Edinburgh could be done in four days. Regular coach services from Lincoln, Louth and Newark to London started about 1784, when the fare from Lincoln to London was £1 11s. 6d. inside and 15s. 9d. outside. By 1791 coaches were running between London and the Humber ferry at Barton, taking three days for the journey, and by 1800 the *Perseverance* ran three times a week between Boston and London. Goods wagons were travelling twice a week from Lincoln to London in 1787, the journey taking about a week, and they could also carry a few passengers. The growth of coach traffic on the Lincoln to Peterborough road led to the erection of the large Greyhound inn at Folkingham.[35]

[34] Rogers, *Lincolnshire*, p. 76; Bagwell, *Transport Revolution*, p. 40; White, 'The Brigg Turnpike Trust', p. 6; Ruddock and Pearson, p. 35; L. T. C. Rolt, *Thomas Telford*, London, 1958, p. 133; *SM*, 16 April 1830, 24 January 1834.
[35] N. C. Birch, *Stamford — An Industrial History*, Lincoln, 1972, p. 28; T. K. Derry and T. I. Williams, *A Short History of Technology*, Oxford, 1960, p. 433; Hill, *Georgian Lincoln*, p. 122; Ruddock and Pearson, p. 35; A. A. D'Orley, *The Humber Ferries*, Knaresborough, 1968, p. 22.

The mail was carried by post boys on horseback until 1784 when the first Royal Mail coach in the kingdom started running between London and Bath. These coaches carried not only the mail but also a number of passengers. They spread to other routes and in 1786 appeared on the Great North Road through Lincolnshire, but not until the Lincoln and London Mail commenced on 5 April 1801, running through Peterborough and Sleaford, did they penetrate further into the county. This service was later extended to the Hull ferry at Barton-on-Humber with a stop at Spital-in-the-Street (fig. 8), but it was discontinued between 1816–22 because of the post-war recession. A second Royal Mail route opened on 5 July 1807 when coaches ran through Boston to Louth, mail being forwarded to other places by the post boys. The horses and coachmen for the Royal Mail coaches were supplied by contractors; but the coaches and armed guards were provided by the postmaster general. The guard was in charge and he sat aloft at the back, resplendent in gold-frogged scarlet coat and gilt-banded top hat, with his long horn in its wicker basket by his side. The mail coaches, light, well-sprung vehicles in their elegant livery of maroon and black coachwork and wheels of post-office red, were the elite service and they set the standard for the other, cheaper, stage-coaches. The proprietors of the other stage-coaches were usually the landlords of the principal inns at which the coach called, such as Daniel Jackson of the Peacock inn, Boston. The mail coaches offered a daily service and many of the other coaches soon changed to the same frequency. [36]

Improvements in coach design allowed the number of outside passengers to be safely increased from four to twelve in 1806, though on mail coaches it was still restricted to three. By about 1820 it was quicker to travel by fast coach than on horseback and thereafter the individual rider was much less frequently seen on the road. Between 1820 and 1845 many other coach services were developed until the opening of railways led to their gradual withdrawal. During the peak years of the coaching era more mail coaches were introduced, including one in 1827 from Louth to Grimsby and another by 1836 from Louth to Sheffield. [37]

Even before the Louth mail coach started there were two stage-coaches running from London to Spilsby and beyond, the *Old Boston Coach* being challenged by the *Lord Nelson* in 1806, but coach

---

[36] Bagwell, *Transport Revolution*, p. 47; Ruddock and Pearson, p. 36; E. Vale, *The Mail-Coach Men of the late Eighteenth Century*, Newton Abbot, 1967, p. 51.
[37] Bagwell, op. cit., p. 49.

Figure 8 *Changing horses at the Spital inn, Spital-in-the-Street, in 1835 on the Barton-on-Humber to Lincoln turnpike road near Caenby corner*

Figure 9 *Deacon, Harrison and Co.'s fly van, which carried goods between London, Stamford, Grantham, Leeds and other towns, as illustrated in the Stamford Mercury in 1822*

services were cut back in the post-war depression. At one time the only coaches into the county were the daily London–Barton mail coach through Lincoln and another three times a week to Nottingham but by the end of 1824 Lincoln alone had two daily coaches to London and Hull, two to Nottingham, one daily to Manchester via Gainsborough, one daily coach to Horncastle and Louth, and the *Champion* to Grantham. In the following years other coaches were added, many operated by London proprietors who built up large numbers. [38]

The Great North Road was the busiest road in the county, and it was an important source of support to Grantham and Stamford. In 1830, the peak year for the coaching trade, forty mail and thirty stage-coaches passed daily through Stamford. [39]

Several coaches also ran to the Humber at Barton. The main ferry on the river ran between there and Hull, and the crown manor of Barton and Hull corporation ran rival services on this route until 1796 when the corporation leased the rival service and sub-let it to the lessee of their own ferry. In 1806 the service was carried by not less than four large boats of forty-five tons burthen and several smaller ones. This was the longest Humber crossing but in the early nineteenth century the availability of coach connections for those who wished to travel beyond the Humber area gave it an advantage over the shorter crossings. In 1814 the steam paddle sloop *Caledonia* started running between Hull and Gainsborough and was soon followed by other steam boats on the Humber. The speed of the steam boats greatly affected some of the coach routes, and for a time a steamer service from Hull connected with coaches at Thorne on the Stainforth and Keadby canal. [40]

Directly opposite Hull was a creek in a remote part of Barrow parish which since 1803 had become known as New Holland. By 1825 a ferry ran from there to Hull and that year the New Holland proprietors purchased the site; they built the Yarborough Arms near the landing in 1826. They started running coaches to the ferry in 1828 but the development of New Holland was impeded by lack of a good road. In 1831 an attempt to run a rival service on the Barton–Hull route and so force down prices on the ferry operated by the unreformed Hull corporation was short-lived, but it stimulated the New Holland proprietors to complete their plans,

[38] I. Faulds, 'The White Hart Inn, Spilsby', *Lincolnshire Life*, 13 no. 4 (1973), p. 29; *SM*, 1 October 1824.
[39] Birch, *Stamford — An Industrial History*, p. 28.
[40] D'Orley, *Humber Ferries*, pp. 21, 23, 25.

purchase a small steamer *Magna Charta* in 1832, enlarge the Yarborough Arms and improve their road to the turnpike inland of Barton. In 1836 the mail coaches were transferred to New Holland and by 1848 no coaches at all ran to Barton waterside.[41]

Coaches from the ferry at New Holland included the *Pelham* to Boston, the *Magna Charta* to Nottingham via Lincoln and the *Age*, which at first connected with Boston and was later changed to Lincoln. During the 1820s and 1830s other short services started within Lincolnshire and to towns in adjacent counties, building up an elaborate network of connections.

Although the number of coaches increased greatly during these years the fare placed them beyond the means of most inhabitants and the numbers catered for were small. The great majority of people would travel very rarely, other than to and from market, and then either on foot or in a slow-moving cart. In 1836 the *Perseverance* coach from Boston to London carried four inside passengers and eleven outside, and other carriages from the town took even fewer. In 1844 the fare from Boston to Nottingham was 12s. inside and 8s. outside. The villages around each market town were served by thirty or so carriers who provided a local service on market days. By the 1840s there were also a few omnibus services, including one operated by the spirited Miss Ann Parker of Grimsby which ran at stated periods of the week between Grimsby and Caistor, and Grimsby and Louth. There were several conveyances between Grimsby and Cleethorpes.[42]

Goods traffic did not increase as much on the roads as passenger traffic because goods could use the improved and extended waterway system. In the eighteenth and early nineteenth centuries the turnpike roads, canals and coastal shipping somewhat complemented each other, each taking a different part of the traffic. The canals and shipping carried bulky low-value goods over long distances while the roads were used by passengers, the mail and goods for which speed was essential (see fig. 9). Practically all mail and stage-coaches kept to the turnpikes, the main exception being the direct road from Lincoln to Grantham.[43]

By the late 1830s the turnpike trusts were at their peak, both in the extent of roads they controlled and their income. The takings at most toll-gates in Lincolnshire continued to rise until the early

[41] A. Harris, 'The Humber Ferries and the Rise of New Holland', *East Midland Geographer*, 15 (1961), pp. 11–19.
[42] N. R. Wright, *The Railways of Boston*, Boston, 1971, p. 4; *SM*, 9 May 1845.
[43] Bagwell, *Transport Revolution*, p. 57; Albert, *Turnpike Road System*, p. 196.

1840s, except those on the Great North Road and the main Lincoln–Peterborough road. In the mid 1830s four of the six Lincolnshire gates with takings of over £1,000 p.a. were on the Great North
Road, the other two being on the main entrances into Lincoln and
Boston. Five gates took between £500 and £1,000, one of them
being on the North Road and another at Cross Keys Wash, but
most took less than £500 and the one next to Langrett (Langrick)
ferry took only £42 p.a. All roads around Stamford were turnpiked
and in 1834 the total takings were £4,062, while around Grantham
only £3,053 was raised. Tolls on roads entering Boston totalled
£2,465 while at Lincoln £2,000 was produced but in the remote
north-east less than £1,000 was received at Louth and only £564 on
the two roads into Grimsby.

As railways were opened road traffic declined and turnpike
takings fell. An act of 1841 allowed turnpikes to be subsidized out of
the parish rates and this provoked the violent 'Rebecca' riots in
south Wales, echoes of which reached Lincolnshire in July 1843
when walls were knocked down on the Great North Road near
Stamford. The trustees of the Lincolnshire section of the Great
North Road tried to use the act in 1846, when the magistrates at
Spittlegate made an order for the parishes through which it ran to
pay £26 per mile, but this was quashed on an appeal to Bourne
quarter sessions and in January 1847 the mortgagees of the road
seized the tolls and the repair of the road fell back on the parishes. In
contrast the trustees of the Rutland section of road managed to clear
their debts and reduce their tolls in 1853.[44]

After the arrival of the railways most turnpikes went into quiet
decline before being abolished about thirty years later. Despite their
shortcomings, with inactive trustees, corrupt toll-collectors, and
evasive travellers, they had managed in some places to provide the
fine new surface needed for the heyday of the coaching age. On
these roads a horse could haul three times as much as on an
unmetalled road. By 1832 the mail coach took only forty-two and a
half hours from Edinburgh to London. Even between 1820 and
1830 the journey from Grantham to London was reduced from
fifteen and a quarter to twelve hours.[45]

[44] SM, 7 July 1843, 29 January 1847, 8 October 1852.
[45] Derry and Williams, Short History of Technology, p. 433; SM, 16 April 1830.

CHAPTER 3

GEORGIAN COMMERCE AND INDUSTRY

THE improvement of roads and waterways during the eighteenth century was only part of a vigorous movement towards an industrial economy, characterized by greatly increased output of coal, iron and textiles, by new processes and machinery, and by the factory system. These trends, slow to gain momentum at first, so accelerated after 1760 and wrought such changes that the term 'Industrial Revolution' was later coined to describe them; yet overnight revolution it was not, and several generations passed before society lost its primarily agricultural base. In Lincolnshire, although it long remained free of heavy industry (which concentrated on the coalfields) and the bulk of the population remained rural, the effects of the revolution were considerable. The industrial districts of the east midlands, Yorkshire and even Lancashire clamoured for the food and wool it produced. Inside the county, too, there were industrial changes. Easier transport by water encouraged specialized industries in appropriate areas; and since Lincolnshire lacked coal and had only limited water power, some industries declined as its needs were met from elsewhere, while others using local materials such as brick clay expanded to serve a wider market, and yet more arose to meet new demands inside the county. In this last class fall the local foundries which were soon to develop into a major industry.

The coal measures of Nottinghamshire and south Yorkshire slope eastwards under Lincolnshire, and although occasional trial bores during the eighteenth and nineteenth centuries found some isolated nodules of coal no economic seams were found at workable depths. As early as 1722 a bore was made in Blue Hill near Spilsby and during the 1770s the duke of Rutland had trials conducted in the vale of Belvoir but the best known incident was John Parkinson's excavation on the moor near Woodhall in 1811, where the mineral properties of the water which filled the abandoned shaft later led to the establishment of Woodhall Spa.[1]

COMMERCE

After 1750 the population of England and Wales began to increase dramatically and from about 1780 Britain started to import corn, as well as increasing agricultural production at home. More than half of the two hundred and fifty enclosure acts affecting Lincolnshire were passed between 1750 and 1780 and the drainage of fenland and enclosure of commons was followed by a gradual increase in arable farming and a decline of pasturage in Lincolnshire. Cattle and sheep could be moved on the hoof but grain had to be carried in wagons and ships; the improvements to the county's waterway system and Boston harbour allowed cereals more easily to be sent inland to Yorkshire and the midlands, or round the coast to London.

Scottish cattle were ferried across the Trent and driven through Lincolnshire to be fattened in the fens, or in Norfolk or Suffolk, for the London market. In the mid 1830s it was said that thirty-four drovers took 182,000 sheep a year from southern Lincolnshire to London while a further fifty-two men drove 26,520 oxen over the same route. Inns on the fen edges, such as the Leeds Gate at Coningsby and the Ferry Boat at Langrick, offered special accommodation for drovers. By the late eighteenth century there was also a considerable traffic westwards across the Trent as Lincolnshire became the granary and the stockyard of the rising industrial areas of the West Riding, Nottinghamshire, Derbyshire, and even to some extent Lancashire. In 1755 because of the shortage of corn in Derby large quantities had been bought in Lincoln and sent by boat via the Fossdyke, the Trent and the Derwent. That market in grain was to expand considerably so that, in 1804, corn was being sent by canal across the Pennines to feed the Lancashire cotton workers. In 1819 over 40,000 tons of corn, much of it harvested in Lincolnshire, were sent over that route. The Yorkshire demand for corn was also being met in the 1850s from Lincolnshire via the Aire and Calder. In 1830 it was said that the meat consumption of Wakefield, Sheffield and Manchester had long been mainly supplied from the markets of Lincoln and Boston. Much of this livestock traffic crossed the Trent or the Humber by ferry or took a long detour to Newark before other bridges were built at Gainsborough and Dunham. In return Lincolnshire imported coal, in the late eighteenth century from

[1] Brears, p. 185; Honeybone, *Grantham*, p. 117.

Yorkshire and later from the developing Nottinghamshire/ Derbyshire coalfield.[2]

The waterways and roads converging on Boston brought to its granaries and quays the produce of the surrounding fens, which was then loaded into ships moored in the centre of the town. In 1811 Boston sent 360,699 quarters of oats to London, more than one third of the total into London that year. In December 1813 it was said that the trade and commerce of Boston had of late 'much increased, is increasing and will considerably increase', following the enclosure of over 40,000 acres of fens, principally occupied as corn land. Throughout the first half of the nineteenth century Boston remained the main commercial town in Lincolnshire and was aptly described as 'Boston for Business'. The growth of trade brought vigour to the town and prosperity to many merchants such as Edward Wilford (b. 1767). Large new granaries were erected beside the haven, invading the select area of South Square and extending into Skirbeck Quarter on the west bank, and the London warehouse (plate III) was erected on Packhouse quay. On the northern edge of Boston the hamlet of Witham Town developed around the Grand Sluice.[3]

The opening of the Louth navigation allowed that town to develop as a small port, to the further detriment of Saltfleet, but its inland position restricted the size of vessels and amount of traffic it could handle. Thirty years later Louth merchants were involved in the Grimsby haven scheme but the trade of Louth flourished until the middle of the century. In 1826 the town had more coal and corn merchants than Grimsby and as many general merchants and rope-makers. As a centre for the collection and export of local produce and the distribution of coal and other imports Louth had the advantage of being at the hub of several turnpike roads.

Water transport facilitated the easier movement of heavy and bulky goods such as coal, wool and grain, commodities which feature in the shield carved on the Sleaford navigation office (fig. 10); warehouses and coalyards were established at the wharfs of Sleaford and Grantham and the Riverhead in Louth as well as around the Grand Sluice at Boston, and Brayford Pool and Waterside in Lincoln. Close by were ropewalks, boatbuilders and sail

[2] P. S. Bagwell, The Transport Revolution from 1770, London, 1974, p. 120; Brears, p. 94; M. J. T. Lewis, Dunham Bridge — A Memorial History, Lincoln, 1978, pp. 9, 12, 13; Boyes and Russell, Canals, p. 264.

[3] H. Porter, Boston 1800 to 1835, Lincoln, 1941, p. 6; idem, Boston 1800 to 1835, II, Lincoln, 1942, p. 88; Pigot and Co., Directory, London, c. 1830, p. 509; D. N. Robinson, The Book of Louth, Buckingham, 1979, p. 61.

Figure 10 *Coat of arms of the Sleaford Navigation Company. It features a stook of corn, the primitive pit-head windlass of a coal mine, a river boat and scales like those in plate II, all symbolizing the commerce of the waterway. The motto is taken from the latin: 'Leve fit quod bene fertur opus'.* (Drawn by M. Clark for this volume, from a photograph of carving on Navigation Office at Sleaford)

makers and industrial premises such as corn mills, breweries, maltings and gas works. Bishopbridge, away from any town, developed similarly after it became the head of the Ancholme navigation. The Trent carried the growing traffic of the midlands past Lincolnshire and from 1802 to 1808 there was a factory at Brampton in Torksey where William Billingsley decorated pottery brought in the white from Staffordshire. The factory was not ready until July 1805 and during that time Billingsley probably worked at a shop in Silver Street, Lincoln. The business was not a financial success and on 15 April 1808 he secretly moved to south Wales.[4]

The waterways were also used by travellers and local people going to market and the Barge inn at Boston Grand Sluice was built on a similar scale to the coaching inns of the town centre. Horse-drawn packets started service on the Fossdyke in 1805 and on the

[4] C. L. Exley, *A History of the Torksey and Mansfield China Factories*, Lincoln, 1970, pp. 9, 15, 20, 52.

Witham in 1809, and steam powered boats appeared in 1814 when a service started between Gainsborough and Hull. In 1816 the Lincoln-built *Witham* started a regular steam packet service between there and Boston and by July 1817 a second steam packet was on that route. Owners of some sailing packets resented the new competition and in 1819 Nathaniel Clayton Snr was fined for running his boat against the *Favourite* steam packet, damaging the steamer. However by 1826 Clayton was master of the *Countess of Warwick*, the third steamer running between Boston and Lincoln. Ten years later William Howden of Boston built the first iron boats for use on the Witham, launching the *Celerity* in 1836 for John West, though by 1842 Nathaniel Clayton Jnr (plate VI) was its master.[5] There were also regular boat services along the navigable drains of south Lincolnshire, between Boston and the scattered hamlets along the drain banks. In 1856 there were fourteen market packet boats which converged on Bargate bridge every Wednesday and Saturday from as far away as Revesby and Hagnaby, and small craft from Donington and Holland Fen congregated at the Black Sluice.

Unsuccessful proposals for railways between Boston and London in 1836 led local people to establish a steam-boat service for cattle between the port and the capital, in conjunction with the St George's company of Hull. They constructed a 'dock' in the haven next to Hob Hole sluice for use by the *Scotia* and started trading in June 1837, but their efforts were unsuccessful and steam traffic was for long dependant on William Teal's *Forager* sailing to Hull once a week.[6] Warehouses and wharves were built beside the new Nene outfall at Sutton bridge and a large village was developed there by William Skelton (1788–1869), steward of the large estate owned by Guy's Hospital, but conversely the creation of Hob Hole drain diverted water away from the Steeping river and exacerbated the decline of Wainfleet as a port.

The growth in port activity and increase in population at Grimsby after the construction of the new dock was not as great as had been optimistically forecast. The town lacked an existing group of merchants or a potential raw material trade and had no transport links to more distant manufacturing areas. Many people regretted building warehouses or leasing land in the 'new town' and wharves

[5] Ruddock and Pearson, p. 24; Stark, *Gainsborough*, p. 209; N. C. Birch, *Waterways and Railways of Lincoln and the Lower Witham*, Lincoln, 1968; SM, 22 April 1836.

[6] N. R. Wright, *The Railways of Boston*, Boston, 1971, p. 2; Porter, *Boston 1800 to 1835*, II, p. 80; M. J. T. Lewis and N. R. Wright, *Boston as a Port*, Lincoln, 1974, p. 11.

along the eastern side of the dock changed hands quickly in the first few years of the century. Gabriel Neve, originally a Louth timber merchant, erected a boiling house on the Humber bank in 1804 and tried to establish a whaling industry in Grimsby but when its vessels were lost in 1813 and 1821 they were not replaced.[7]

Fishing was important in Boston and Cleethorpes at the turn of the century, but not at Grimsby until after 1850. At Cleethorpes in the 1820s about twenty boats and fifty men went fishing regularly for oysters on the Yorkshire and Lincolnshire coasts, in the English Channel and around the Isle of Wight. On their return the oysters were deposited in pits which were overflowed by the tide, and large quantities were sent weekly to the markets of Hull, York, Leeds and Sheffield. Passengers and light or perishable goods could travel more quickly by coach than by water and in 1831 Boston shrimps were sent by coach to London, the cost of their carriage coming to over £1,000 (see plate VII). The former traffic in wildfowl, geese and cranberries declined as the fens were enclosed and put to more intensive production.[8]

The coach services which developed along the improved roads brought more travellers into Lincolnshire and allowed its coastal sand dunes and wide beaches to become better known by the leisured classes. Inns had to change to cope with the increasing traffic, adding stables and coach houses as well as accommodation for the passengers. The George Hotel in Grantham was built in 1780, the George at St Martin's, Stamford was enlarged between 1785 and 1792 at a cost of over £1,830, and the pretentious Stamford Hotel was built in 1810–13 though it remained empty until 1825. By 1826 there were more people running hotels and taverns in Grantham than were engaged in any other single trade. In the 1790s Thomas Hawkes said that Spalding was 'much frequented by those who come from Leicestershire etc. for sea bathing at Freestone, Skegness or Cleythorpes', and by 1826 Freiston Shore and Skegness each had two hotels while Cleethorpes and Saltfleet had one each in addition to lodgings in cottages.[9]

Travellers by stage-coach could get to Boston more easily than to the North Sea coast and machines were provided for bathing in the haven at Skirbeck as shown in plate VII as well as at Freiston Shore on the Wash itself. In 1842 J. Parrott of the Pudding Pie House,

[7] G. Jackson, *Grimsby and the Haven Company*, Grimsby, 1971, pp. 38, 43, 47.

[8] Porter, *Boston 1800 to 1835*, p. 49; White, *Directory*, 1826, pp. 77, 102.

[9] B. Street, *Historical Notes on Grantham*, Grantham, 1857, p. 68; RCHM, *Stamford*, pp. 105, 135; Honeybone, *Grantham*, p. 56; N. R. Wright, *Spalding — An Industrial History*, Lincoln, 1973, p. 48.

Skirbeck, rebuilt the bathing house on the old site 'contiguous to the sea' which had been 'well patronized' during the previous fifty years. The Coach and Horses at Freiston Shore was kept by Mr and Mrs Plummer from 1798, and when Richard Fowke of Leicester left after a visit in 1805 there were thirty-two visitors there, but there could be as many as a hundred and twenty. In 1821 a coach service ran three days a week from Nottingham to Boston, 'where gentlemen might have saddle horses and ladies a horse and gig and careful drivers to any of the shore houses at Freiston' and within five years there was a daily coach service between Boston and Freiston Shore. By the 1840s there was a regular two-day race meeting each summer and it was still popular in the 1860s.[10]

For those who wished to visit the North Sea the nearest resort was Skegness, which had bathing machines by 1805. The Vine was an old hotel which had 'commodious caravans, with docile horses and careful attendants' and by 1826 there was a new hotel taken over in 1830 by J. Hildred, who ran a daily coach service to the Peacock in Boston. In 1821 the Dolphin Hotel was built at Cleethorpes and by 1844 there was a coach three times a week to Lincoln. Some years before 1826 a hotel was built above the beach at Saltfleet and Sutton-on-Sea was also an 'improving bathing-place'. Public interest in mineral water cures was reflected by the erection of baths at Woodhall near Horncastle in 1836, and a bath-house at Braceborough near Stamford in 1841. By 1838 there were so many visitors taking the waters of Woodhall Spa that Thomas Hotchkin erected the Victoria Hotel with a suite of cold, warm and shower baths, a pump room and reading rooms, and grounds laid out with shrubberies and serpentine walks. In July 1843 a coach started running daily between Horncastle and Skegness, so that the afflicted might partake of both sea bathing and mineral waters, but the real development of the spa came after 1875. By the middle of the nineteenth century Lincolnshire resorts could still count their visitors each summer only in hundreds; not until the 1870s and 1880s did railways bring massive crowds.[11]

MERCHANTS AND BANKERS

Enclosures, drainage works, and canals were expensive undertakings but their completion and the consequential growth of

[10] SM, 3 June 1842, 17 June 1825; H. Porter, Boston 1800 to 1835 continued to 1868, Lincoln, 1943, p. 229; Lincolnshire Echo, 29 November 1974.
[11] SM, 16 July 1830, 26 August 1836, 11 August 1837, 23 June 1845, 14 July 1843; White, Directory, 1826, p. 168; 1856, pp. 753, 872.

F

commerce brought great rewards, as the Ellisons of Sudbrooke had found. Many local merchants and lawyers made fortunes during the reign of George III, particularly in Boston which was the main commercial town. During this time the dominant family were the Fydells, headed by Richard (1710–80) and his son Thomas (1740–1812). Thomas was involved in all aspects of Boston's affairs but the family were rising into the gentry and after 1812 his son Samuel Richard (1771–1868) became an absentee landlord, living on a country estate in Rutland.

For fifty years after 1780 all events in Grimsby were affected by the contest between George Tennyson (1750–1835), inheritor of the Clayton interest, and the ambitious Charles Anderson-Pelham (1749–1823) of Brocklesby, the main landowner in north-east Lincolnshire, who was created Baron Yarborough in 1794. Tennyson's second son Charles (1784–1861) pursued a political career and was a privy councillor from 1832, adding d'Eyncourt to his name and enlarging Bayons Manor to a fantastic moated Gothic castle. His nephew Alfred Tennyson (1809–92), poet laureate in succession to Wordsworth in 1850, was created a baron in 1884. [12]

Drainage, enclosure, turnpikes and other projects generated work for solicitors and land agents such as Samuel Tunnard (1750–1818) of Boston and Benjamin Handley of Sleaford. Corn merchants and maltsters such as Samuel Sandars of Gainsborough also prospered and invested in breweries, maltings and other industrial enterprises. Even John Grundy the engineer engaged in commerce; adjoining his house on the Welland bank in Spalding he owned warehouses, timber yards and an oil mill. He also owned the sloop *The Good Intent*, which voyaged as far as the Baltic for timber. [13]

Boston's commercial activities were helped in 1754 when William Garfit (1700–83), a Boston merchant, opened the first bank in Lincolnshire; at the same time Joseph Pease (1688–1778) of Hull opened the first bank in Yorkshire, which could also serve north Lincolnshire. It was to be twenty-one years before another bank opened in Lincolnshire, but during the late eighteenth century several prosperous merchants, lawyers and brewers undertook some banking functions and these formed the basis of many banks founded in Lincolnshire between 1780 and 1810; in some cases the

---

[12] Jackson, *Grimsby and the Haven Company*, pp. 3, 4; A. Wheatcroft, *The Tennyson Album*, London, 1980, pp. 13, 16.
[13] J. H. Hopper, 'Lincolnshire Worthies No. 6 — The Two John Grundys', *Lincolnshire Life*, 20 no. 3 (1980), p. 25.

banking business got quite large without being separated from the merchants' other activities.

The second bank in Lincolnshire was opened in 1775 by Abel Smith of Nottingham, Richard Ellison, lessee of the Fossdyke and John Brown of Lincoln. Brown, a mercer and ex-mayor of Lincoln, was already Ellison's agent in the city. Garfit, Claypon and Co. of Boston (as the firm became in 1774) and Smith, Ellison and Co. of Lincoln were the main banks in nineteenth-century Lincolnshire and remained independent until 1891 and 1902 respectively. By 1799 Smith, Ellison and Co. had notes worth £116,000 in circulation. Other banks were opened in Louth in 1775 and Boston in 1783 and others followed in the 1790s. Henry Gee (1761–1845) had arrived in Boston in 1781 and joined Henry Clarke to trade as merchants and brewers and, from 1783, as bankers. Later they owned a fleet of sailing ships in partnership with William Ingelow, who opened his own bank in 1805.

It was a sign of Boston's vigorous commercial activity that by 1790 there were four banks in the town and six between 1805 and 1814, a greater number than in any other Lincolnshire town. Abraham Sheath and his sons founded the Skirbeck Quarter Bank in 1789 and were also partners with others to form banks in Lincoln, Spilsby and Wisbech as well as a branch in Holbeach. Their Lincoln bank was opened in 1806 in partnership with John Steel and John Wray; apart from a previous partnership of Steel and Mackeness this was the only challenge to Smith, Ellison and Co.'s monopoly in Lincoln until the 1830s. The other three Boston bankers were also merchants and shipowners. In the 1790s banks were opened in Grantham, Stamford, Gainsborough, Sleaford and other towns, including Peacock, Handley and Co., who opened premises in Sleaford in 1792, and a Stamford bank which later became Eaton, Cayley and Co. In 1806 Peacock, Handley and Co. opened a separate bank in Newark and by 1826 had a branch in Bourne. [14]

Several merchants went into banking during the Napoleonic wars but collapsed in the face of economic difficulties. Hornby and Esdaile of Gainsborough went bankrupt as early as May 1803, Manners and Scott of Grantham closed in 1811 and Marris and Nicholson of Barton-on-Humber failed in 1812, but worse disaster occurred in 1814 when several banks went down like dominoes. Samuel Barnard's bank in Boston stopped payment on Monday 27 June 1814 and the alarm caused a run on other banks in the town and elsewhere.

[14] S. N. Davis, *Banking in Boston*, Boston, 1976, p. 16; *Holden's Directory*, London, 1805–7.

Sheaths of Boston stopped payment on 29 June and their other partnerships also collapsed; it was said that the various banks in the Sheath group had notes circulating to the value of £500,000 at the time of the collapse. Less than a week later the Stamford bank of A. W. Bellairs and Son closed, followed by Leicester and Derby banks in which they were partners and, the next day, by Edwards and Harper of Stamford. Edward Wilford of Boston survived a few more months but then he closed on 13 January 1815. Sheath's Wisbech partnership managed to pay 20s. in the pound plus three per cent interest but customers of other banks were not so fortunate. Many of the firms to survive 1815 continued in business until they were respectably amalgamated with other banks after 1890.[15]

In the depression after 1815 the need to alleviate the hardship of the working class became vital and one consequence was the Trustee Savings Bank Act of 1817 by which working men and small tradesmen could bank their savings with trustees and earn a little interest. The Lincoln Trustee Savings Bank had been set up in 1816 and by 1819 other such banks were established in ten Lincolnshire towns. The trustees were drawn from the country gentry and the professional classes and the administration was often done by employees of private banks. In the early days each savings bank was open perhaps twice a week for an hour or so in a public building such as the town hall in Barton, Louth or Gainsborough or the national school as at Lincoln and Market Rasen. After 1826 joint stock banks could be set up anywhere in England and the Stamford and Spalding Banking Co. opened premises in those towns in 1832, in 1836 adding Boston to their title. In August 1835 the Lincoln and Lindsey Banking Co. opened their head office in Lincoln and soon had branches in Louth, Horncastle, Gainsborough and Brigg; they decided not to open a branch in Grimsby as it was too far from the head office. At the same time a Hull Banking Co. opened branches throughout north Lincolnshire, including one in Lincoln in 1835, but after 1839 the Hull company withdrew from all Lincolnshire towns except Grimsby and Barton-on-Humber. The fourth joint stock bank in the county was the National Provincial, which had branches in Boston, Spalding and Long Sutton. Over the years branches of banks based in adjacent counties were opened in towns like Stamford and Grantham but not until the final years of the century did other banks penetrate deep into the county.[16]

[15] Porter, *Boston 1800 to 1835*, p. 165; *SM*, 8 July 1814.
[16] Davis, *Banking in Boston*, p. 28; Hill, *Georgian Lincoln*, p. 205; W. F. Crick and J. E. Wadsworth, *A Hundred Years of Joint Stock Banking*, London, 1936, pp. 209, 254.

Provincial banks were entitled to print their own notes, unless they had an office in London, and for most of the nineteenth century local notes would be more familiar than Bank of England notes. In December 1848 Smith, Ellison and Co. had notes worth £80,040 in circulation, more than any other private bank in England or Wales, and only six joint stock banks had a larger circulation. At the same time Garfit, Claypon and Co. were ninth in the list with a circulation of £61,036 and Peacock and Handley were thirteenth with £49,112. The two joint stock banks based in the county each had note issues of about £51,000 and other notes were circulated by Eaton, Cayley and Co. of Stamford and Hardy and Co. of Grantham.[17]

BOAT BUILDING

Many of the sailing vessels employed in the coastal and waterway traffic of Lincolnshire were built in small yards located around the Wash or the Humber and their associated waterways. Many of the yards covered less than an acre and there were often family connections between them; the labour force also moved between yards so there were scattered communities of boat-builders working in the ports and waterways around the Wash and the Humber. At different times members of the Goodwin family had yards in Spalding, Boston and Deeping St James, while in the north branches of the Wray family had yards at Burton Stather and Louth for most of the nineteenth century. The Richardsons and Keightleys were boat-builders at Boston over several generations. About 1800 new and larger yards were opened. One established at Alkborough on the Trent about 1788 moved to Burton Stather in 1800 where a slipway was built at a cost of £1,000 and houses were erected for the men; this large yard was operated by the Wray family until late in the nineteenth century.

At Grimsby the Haven Company saw the creation of shipyards as a corollary of their new dock and in July 1801 gave land to John Julius Angerstein, their principal shareholder, as a site for a dry dock. It cost him £10,000 and was ready early in 1804, but he could not find an occupier so Lord Yarborough delayed building one on his own land. In 1807 the company built a shipyard themselves but ship building failed to develop and the yards were used mainly for repairs. On 11 March 1814 two brigs were launched at Grimsby on the same day, one from Angerstein's yard and the other from the company's yard operated by Gabriel Neve, but in the previous

[17] *SM*, 29 December 1848.

thirteen years only twelve ships had been launched in Grimsby, with an average weight of fifty-two tons. In Boston ship building revived spontaneously after 1804, following a long period in the doldrums. The main yard in the town was at the end of White Horse Lane, occupied by Banks and Richardson in 1825, but two groups of small yards on the east bank of the haven were occupied by various boat-builders. Ships of 250 tons, 340 tons, 414 tons, even (in 1810) one of 600 or 700 tons were built, as well as smaller schooners and iron steamers for the Witham service. One of the principal Lincolnshire boatyards was Smiths of Gainsborough, run by John and Henry Smith in 1817 when vessels of 600 to 800 tons were said to be frequently launched there. Their craft included the steam packet *Pelham* launched in 1828 for the Hull–Grimsby service and the 77-foot iron steamer *Eclipse* launched in May 1837 for the Boston–Lincoln run.[18]

Many clinker-built sloops for the Humber and keels for the connecting waterways, up to seventy feet in length, were built around Knottingley and other places on the canal system west of Goole. There were always more keels built than sloops as the former were more suitable for the restricted widths of the inland waterways and the size of most boats came gradually to match that of the locks on the route for which they were built. The Lincoln ketches built on Brayford, for example, were slightly longer than Humber keels. Joseph Shuttleworth was established as a boat-builder in Lincoln by 1805 and on 26 May 1816 Shuttleworth and Robinson launched the *Witham*, the first steam packet to ply between Boston and Lincoln; in 1834 a dry dock was added to the yard.[19]

TEXTILE INDUSTRIES

The falling price of raw cotton and the development of new machines meant that from the 1780s cotton ceased to be a luxury, and by the early 1800s there was a general preference in all ranks of society for cotton goods rather than the wool or linen that had previously enjoyed a price advantage. A whole range of closely interlinked inventions had freed the textile industry from its medieval shackles, though it was the organization of factories powered first by water and later by steam that allowed the potential of the inventions to be realized.

[18] Jackson, *Grimsby and the Haven Company*, pp. 31, 39; *SM*, 11 March 1814, 2 May 1828, 2 June 1837; Lewis and Wright, *Boston as a Port*, p. 12; Stark, *Gainsborough*, p. 209; Gillett, *Grimsby*, p. 207.
[19] *Holden's Directory*; Ruddock and Pearson, p. 24; Hill, *Victorian Lincoln*, p. 100.

The Revd Edmund Cartwright (1743–1823), a Leicestershire rector and prebend of Lincoln Cathedral, developed the predecessor of the power loom in 1785 when he set up a cotton weaving and spinning factory in Yorkshire. In 1788 his older brother Major John Cartwright, the radical reformer, settled on his newly-acquired Brothertoft estate near Boston and also established the Revolution Mill at Retford. This was a worsted mill containing one of the first and largest steam engines in the east midlands.[20]

However the use of power in the spinning and weaving of traditional fabrics like wool and flax was more difficult and followed about twenty years behind cotton. A carding machine to prepare short wool for cloth began to be power-driven in the early 1770s in Yorkshire but in the production of both worsted and linen it was the preliminary process, the combing, which proved most difficult to mechanize. Edmund Cartwright made the first attempt to solve the problem in 1792 but it was 1827 before the first successful machine was patented in Britain. Mr Chaplin established one of Cartwright's steam-driven wool-combing machines at Raithby near Louth but 'he lost a great deal of money' and by 1797 nothing remained of it.[21]

Lincolnshire was a major source of long wool for the worsted makers of Yorkshire and East Anglia and flax was grown in the Isle of Axholme and the fens, so the growers of the county were adversely affected by the rise of cotton. Around Burton Stather people earned no more than 3d. a day in 1797 for spinning flax and weaving linen but in Holland Fen women could earn about 6d. a day for spinning it. Flax yarn from Russia was also imported into Spalding to be worked by cottage weavers. Attempts had already been made to bring workers together in factories in Lincolnshire, as when William Hornby leased Gainsborough Old Hall about 1760 and tried unsuccessfully to set up a coarse linen manufactory. Coarse linen products included sacking, canvas, sail cloth and mail bags. From 1773 until about 1780 Hussey Hall in Boston was leased by a sailmaker, and an adjacent building was occupied as a sacking factory until about 1800.[22]

In contrast to these rented premises the Newark merchants John Wriglesworth and John Jalland had by 1805 established a new

[20] D. Smith, *Industrial Archaeology of the East Midlands*, Newton Abbot, 1965, p. 95; Hill, *Georgian Lincoln*, p. 166.
[21] T. K. Derry and T. I. Williams, *A Short History of Technology*, Oxford, 1960, p. 569; Young, *General View*, p. 456.
[22] Young, *General View*, p. 456; Porter, *Boston 1800 to 1835*, II, p. 80; Stark, *Gainsborough*, p. 419; Thompson, *Boston*, p. 244.

Figure 11   *Wriglesworth, Jalland and Co.'s water-powered textile-mill at Claypole, near Newark*

four-storey brick mill (shown in fig. 11) at Claypole, just inside Lincolnshire, which in 1809 was producing sacking and sail cloth. In 1825 the Ordnance Survey identified it as a cotton mill or flax mill, but it later became a corn mill and parts of the building still remain.

In August 1813 a sacking factory was advertised to let near the Grand Sluice in Boston, consisting of a weaving shed with four looms, a heckler's shop with three sets of hecklings, a starch shop with three frames, a spinning shed and a rope or twine walk. During the 1820s and 1830s there were also manufacturers of coarse linen in Boston, beside the waterways and on the Isle of Axholme, and damask table cloths were woven in Boston, Lincoln and Stamford. In 1836 Mrs Knight established a linen factory at Stamford, which by the following April employed about seventy women and had sixteen looms at work producing drabbet, a drab twilled linen used for smock frocks. Her business did not last but Benjamin Singleton's flax business established in Lincoln by 1805 developed into oil cloth and cover making, which prospered when the railways arrived.[23]

As well as flax there was also some spinning and weaving of worsted in Lincolnshire and towards the end of the eighteenth century there were voluntary efforts to increase the production and use of wool in the county and so help the graziers. Competition

[23] *SM*, 13 August 1813, 8 July 1835, 7 April 1837.

from Scottish and Irish wool had been gradually reducing the profitability of wool growing since the 1720s but the importing of soft merino wool and the change to cotton made the situation even worse. The price of wool dropped greatly in the early 1780s and when Benjamin Kent of Boston ceased manufacturing coarse woollen or stuff goods in 1791 after nearly thirty years he was said to be the last person engaged in woollen manufacture in the town. Attempts by graziers to remove a ban on the export of wool were rejected by parliament. Few ships left the Lincolnshire or Yorkshire coast towns without having one or two sacks surreptitiously stowed away in their holds but smuggling was risky and could only move a fraction of the clip.[24]

In the early 1780s a Society for the Promotion of Industry was formed in eastern Lincolnshire under the leadership of the Revd R. G. Bowyer, vicar of Willoughby near Alford. They offered premiums to encourage young children to knit hosiery at home and set up spinning schools, supported by parish funds, for children over eight. In November 1785 the Friends of the Society of Industry inaugurated the Stuff Ball at Alford as a further encouragement to the use of wool, the ladies being requested to wear gowns of wool grown and manufactured in Lincolnshire. This soon became the leading social event in the county and was moved to the Bail of Lincoln in 1789. The availability of cheap yarn brought some weavers to the county and the society subsidized the establishment of a dyer and finisher at Louth. Their products included blankets, flannel horse cloths and stable waistcoats. At the same time the warden and six assistants of Louth promoted the establishment of a water-powered worsted mill on the river Lud. They provided the site at a nominal rent and £1,000 to cover the cost of the buildings, but it was in difficulties until the 1800s. It soon came to depend on the production of carpets and blankets rather than worsted and this was of little benefit to the graziers because the price of wool used in carpet making was lower than that of combing wool. In 1836 a steam engine was installed and the factory was said to employ over a hundred people 'at good wages' but after the corporation was reformed the carpet factory went into decline and in 1838 it employed only twelve. Despite its reduced circumstances it kept going until after 1872.[25]

[24] J. A. Perkins, *Sheep Farming in Eighteenth- and Nineteenth-Century Lincolnshire*, Lincoln, 1977, pp. 12, 19, 23; Thompson, *Boston*, p. 254; Hill, *Georgian Lincoln*, p. 117.
[25] Perkins, op. cit., pp. 24, 25, 28, 29; Hill, *Georgian Lincoln*, pp. 16, 120; *Lincolnshire Echo*, 4 November 1974.

Lincolnshire lacked coal or the great water power available in the Pennines and neither its cottage spinners and weavers nor its small mills could compete with Lancashire and the West Riding. Farmers and landowners needed more labourers as pasturage was converted to tillage and they feared that sedentary factory work might make children puny and unfit for agricultural labour. The momentum went out of the Society of Industry and in 1794 the last of the spinning schools closed.[26]

The spinning of worsted continued in several parish workhouses until the 1820s and several weavers scraped a living in the county. At Louth in 1795 the 'farmer of the poor house of industry' was a 'woolcomber and manufacturer of worsted' who employed 'some of the poor in combing wool, spinning and knitting worsted'. In 1826 George Barber, governor of Winterton workhouse, was also a stocking manufacturer. When the price of coarse Lincolnshire long wool was particularly low in 1808 George Whitworth established a factory in Caistor to make it into rope, but the factory closed when prices rose. John Parkinson established the weaving of crapes and bombazines at his new town of New Bolingbroke in 1824. By July two thousand yards of stuff had been finished off and he planned to manufacture linen as well but by January 1827 he was bankrupt and the mill closed. In 1826 there were still makers of spinning wheels in Old Bolingbroke and Swineshead and some individual weavers of flax and worsted continued on a small scale for a few decades, but during the 1830s power looms started to be introduced in the worsted mills of the West Riding and the Lincoln jersey school closed in 1831. By the 1830s cotton had clearly replaced wool and ladies at the Stuff Ball were no longer expected to appear in stuffs. In the village of Appleby the last cottage flax-weaver ceased in 1842 and most production of woollen cloth in the county had also ceased by then. Other textiles were tried but no more successfully. By 1816 George Gouger had opened a steam-powered silk-throwing factory in Stamford where he employed about three to four hundred women and children in 1822, but that ceased sometime after 1826. Attempts were made to establish the making of Nottingham lace at Stamford in 1823 and Boston about 1830.[27]

[26] Perkins, op. cit., pp. 25, 27.
[27] Ibid., pp. 25, 26, 29, 30; White, *Directory*, 1826, pp. 72, 195, 203; G. J. Fuller, 'Development of Drainage, Agriculture and Settlement in the Fens of South-East Lincolnshire during the Nineteenth Century', *East Midland Geographer*, 7 (1957), p. 11; *SM*, 17 January 1823, 9 July 1824; Derry and Williams, *Short History of Technology*, pp. 565, 566; H. E. Dudley, 'Linen Weaving at Appleby', *Lincs. Mag.*, 1 (1932–34), p. 246; W. O. Massingberd, 'Industries', in VCH, *Lincs.*, pp. 387–88.

OTHER INDUSTRIES

In the early nineteenth century the dressing of rabbit skins to line robes, tippets and muffs and to produce down for hats provided employment for most people in Brigg, employing women and girls mainly, and in 1810 the warrens around the town were said to be greater than in any other locality in England. In 1826 Brigg was still the main provincial town engaged in this trade but enclosure of the warrens quickly destroyed the industry. In January 1847 one of the two remaining furriers in the town closed his factory and although two were listed in 1856 the trade was extinct by 1872. The growing of woad for use as a dye and mordant required processing in woad mills and there were a few of these on Lincolnshire farms at different times. Major Cartwright built one on his Brothertoft estate towards the close of the eighteenth century, which had the refinement of water access, and later there were ones on Tattershall Road, Boston and near St Nicholas's church at Skirbeck. The shell of a later one still remains at Algarkirk. [28]

Even after the enclosure of the fens some geese were still kept and in 1826 there were still feather and quill merchants in Boston, Spalding and Stamford. Feathers for beds needed purifying and from about 1830 Timothy Anderson had premises in Bridge Street, Boston where the drying room was heated to 90–120 degrees. The smell from this process was a great annoyance to the neighbourhood and in April 1842 Anderson moved to new premises out towards the end of West Street, where the railway level crossing now is. Anderson shortly died and the premises were operated by Richard Naylor from May 1843 until they were demolished in 1848. [29]

Some other industries declined as improved communications and the availability of greater power allowed their concentration in particular centres. The country potteries producing course earthenware in the Old Bolingbroke area were finished once access to east Lincolnshire was made easier. Samuel Langley, a 'harmless potter', was buried at Old Bolingbroke in 1793 and potting only continued a few years longer in East Keal, in conjunction with the making of bricks and tiles. There was a coarse potter in Barton-on-Humber by 1841 and some brick and tile makers also produced flower pots, sanitary pipes and similar items during the 1850s. [30] During the late

[28] Massingberd, 'Industries', pp. 387–88; SM, 29 January 1847.
[29] SM, 10 March 1842, 15 April 1842, 26 May 1843.
[30] R. H. Healey and E. H. Rudkin, 'Lincolnshire', in The English Country Pottery. Its History and Techniques, ed. P. C. D. Brears, Newton Abbot, 1971, p. 194; White, Directory, 1842, p. 584; White, Directory, 1856, pp. 689, 693.

eighteenth and early nineteenth centuries there were several watermills producing paper in Lincolnshire, particularly in Tealby near Market Rasen where four were listed in 1826. But the number of paper-makers in England declined as the Fourdrinier and other machines became more common and after 1840 the only one in Lincolnshire was the Houghton mill at Grantham.

For many years a considerable number of inhabitants of Horncastle were employed in tanning leather but this trade began rapidly to decline in the closing years of the eighteenth century and by 1826 there were only two tan-yards left in the town. There and in other towns such as Stamford and Lincoln tanning continued at a reduced level during the nineteenth century and met much of the local demand for boots, shoes, saddles and harness.[31]

The demand for some other products was also met by local manufacturers. The taking of snuff had largely displaced the smoking of tobacco but some pipemakers still worked at their humble trade in Lincoln and Gainsborough; by 1776 John Naylor had moved from Lincoln and was making pipes in Boston. After 1815 there was a return to smoking. The number of makers in Boston increased and the industry restarted in Stamford and other towns, but, perhaps as a consequence of this new competition, there were fewer makers in Lincoln. At least one learnt his trade in Lincoln and moved to Gainsborough in the 1820s. In 1821 changes in duty on tobacco encouraged home production and by 1822 George Archer Bellwood of Gainsborough was listed as a 'tobacco manufacturer', converting the imported cured leaf into a form suitable for the smoker. By 1826 so were the Gambles, leading Gainsborough merchants, and other tobacco factories were established in Boston in 1834 and in Lincoln by 1842.[32]

Other commodities which, like wool and corn, were supplied to a larger market beyond Lincolnshire, came newly into large-scale production. After about 1775 brick was used for cottages as well as in finer houses and public buildings, and to meet local needs permanent brickyards were established on the edge of towns with suitable clay. By 1826 there were five brick-makers at both Boston and Louth, three at Grimsby and two each at Lincoln and some other towns. A third was established at Lincoln in 1828, clay being brought by boat from Bardney to a field near the Stamp End lock.

[31] White, Directory, 1826, p. 145.
[32] P. Wells, 'The Clay Pipe Makers of Boston', in Aspects of Nineteenth-Century Boston and District, Boston, 1972, p. 14; J. E. Mann, Clay Tobacco Pipes from Excavations in Lincoln 1970–74, London, 1977, p. 58; N. R. Wright, 'Tobacco Manufacturing in Lincolnshire', Ind. Arch., 7 no. 1 (1970), pp. 1, 6, 7.

From the 1820s the brickyards on the south bank of the Humber increased in size and number, far beyond local needs, and an extensive brick and tile industry developed to meet the needs of a wide area served by water transport. They had reserves of high-quality clay and could supply not only the growing towns of the industrial districts but also East Anglia and London.[33] By 1855 there were five yards in Barton-on-Humber, five at other places on the south bank of the Humber, one on the Trent and six along the Ancholme between Brigg and South Ferriby.

The limestone quarries at Haydor and Wilsford in Kesteven flourished as their stone was used in new churches and public buildings erected in the nineteenth century. John Woolstone's quarry at Stamford was established in 1830 and in 1843 Charles Kirk, a Sleaford architect and builder who already had lime kilns at Bully (alias Boiling) Wells, opened a new quarry at Wilsford. Similarly the chalk of the Wolds was exploited where it reached the Humber; at Barton there were at least two quarries, each with their own wharf on the river. James Craburn's quarry was established about 1796, and in 1827 the chalk was used for repairing tidal river and sea banks, for making and repairing roads, for lime, marling land and the manufacture of Paris white. At that time there were at least four manufacturers in the town producing whiting, a domestic cleaning product mixing chalk and glue size to form balls. On a smaller scale there were also whiting manufacturers in Alford and Boston. Starch was also produced in Barton-on-Humber at this time.[34]

Brewing became increasingly concentrated in large breweries and the numbers of these increased during the early nineteenth century. In 1826 there were twenty-eight in the ten main Lincolnshire towns and this increased to over fifty in 1856. The brewers acquired direct control over increasing numbers of public houses. In 1825 Hartleys of Boston owned houses in Lincoln and Sleaford and in 1843 another Boston brewery owned over twenty in and around the town. Firms such as Mowbrays of Grantham, Dawbers

[33] M. W. Barley, *The English Farmhouse and Cottage*, London, 1961, p. 246; Lincolnshire Library, 'Industry II', p. 26; L. Elvin, *Lincoln as it Was*, II, Nelson, 1976, p. 3; S. A. Holm, *Brick and Tile Making in South Humberside*, Scunthorpe, 1976, p. 2.

[34] *SM*, 26 May 1843; D. Purcell, *Cambridge Stone*, London, 1967, pp. 66–68; Barton-on-Humber Local History Class, *Barton-on-Humber in the 1850s. Part Two. The Town and the People*, Barton-on-Humber, 1978, p. 53; White, *Directory*, 1826, p. 69; Porter, *Boston 1800 to 1835*, II, p. 80; G. B. Wood, *The Industrial Archaeology 1880–1980 of Alford*, Alford, 1980, p. 2.

Figure 12   *Union oil mill beside the Trent at Gainsborough in 1823*

of Lincoln and Phipps of Stamford were founded about this time and grew during the nineteenth century. Samuel Barnard and the Buggs of Spalding were all brewers who went into banking. The number of maltings also increased, particularly in Grantham, Stamford, Horncastle, Louth and other towns with good water communications. In reaction to drunkenness the temperance movement indirectly led to the manufacture of non-alcoholic 'mineral waters'; for example, the Grantham Soda Water Manufactory was established in 1835.[35]

The crushing of seeds to produce oil became concentrated in ports on the east coast of England, particularly Hull, as imported supplies from Europe and the middle east gradually replaced indigenous seeds. Mills appeared on the banks of the Trent, at Gainsborough in 1787 and two at Owston Ferry in 1799. From the late eighteenth century more and finer oil was needed for lubricating machinery, for mixing with paint, for weaving, and for other industrial and domestic uses. Several new mills were established in Gainsborough, Owston Ferry, Brigg, Grimsby and other places in north Lincolnshire, as well as at Sleaford and Spalding in the south of the county. More oil and fat was also needed for household soap

[35] *SM*, 14 January 1825, 14 July 1843, 27 April 1849.

and candles. By 1784 hard soap had largely replaced soft soap and thereafter this industry, too, became concentrated in the ports, although some country grocers such as Edward Collingwood of Corby Glen continued to make their own soap and candles for some time.[36]

Soap boilers had been long established in Gainsborough and when a new prison was built in Kirton-in-Lindsey the old one in Gainsborough was sold in 1792 to a soap boiler for £410. However, soap-making in Gainsborough did not long survive the death of this proprietor and seems to have ended in the town during the early 1830s. Because soap-making was an objectionable process, Thomas Collingwood's soap works in 1826 was not in Lincoln but at Washingborough three miles away. There were then other soap makers in Louth, Stamford and Spilsby.[37]

CRAFTSMEN

Many industries involved the use of traditional techniques but some gave more opportunity for the use of skill and innovation. Stamford clock-makers such as John Wilson could produce long-case clocks conforming to the best designs of London tradesmen and there were so many clock-makers in the provinces that some local cabinet-makers could specialize in the production of case-work. Some clock-makers also produced barometers. The improved road surfaces encouraged the greater use of private carriages and by 1826 Boston, Stamford, Grantham and Louth each had two coach-makers working in the town. Harrison's bell-foundry opened premises in Barton-on-Humber in 1770 and a few years later closed their original factory in Barrow. From about 1780 it was run by James Harrison (c. 1760–1835), who cast bells for Lincolnshire and as far afield as Newcastle, but after his death the foundry was demolished.[38]

Millwrights like John Saunderson of Louth built and improved windmills and watermills, and were masters of many trades from

[36] H. W. Brace, *History of Seed Crushing in Great Britain*, London, 1960, pp. 13, 27, 30, 37; *SM*, 4 August 1843; L. Gittins, 'Soapmaking and the Excise Laws, 1711–1853', *Industrial Archaeology Review*, 1 no. 3. (1977), p. 274; D. I. A. Steel, *A Lincolnshire Village. The parish of Corby Glen in its historical context*, London, 1979, pp. 162–64.
[37] *LAOR* 8, p. 33; *LAOR* 13, p. 9; J. S. English, 'Street Names and the Industrial Archaeologist', *LIA*, 7 no. 2 (1972), p. 21; Gittins, 'Soapmaking and the Excise Laws', p. 265.
[38] L. Tebbutt, *Stamford Clocks and Watches*, Stamford, 1975, foreword; T. North, *The Church Bells of the County and City of Lincoln*, Leicester, 1882, pp. 63, 66, 67.

carpentry and smithing to gearing wheels with wooden cogs and dressing millstones. They were the predecessors of Lincolnshire's nineteenth-century engineering firms such as that founded by the Skirbeck millwright William Wedd Tuxford (1781–1871). Improvements in iron-founding during the industrial revolution led to technological innovation in English windmills, such as the fantail with its small gears, the patent sail with its numerous small castings, and the much larger shafts and gears inside the mill itself, so that millers could manage larger and taller mills. The fantail was an automatic device which moved the cap of the mill as the wind changed direction so that the mill sails were always facing into the wind; patent sails could be set by the miller from inside the mill while they were still in motion, and included an automatic device to reduce the dangerous effects of excessive winds. Lincolnshire was one of the counties where these improvements were most widely adopted and after the introduction of patent sails by William Cubitt in 1807 the tall brick tower mills with their fantail, patent sails and distinctive ogee cap and ball finial overwhelmed the old post mills and smock mills of the county. It was in Lincolnshire, too, that windmills with more than four sails were most commonly to be found; preserved examples can still be seen at Boston, Sibsey, Heckington and other places, as well as a post mill at Wrawby and a small tower mill at Lincoln. Rex Wailes has said that the tall Lincolnshire multi-sailed mills were the finest tower mills ever built in England.[39]

ENGINEERING

Early iron foundries in Lincolnshire undertook a variety of work but it was the development of agricultural thrashing machines and later portable steam engines which raised them from millwrights or blacksmiths with half-a-dozen hands into substantial firms. The first really useful thrashing machine to break the husk of corn and release the grain was developed by Andrew Meikle in 1786 and subsequently many were made and fitted in barns in Scotland and northern England. They could be operated by hand or later by water wheels or horse gins.[40]

William Howden (1774–1860) served his apprenticeship with Joseph Conacher, engineer and millwright of Edinburgh, and about 1790 made working models of thrashing machines which Sir

[39] R. Wailes, *The English Windmill*, London, 1954, pp. xxii, xxiii, 54, 64, 66, 95.
[40] W. Tritton, 'The Origin of the Thrashing Machine', *Lincs. Mag.*, 2 (1934–36), pp. 7, 9.

Francis Kinloch presented to the Agricultural Society at Bath and sent to America and Russia. Later Howden worked for John Rennie at Blackfriars in London before moving to Boston, where he set up the Grand Sluice iron works in 1803. In May 1805 John Pinder, 'millwright, founder and thrashing machine manufacturer' moved from Bawtry to Gainsborough and later other makers set up in the county, including Richard Gray in Boston by 1810 and James Coultas in Grantham by 1811. Winnowing machines were also developed. They were so expensive that only the prosperous tenant or landlord could afford to install them, and they only slowly came into use.[41]

Early machines were immobile but farmers were interested in one that could be transported to serve different farms. In 1811 the Boston Agricultural Society offered a premium of twenty guineas to the first person in the neighbourhood who should use a well-constructed portable thrashing machine capable of being easily removed from place to place, set at work without difficulty and properly adapted to thrashing cole seed and corn. Thrashing was back-breaking work but it was the only indoor work for agricultural labourers during the winter and there was resistance to the introduction of machines, that broke into rick-burning and threatening letters to farmers in the winter of 1830–31. Parallel to the development of a portable thrashing machine was the slow introduction of steam engines into Lincolnshire. By May 1800 Charles Lowe of Boston had one of the first in the county, attached to his newly-built tower windmill near the Black Sluice. Gardiner and Ayre had one in their oil mill at Spalding in 1816 and about then one made by Davy Brothers of Sheffield was installed for drainage at Torksey. Other steam drainage engines followed at Sutton St Edmunds about 1817, a massive pair at Pode Hole in 1825 and one, still preserved, at Spalding marsh in 1833. Many of these early engines were made at Butterley in Derbyshire and it was not until the 1840s that steam engines and thrashing machines were made in large numbers in Lincolnshire.[42]

---

[41] *Lincolnshire Chronicle*, 28 September 1855; R. H. Clark, *Steam Engine Builders of Lincolnshire*, Norwich, 1955, p. 60; R. Craddock, 'Mills and Milling — Some Observations', *LIA*, 4 no. 4 (1969), p. 54; Tritton, 'Origin of the Thrashing Machine', p. 11; Young, *General View*, pp. 93–97.

[42] Porter, *Boston 1800 to 1835*, II, p. 87; *SM*, 10 December 1830; Craddock, 'Mills and Milling', p. 54; Wright, *Spalding — An Industrial History*, p. 37; G. L. Nutt, 'Early Rotary Pumps', *Lincs. Mag.*, 1 (1932–34), p. 185; R. L. Hills, *Machines, Mills and Uncountable Costly Necessities*, Norwich, 1967, p. 94.

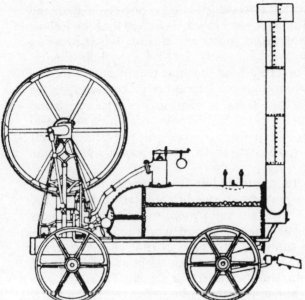

Figure 13   *The first
portable steam-engine to be
made by William Howden at
his Grand Sluice iron works,
Boston, in 1839. (Repro-
duced, with permission,
from W. J. Hughes,* A
Century of Traction Engines)

Figure 14   *A view of the Boston and Skirbeck iron works of William Tuxford
and Sons beside the Maud Foster drain in 1854. The top of Tuxford's windmill
also appears in plate VII, and the cap and sails of the mill were in 1892 removed to
Heckington mill, which is still preserved*

Before then Howden had produced the first steam engine to be made in Lincolnshire, for a small packet boat which steamed from Boston to Lincoln on 14 December 1827, and in subsequent years he made and installed engines in several other vessels at his riverside works.[43]

John Green, a coach-builder of West Street, Boston, spent a great deal of time and money between 1831 and 1833 on designing and building a steam carriage to run on the regular turnpike road. Despite the doubts of his friends he was sure that in a little time 'instead of a gentleman having his horse harnessed to go a journey, he will light up a fire in his carriage, and travel with greatest ease and safety'. By October 1833 he was building a second one so that both could run on a regular service he hoped to start between Newark and Lynn, via Boston, but his scheme did not materialize and in 1836 he moved to Doncaster.[44]

In contrast to self-moving engines Howden gave his attention to portable ones, making the first in Lincolnshire in 1839 (fig. 13). It was mounted on an oak chassis that could be pulled from one job to another by horses. The pioneer machine was exhibited at the Lincolnshire agricultural show at Wrangle in 1841 and thereafter it drove a scoop wheel in an adjacent fen for many years. By a belt round their fly-wheel portable engines could power thrashing machines and other farm equipment such as saw benches, corn mills and chaff cutters as well as drainage wheels.[45]

The next ironfounders to produce portable engines in Lincolnshire were William Wedd Tuxford of Boston and Nathaniel Clayton of Lincoln, who were both said to have got their ideas from Howden's machine. The Tuxford family were millers and flour dealers and William erected a large eight-sail tower mill (plate VII and fig. 14) in 1813 in the parish of Skirbeck. In 1824 he had started to give attention to the 'reeing' or sifting and cleaning of wheat and this eventually led to a machine patented in 1830. In 1826 he decided to make the castings for the machine in the workshop attached to his mill and from these beginnings came the Boston and Skirbeck iron works shown in figure 14. During the 1830s many small works were making improvements and alterations to thrashing machines and in 1839 it was suggested to Tuxford that he apply steam power to his own reeing and dressing machine. A design and even working models were prepared but the project hung fire until

[43] Clark, *Steam Engine Builders*, p. 60.
[44] White, *Directory*, 1826, p. 85; *SM*, 11 October 1833, 24 June 1836.
[45] Clark, *Steam Engine Builders*, p. 61.

1842 when a full-sized prototype was completed. This combined portable engine and thrasher mounted on one frame with its own wheels was exhibited at the 1842 meeting of the Royal Agricultural Society of England at Bristol. This layout was not altogether a success and in the autumn of 1842 the Tuxfords separated the two components, thus producing the first portable steam thrashing set.[46]

These were the basic elements of the thrashing sets which were to be produced in their thousands by makers in Lincolnshire and elsewhere over the next hundred years. Details were changed, size increased, the portable gave way to the traction engine and a straw elevator was added but the basic concept remained the same. The use of steam allowed larger and more powerful thrashing machines to be built, and portables could move outside the barn and work in the stackyard next to the corn ricks. Seven sets were made to Tuxford's original design, the first going to Robert Roslin of Algarkirk, and a further twelve sets were produced to a modified design.

Between 1760 and 1845 there was an increase in the number of windmills grinding corn in the county and by the latter date Lincoln and Boston each had about a dozen, some of which were starting to add steam engines for use in calm periods. The first mill dependent on steam alone was erected in Lincoln in 1836 by Keyworth and Seely and others followed, the Victoria mill in Brigg being converted from wind to steam in 1843 and the South Holland mills being built in Spalding in 1845.[47]

Lincolnshire engineering started in Boston but during the 1840s the foundations were laid in Lincoln, Grantham and Gainsborough of other great firms which were to eclipse the Boston pioneers. About 1843 the first steam engine boiler was made in Lincoln and installed in Edward Rudgard's porter brewery; and during the decade small businesses of agricultural machine makers and general smiths were started in St Swithin's parish by Proctor and Burton, Richard Duckering and Watkinson and Robey. The first foundry on Waterside South had been set up by James Chambers by 1833. More important than these was the Stamp End iron works established in 1842 by Nathaniel Clayton (1811–90) and his brother-in-law Joseph Shuttleworth (1819–83), shown in plates V and VI. Clayton had begun work at the Butterley iron works but

---

[46] Ibid., pp. 113, 115; *SM*, 18 August 1871; Tritton, 'Origin of the Thrashing Machine', pp. 53, 54; Wailes, *The English Windmill*, p. 100.
[47] *SM*, 9 September 1836, 16 December 1836, 7 April 1843.

returned to Lincoln to work for his mother as a packet captain following the death of his father. The new firm took over Shuttleworth's boatyard and reclaimed one and a half acres of low land west of their dock. They started with twelve men, two forges and a lathe and undertook a variety of work, making their first portable engine in 1845. They had wealthy sleeping partners and invested heavily in the development of portable engines, being the first to produce a portable with horizontal cylinders on top of the boiler, which became the general arrangement. In 1815 Richard Hornsby (1790–1864), in partnership with Richard Seaman until 1828, had established a business in Spittlegate, just south of Grantham, producing horse-powered thrashing machines, winnowing machines and seed drills. Iron and brass foundries were added, their range of products increased and their first portable engine was made in 1849.[48]

The attempt to establish textile manufacture in Lincolnshire had been unsuccessful, but engineering firms producing equipment for farmers soon established international reputations and during the second half of the century supplied agricultural machinery and steam engines to eastern Europe, South America and many parts of the British empire.

[48] VCH, Lincs., p. 119; Hill, Victorian Lincoln, p. 121; LAOR 26, p. 47; P. A. Wright, Traction Engines, London, 1959, p. 6; B. Newman, One hundred years of good company, Lincoln, 1957, p. 61; M. Pointer, Hornsby's of Grantham 1815–1918, Grantham, 1976, p. 3; Clark, Steam Engine Builders, p. 53.

CHAPTER 4

GEORGIAN TOWNS

THE Industrial Revolution generated rapid — sometimes explosive — urban growth, the effect both of a population boom and of the concentration of industry into towns. Change was everywhere, not merely technical, but social, cultural, economic and environmental; and though it placed a heavy and inevitable strain on political and social institutions, it was accommodated in the end by evolution, not revolution. The towns expanded with new housing, often jerry-built; water supply, health care and education were raised at least a little above their previous quite inadequate level; electoral and municipal reform was at last achieved; religious dissatisfaction was met by the upsurge of nonconformism; a new middle class arose, and English society became less aggressive and brutal, and more inhibited and prejudiced. Although the upheavals of the Industrial Revolution left their deepest mark on the textile communities and such great conurbations as Manchester and Birmingham, some of Lincolnshire's towns did not escape similar urban problems, albeit on a smaller scale.

GROWTH OF POPULATION

The years 1760 to 1850 were one of the most exciting periods of change in Lincolnshire. The number of inhabitants was increasing rapidly and figure 15 shows that until 1850 about 30 per cent of the people lived in the towns. Over the surface of Lincolnshire there were about thirty-six market towns ranging in size from Wragby with 410 inhabitants in 1801 to Lincoln with 7,197 people, but most of the towns were small. Only eight had more than 2,000 inhabitants including Lincoln, Boston and Stamford, which each had over 5,000, but even small places were commercial and social centres for their area. Figures 16 and 17 show that each of the seven main towns was growing at a similar rate between 1750 and 1851 and by the latter date there were ten towns with over 5,000 inhabitants.

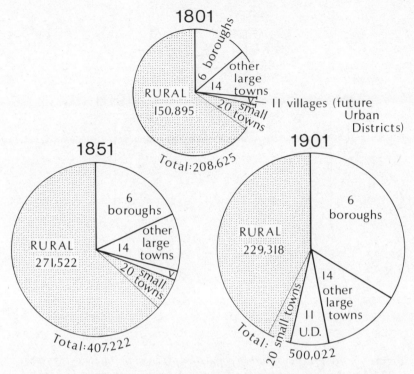

Figure 15 *Distribution of total population of Lincolnshire, urban and rural, 1801–1851–1901. The three unshaded segments represent the urban population of the county, and broadly match the categories in figure 1*

Boston and Lincoln were the two largest towns throughout this period. In 1750 the river port of Gainsborough was third in size but by 1851 it had been overtaken by Grantham, Stamford, Louth, Spalding and even Grimsby. For most of this period Grimsby was a very small place and even the opening of the dock in 1800 produced only a temporary quickening of the pace at which its population increased. Hull continued to be the most important town for much of north Lincolnshire. Boston was the fastest growing town in the county and from about 1806 to 1852 its population exceeded even that of Lincoln. Boston's growth was most vigorous between 1801 and 1821 while the East, West and Wildmore fens were being reclaimed, whereas Grantham and Stamford grew most rapidly in the late eighteenth century as traffic increased on the Great North Road. Louth grew fastest after 1811 and by 1841 was the third

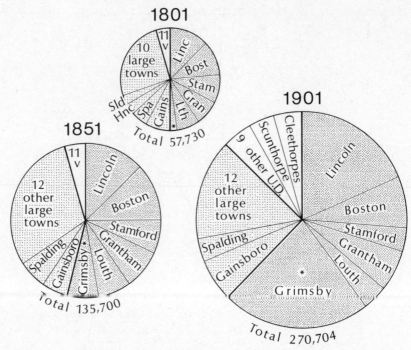

Figure 16   *Distribution of urban population of Lincolnshire, 1801–1851–1901. This is a more detailed analysis of the unshaded section of figure 15. The main divisions represent the six boroughs, fourteen other large towns, and eleven villages which were later created into urban districts*

Sld = Sleaford   Hnc = Horncastle

largest town in the county. Outside the towns the fastest rate of population growth was in the coastal villages of Cleethorpes and Skegness, but although Cleethorpes had 1,034 people in 1851, Skegness, Sutton-on-Sea and Mablethorpe each had only about 350 residents, mainly engaged in farming and a little fishing.

One of the few towns in decline was the old port of Saltfleet, which suffered from the declining profitability of grazing long wool sheep on the coastal marsh and from the opening of a navigation direct to Louth. Saltfleet market ceased about 1790 and the continuing poverty of the area led many people to emigrate. In the 1830s a local clergyman considered that Saltfleet was 'for its size . . . probably the worst place in England. A neighbouring clergyman who . . . had known it for fifty years habitually called it Little Sodom'. A hotel was erected on the beach, but in the late nineteenth

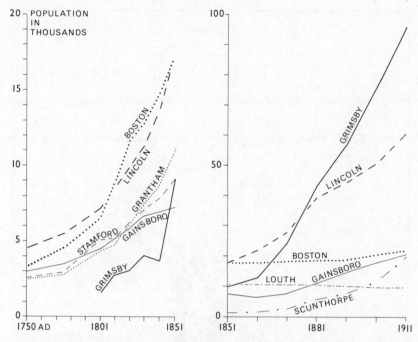

Figure 17 *Population of main Lincolnshire towns 1750–1851. For the purpose of this diagram Lincoln includes Bracebridge, Boston includes Skirbeck, Stamford includes St Martin's*

Figure 18 *Population of main Lincolnshire towns 1851–1911. For the purposes of this diagram Grimsby includes Clee and Cleethorpes, Lincoln includes Bracebridge and Boultham, Boston includes Skirbeck*

century it was neighbouring Mablethorpe which blossomed into a popular resort.[1]

NEW HOUSING

As their population rose, the centres of Boston, Gainsborough and other towns became more congested as new houses filled court-yards and gardens. It was several years before building sites within the towns were exhausted and development started encroaching on the surrounding fields. The amount of growth in each town was mainly dependent on economic factors but the shape of the town was influenced by land ownership. Owners of some fields built as

[1] White, *Directory*, 1872, p. 422; J. A. Perkins, *Sheep Farming in Eighteenth- and Nineteenth-Century Lincolnshire*, Lincoln, 1977, p. 32.

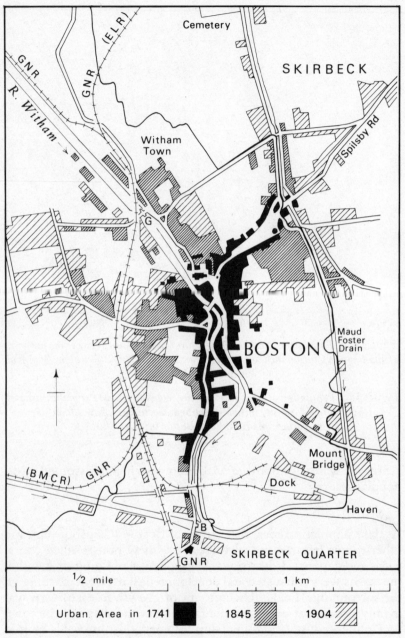

Figure 19   *Boston — growth of urban area 1741–1904*
G = Grand Sluice   B = Black Sluice

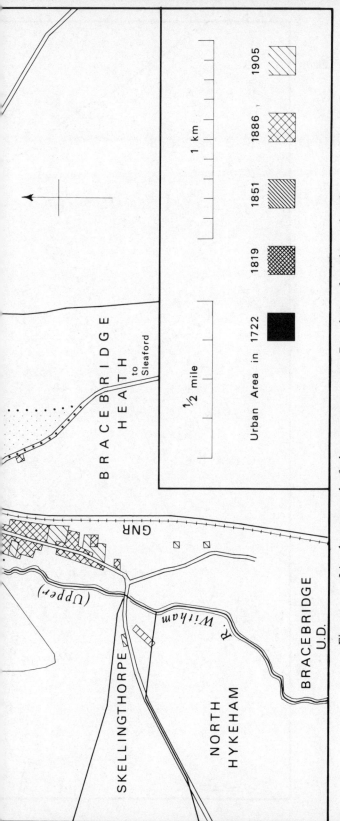

Figure 20 Lincoln — growth of urban area 1722–1904. Boundaries of parishes within the city are omitted for clarity. The urban part of Bracebridge, west of the railway line, became an urban district in 1898 and was separated from Bracebridge Heath

C = Cathedral

SKELLINGTHORPE

(Upper)

GNR

BRACEBRIDGE HEATH

to Sleaford

R. Witham

NORTH HYKEHAM

BRACEBRIDGE U.D.

Urban Area in 1722

1722   1819   1851   1886   1905

½ mile

1 km

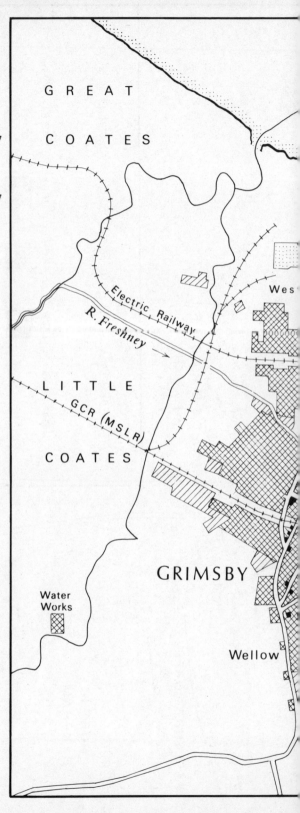

Figure 21 *Grimsby —
growth of urban area
1760–1905: N = New Town
of c.1800*

1. Old Dock 1798–1800
2. Royal Dock 1846–52
3. Tidal Basin 1846–52
4. No.1 Fish Dock 1855–57
5. No.1 Fish Dock
   Extension 1866
6. Union Dock 1873–74
7. No.2 Fish Dock 1876–77
8. Alexandra Dock
   1878–80
9. No.2 Fish Dock
   Extension 1897–1900

GREAT

COATES

Electric Railway

R. Freshney →

LITTLE

GCR (MSLR)

COATES

Wes

GRIMSBY

Water
Works

Wellow

3

4

2

5

7

9

6

New Clee

8

New
Cleet

Marsh

1

N

Sidney
Park

Grant
Thorold
Park

Cemetery

C L E E

People's
Park

Old
Clee

G N R

Weelsby

(E L R)

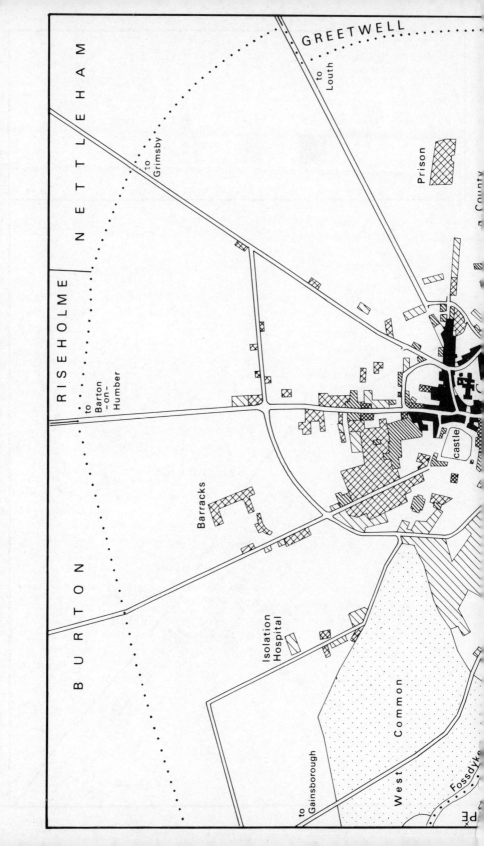

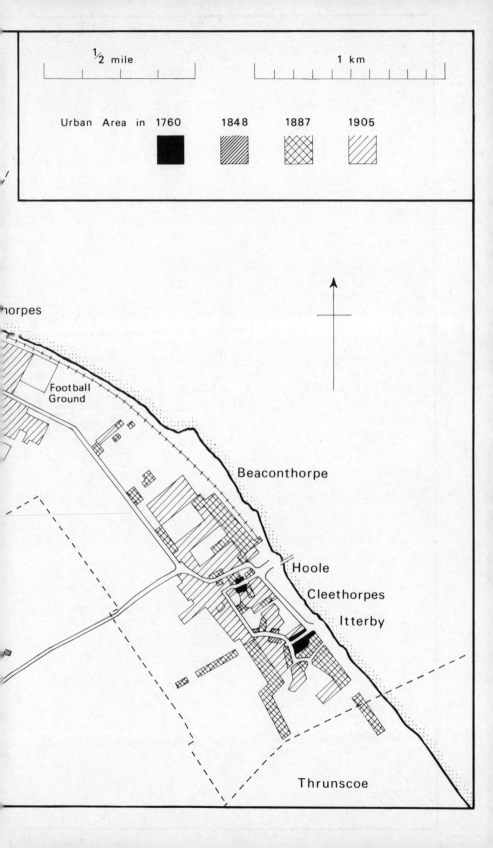

½ mile

1 km

Urban Area in 1760   1848   1887   1905

horpes

Football
Ground

Beaconthorpe

Hoole

Cleethorpes

Itterby

Thrunscoe

many houses as possible on their property but others, such as the Fydells of Boston, kept some land in the town centre in agricultural use until the twentieth century.

Figure 19 shows that the outward development of Boston spread over three main areas and into the adjacent parish. Witham Town developed as a distinct hamlet near the Grand Sluice and in the early nineteenth century houses grew between there and the market-place, including a riverside terrace in Witham Place. At the same time other new areas were developed in the vicinity of Pen Street and Liquorpond Street. The growth of Boston also spread over into Skirbeck and Skirbeck Quarter, which were part of the parliament-ary borough but not the municipal borough. By 1851 there were 14,733 people living in the municipal borough and 2,386 just outside, particularly in Skirbeck, which was ideal for retired farmers and businessmen, being close to Boston without the bur-den of 'excessive rates and impositions'. Some industrial housing developed around Tuxford's iron works in the southern part of the parish.[2]

In the first half of the nineteenth century most growth in Lincoln (fig. 20) was on the gentle slope north of the Witham, extending east towards Stamp End and west towards the Brayford. However, until the 1840s development did not spread far beyond its medieval extent, the main exception being in St Nicholas's parish north of the castle, which started to grow in the 1820s. Similarly the outward growth of Gainsborough did not start until the 1820s and was then on a small scale, mainly in Spring Gardens at the east end of Lord Street (fig. 22).

The borough of Grantham had only a small acreage and after 1800 the town spread first into Little Gonerby on the north and later into Spittlegate on the south (fig. 23). From the 1820s Spittlegate grew more rapidly than either Little Gonerby or the borough, largely because of the presence of Richard Hornsby's iron works. By 1851 the borough had just 5,375 inhabitants while Spittlegate and Little Gonerby together had 5,428 people. The outward growth of Louth was eastwards towards the Riverhead particularly after 1793, when James Street was laid out by the corporation to link the two areas; and southwards towards the old quarry, which after 1802 was used for fairs and a livestock market (fig. 24). When the dock at Grimsby was opened in 1800, the corporation laid out a grid of streets along its eastern side (fig. 21) and granted building plots to the freemen. Each plot was twelve yards by thirty, and any

[2] *SM*, 18 February 1825.

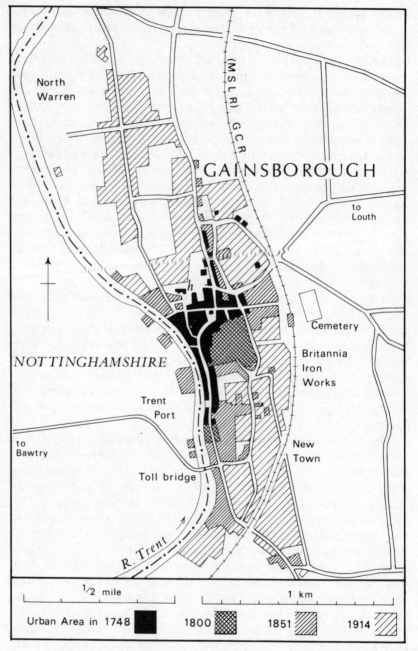

North
Warren

(M S L R) G C R

GAINSBOROUGH

to
Louth

h

NOTTINGHAMSHIRE

Cemetery

Britannia
Iron
Works

Trent
Port

to
Bawtry

New
Town

Toll bridge

R. Trent

½ mile		1 km	

Urban Area in 1748 ■   1800 ▨   1851 ▧   1914 ▨

Figure 22   *Gainsborough — growth of urban area 1748–1914*
h = Old Hall

not taken by Christmas were then offered to non-freemen. The corporation erected an obelisk and a cistern in the space left for a central market but development was spasmodic. The area survived a temporary crisis in 1819 but in the 1830s the population of Grimsby fell and people began to return to the old town in a steady stream. By 1841 the population of Grimsby was 'roughly what might have been expected had the dock never been built (assuming a rate of growth in Grimsby similar to that in the other Lincolnshire towns)'.[3]

The delay in enclosing the open fields of Stamford largely confined development within the line of the old walls, together with a small area of Scotgate just north of the town, but after 1800 encroachments were made on the manorial waste along the northern edge of the town (fig. 25). By 1828 there were about one hundred cottages and in 1845 there were 380 houses as well as a Strict Baptist chapel built in 1834. In the 1840s the Blackfriars estate was laid out between the town and the Welland, but many plots there were used as gardens by the owners of old houses within the medieval boundaries.

New developments on the edges of towns were often more homogeneous than in the town centres, lacking the mixture of social classes where houses, shops and workshops were cheek by jowl. Some areas were occupied by professional and business men and others became the slums of the poor, such as the Lincoln Lane area in Boston, which was the main part of the town to be affected by the cholera outbreak of 1849. In Grimsby in 1848 the worst slums were in the new town and many plots of 360 square yards had between nine and sixteen slum houses on them.[4] Many Irish families came to Lincolnshire seeking work on the land and some settled in the county. Distinctive Irish communities occupied poor accommodation at North Street in Boston and Irish Hill in Louth, which were the sites of some of the first Catholic churches established in the early nineteenth century.

ARCHITECTURE

In these growing towns the buildings and streets followed popular fashions, albeit a little behind the time, and adopted and applied classical elements. Terraces allowed palatial proportions to be

---

[3] *The Louth Riverhead*, ed. I. S. Beckwith, Louth, 1976, p. 10; Robinson, *Louth*, p. 81; G. Jackson, *Grimsby and the Haven Company*, Grimsby, 1971, pp. 44, 46; Gillett, *Grimsby*, p. 182.

[4] RCHM, *Stamford*, pp. xliv, 69; Gillett, *Grimsby*, pp. 216–17.

applied to a number of distinct houses as in Stamford and Spalding, and small detached or semi-detached villas lined the roads out into the country. The revival of Stamford after 1720 made it one of the loveliest Georgian towns in England, though the preservation of its open fields allowed no spacious crescents and few grand terraces, the main exception being Rutland Terrace, built 1829–31. The ninth earl of Exeter (1725–93) was responsible for systematic rebuilding, to a uniform design, in a series of individual buildings: seven blocks of new houses were built in St Mary's Hill and St Mary's Street and other houses were improved.[5]

The growing prosperity of merchants and professional men resulted in fine houses being built in several towns, usually in brick. About 1800 a fashion developed for stucco on domestic buildings, to give brick houses the appearance of stone at a cheaper cost, but most houses had red brick walls and pantile roofs. Fashionable houses also had ornamental iron work on balconies and some examples survive in Lincoln. At the same time assembly rooms, theatres, a county hospital, lunatic asylum, several large work-houses and other large public buildings were being erected, many in a classical style. The corporation building in Boston was built in 1772; seven years later Stamford had a new town hall. Some older properties also had their street fronts refaced in the fashionable style.[6]

URBAN PROBLEMS

The growing towns also started to experience the first significant changes to their internal street plans, buildings being cleared for new streets in Boston and Louth, and the medieval gates of Stamford and Lincoln being removed to ease traffic flow. Between 1772 and 1822 the whole western side of Boston market-place was rebuilt. Much development in all the main Lincolnshire towns was either in narrow alleys or in courtyards entered by passages through buildings on the main streets (see plates XV and XVI). As the population continued to increase steadily the overcrowding worsened, though numbers were not as great as in Nottingham or other industrial cities. The situation in Stamford was particularly difficult because of the delay in enclosing the commons. St Martin's parish was enclosed in 1796, but much land was added to Burghley Park and none was left for any large development south of the

---

[5] RCHM, *Stamford*, p. lxxxii.
[6] Honeybone, *Grantham*, p. 87; M. Aston and J. Bond, *The Landscape of Towns*, London, 1976, p. 167.

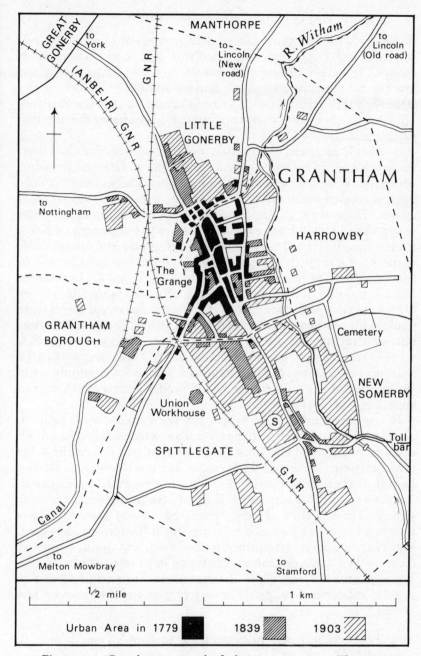

GREAT GONERBY

MANTHORPE

to
York

R. Witham

to Lincoln
(New road)

to Lincoln
(Old road)

G N R

(ANBEJR) G N R

LITTLE
GONERBY

GRANTHAM

to
Nottingham

HARROWBY

The
Grange

GRANTHAM
BOROUGH

Cemetery

NEW
SOMERBY

Union
Workhouse

S

Toll
bar

SPITTLEGATE

G N R

Canal

to
Melton Mowbray

to
Stamford

½ mile	1 km

Urban Area in 1779 ■   1839 ▨   1903 ▨

Figure 23   *Grantham — growth of urban area 1779–1903. The outer boundaries of Grantham parish and townships are shown in figure 2. The outer boundary shown on this map was established by the Grantham Borough Extension Act of 1870*

S = Spittlegate iron works

Welland. With the outbreak of war in 1793 the price of land, materials and wages rose and standards of size and construction dropped to keep working class houses cheap. Standards remained low for much of the nineteenth century and the problem was not effectively tackled until late in Victoria's reign. In 1845 tenements in Lincoln were being built with no foundations and very thin internal partitions.[7]

As people gathered in towns in greater numbers than had been known before it became difficult to obtain wholesome drinking water and to dispose of sewage. Not only was water in short supply but it was often polluted because of the inadequate sewage arrangements. There were conduits in Grantham and Lincoln but most water was obtained from private wells and public pumps or direct from rivers. Boston obtained much of its fresh water from the roofs of the town, caught in gutters and carried to cisterns in each yard. In the droughts of 1819 and 1826 it was brought by packet boats from Lincoln and sold in Boston market-place for 1d. a bucketful, and by carts from the nearest source ten or sixteen miles away. Bores were made in the market-place in 1783–85 and 1826–28 in search of water but with no success. By 1826 Gainsborough had a waterworks, where a steam engine raised water out of the Trent, and in 1837 the marquess of Exter provided Stamford with a water supply from Wothorpe but not until the 1840s did modern waterworks start to appear in Lincolnshire towns.[8]

It was even later before proper sewage systems were built. In Sleaford sewage flowed into the river from which much of the town drew its water, and the Mowbeck in Grantham served the same dual function. These and open drains like the Barditch in Boston helped to spread disease. In 1832 cholera descended on England. There were 246 deaths in Hull but Lincolnshire escaped more lightly. There were forty-one deaths out of 223 cases in Gainsborough between 5 June and 2 August but at Boston only five died, plus two on vessels quarantined in the Wash, and two at Grimsby. Temporary boards of health were set up in Boston, Louth, Gainsborough and Lincoln while the emergency lasted and for a few months established hospitals in warehouses and employed a few nurses.[9]

[7] RCHM, *Stamford*, p. xliv; Aston and Bond, *Landscape of Towns*, p. 169; *SM*, 14 February 1845.

[8] H. Porter, *Boston 1800 to 1835*, Lincoln, 1941, pp. 88, 89; Thompson, *Boston*, pp. 98, 667; White, *Directory*, 1826, p. 117; Rogers, ed., *Stamford*, p. 109.

[9] Gillett, *Grimsby*, p. 216; White, *Directory*, 1856, p. 167; *SM*, 6 July 1832, 13 July 1832, 20 July 1832, 20 April 1832, 4 May 1832, 9 November 1832.

TOWN IMPROVEMENTS

After 1748 improvement commissioners were established in some English towns by local acts of parliament to deal with some of the problems of urban areas. Commissioners responsible for lighting and watching were established in Gainsborough, Boston and Lincoln by acts of 1769, 1776 and 1779 respectively. They could widen and improve streets, lay down pavements and remove encroachments, have the streets cleaned and lighted, and employ watchmen to patrol at night. The expenses of the Gainsborough commissioners were defrayed by a levy on coal landed at the port, an impost which had earlier been used to pay for the rebuilding of All Saints church. Even though later acts widened their powers and increased their revenues, their activities were still somewhat restricted. The maximum rate which the Lincoln commissioners could levy under their 1791 act was 6d. and this prevented any expensive schemes. Improvement commissioners were not appointed in other Lincolnshire towns until the 1820s. Many commissioners were appointed in each town but effective control was exercised by a few active members and after the reforms of the 1830s their non-elective character was an anachronism. Grimsby corporation made a start on paving and lighting parts of their town in 1800, twenty-four lamps being placed in the streets, but the town did not prosper and the lighting was abandoned in 1829. Elsewhere the laying of pavements and other improvements depended on voluntary action by the inhabitants, either collectively or individually; in 1847 it was complained in Alford that 'the abrupt termination [of pavements] every here and there cause an unsightly appearance, and in some cases a dangerous stumbler for the pedestrians'. [10]

Fire-fighting equipment such as buckets, fire-hooks and engines might be paid for by public funds but volunteers were still relied on to use it when the need arose. Sometimes insurance companies contributed towards the cost of the equipment, but they expected some preference for their policy holders in the event of fire. Another source of funds was to charge for each turn-out, particularly if the equipment went into another parish. Street lighting was difficult as it depended on oil lamps until the 1820s, and even then they were lit only during the winter months. By 1805 Lincoln

---

[10] L. Golding, *Local Government*, London, 1959, pp. 13, 14; White, *Directory*, 1856, pp. 163, 274; White, *Directory*, 1872, p. 810; Hill, *Georgian Lincoln*, pp. 210, 240; I. S. Beckwith, *The Industrial Archaeology of Gainsborough*, Gainsborough, 1968, p. 7; Gillett, *Grimsby*, pp. 183, 209; *SM*, 22 January 1847.

H

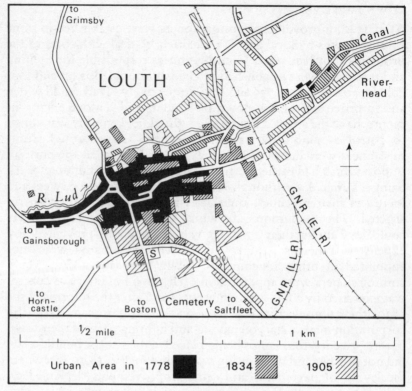

Figure 24   *Louth — growth of urban area 1778–1905*
S = sheep market established in former quarry

had 146 lamps which were lit for sixteen nights a month for four months, and the Boston and Gainsborough commissioners also had responsibility for lighting.[11]

A great improvement was made in the quality of street lighting when gas lamps were introduced. Stamford gas works was completed in 1825, only eleven years after London was lit by gas, and Boston, Gainsborough and Louth followed in 1826. By 1845 sixteen Lincolnshire towns had the benefit of gas, provided by local companies from works usually located near a waterway for their supply of coal. The gas was used only for lighting and the companies' largest consumer was the body responsible for lighting the

[11] *SM*, 11 January 1810.

public streets. The forming of the Louth gas company in 1825 was accompanied by the establishment of improvement commissioners for the town, and similarly the Lincoln commissioners enlarged their powers when the Lincoln gas company was authorized. Finally commissioners were established in Stamford at the late date of 1841.[12]

EDUCATION

By the second half of the eighteenth century the charity school movement had lost much of its impetus and further improvements in education in Lincolnshire towns did not come until the close of the Napoleonic wars.

Throughout this period the effectiveness of the grammar schools declined, as the value of their endowment income for free pupils was eroded and their classical curriculum became inadequate for the needs of a commercial and industrial society. In 1835 the Stamford School was said to be of little use to the inhabitants. Many grammar schools had only a single room or lodged in part of the parish church, and Carre's School in Sleaford went into abeyance for twenty years after 1816. Even at Boston grammar school with a building of its own the number of pupils fell to nil at one time. Grimsby grammar school was held in the old chantry house, but was more fortunate than most because in 1804, when the completion of the dock had increased the value of the corporation's property, they increased the master's salary from £40 p.a. to £140 together with a rent-free house; in 1827 the corporation spent further sums on education and established a preparatory school and two dame schools. Where grammar school masters took in boarders and taught commercial subjects for a fee the free scholars took second place. After 1800 schools in Lincolnshire were adversely affected by improved communications, which made it easier to send boys out of the county. The grammar schools and charity schools were clearly inadequate at a time when technological developments in industry and agriculture were calling for a better educated work force. Private venture schools such as Hardwick's Academy in Castlegate, Grantham, were developed for the education and upbringing of the sons and daughters of the middle classes. For poorer children Sunday schools were established in Horncastle in 1780, Lincoln in 1785 and Boston in 1792. By 1833 there were 543 Sunday schools in the county, attended by 31,861

[12] White, *Directory*, 1856, pp. 104, 243, 884; *SM*, 17 June 1825.

children. At first the teachers were paid, but as new day schools developed so Sunday education became concentrated on the inculcation of morals and religion by voluntary enthusiasts.[13]

Great impetus to the education of the poor in England was given by Dr Andrew Bell (1753–1832) and Joseph Lancaster (1778–1838), who each advocated setting up schools by public subscription, to be operated on the 'monitorial' system with older children teaching the younger. Dr Bell's scheme became associated with the Church of England and was espoused by the National Society formed in 1811, while Methodists and other nonconformists supported Lancaster's system, encouraged by the British and Foreign School Society formed in 1812. In some towns where they had sufficient support the Methodists established day schools of their own. In response to a circular issued by the bishop of Lincoln in September 1814 it appeared that in only nine parishes in the diocese had schools been founded on National lines. These included Grantham, Lincoln, Gainsborough and Horncastle, and in the next eight years National schools were established in the other boroughs and smaller towns such as Alford, Caistor and Market Rasen. In Horncastle and Boston the promotion of the National school was in response to proposals by nonconformists to establish British schools. National schools were always more numerous and by 1841 there were still only five British schools in the whole of Lincolnshire. By 1845 the Methodists had seven day schools in the county, in Wainfleet, Lincoln, Gainsborough and four country villages, and Baptists had a day school in Coningsby before 1839 and opened one in 1842 at Witham Green, Boston, for the use of all denominations.[14]

The establishment of new schools under the aegis of the National Society stimulated activity among the small grammar schools of the county, with the erection of new buildings at Holbeach, Sleaford and elsewhere and the rebuilding of masters' houses at towns such as Boston and Spalding. In 1827 Grimsby corporation

---

[13] White, *Directory*, 1872, p. 204; T. and E. Kelly, *Books for the People. An Illustrated History of the British Public Library*, London, 1977, p. 59; Honeybone, *Grantham*, p. 223; J. N. Clarke, *Education in a Market Town: Horncastle*, Chichester, 1976, p. 4; Hill, *Georgian Lincoln*, p. 71; Brears, p. 165; S. J. Curtis and M. E. A. Boultwood, *An Introductory History of English Education since 1800*, London, 4th edn 1966, p. 53.

[14] S. de Winton, 'The Coming of the School Board', in *The First Stone and other papers*, Boston, 1970, p. 12; Clarke, *Education in a Market Town*, p. 8; Thompson, *Boston*, p. 294; *SM*, 24 March 1843; R. C. Russell, *A History of Schools and Education in Lindsey, Lincolnshire 1800–1902*, IV, Lincoln, 1967, p. 13.

erected a preparatory school for ninety children to supplement the grammar school.

Only two more National schools were opened in Lincolnshire between 1822 and 1839 but each of the large union workhouses erected in the 1830s had a school for pauper children. The establishment of the Lincoln Diocesan Board of Education in 1839 led to the provision of many more National schools in the next fifteen years. The board also opened a small diocesan training school for masters in 1841 as the predecessor of the present Bishop Grosseteste College.

Mechanics' institutes, which had their origin in Edinburgh, Glasgow and London in the early 1820s, were established in several Lincolnshire towns in the mid 1830s. W. S. Northouse and other radicals succeeded at their second attempt to form one in Lincoln in 1833, merging with the New Permanent Library and taking

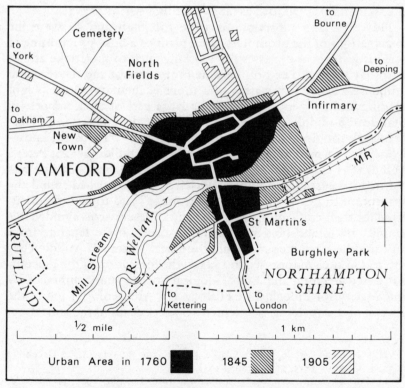

Figure 25   *Stamford — growth of urban area 1760–1905. Until 1832 the county boundary followed the river Welland, and St Martin's was in Northamptonshire*

premises in the ground floor of the Greyfriars, now the City and County Museum. It was at first envisaged as the 'Lincoln and Lincolnshire mechanics' institute', and at its first AGM on 4 December 1834 reference was made to 'the branches to which it has given birth'. During 1834 other mechanics' institutes were established in Louth and Horncastle, the latter being known until January 1836 as the 'Horncastle Society for the acquirement of useful knowledge'. One formed in Grimsby in October 1835 was specifically described as a 'branch of the parent institution at Lincoln'.[15]

Between 1836 and 1838 other mechanics' institutes were formed in Market Rasen, Boston and Epworth. That at Boston was formed in April 1837 with the declared object 'to unite the exertions of persons of all classes, creeds and parties in the cultivation and diffusion of useful knowledge, excluding politics and controversial divinity'. It was their intention to have accommodation for lectures and mutual instruction with a library, museum and philosophical (i.e. scientific) apparatus, as far as the funds permitted.[16]

However, the subscriptions were too high and so were the expectations of the promoters, who planned a busy programme of serious lectures and classes for working men to undertake after a hard day's work. Lectures became more general and the teaching emphasis changed to classes of a more elementary nature. Light reading and conversation became a large part of their activies. In Stamford a middle class 'institution for the dissemination of literary, philosophical, scientific, mechanical and other useful knowledge' was formed in 1838 and erected a large building on St Peter's Hill in 1841–42, but in 1846 the Stamford mechanics' institute was formed because 'the humbler classes of the town had found the institution to be "overlaid with patronage" and to be little calculated for their edification or amusement'. Other towns avoided this conflict by establishing mechanics' institutes quite separate from any middle class literary or philosophical society.[17] Middle class interest in such matters led in 1844 to the formation of the Lincolnshire Architectural and Archaeological Society (now embraced by the Society for Lincolnshire History and Archaeology) and to the revival of the Spalding Gentlemen's Society at about the same time.

[15] Hill, *Victorian Lincoln*, p. 147; Clarke, op. cit., pp. 130–31; *SM*, 12 December 1834, 30 October 1835, 11 December 1835.
[16] H. Porter, *Boston 1800 to 1835 continued to 1868*, Lincoln, 1943, p. 118; *SM*, 5 May 1837.
[17] White, *Directory*, 1856, p. 889; *SM*, 14 April 1848.

THE OLD POOR LAW

Relief of the poor remained a parish responsibility but in 1782 Gilbert's Act allowed them to join in unions and appoint guardians to deal with the poor in a number of parishes. One such union was formed by rural parishes around Lincoln and leased a former glue factory on the hill-top behind the castle for a house of industry where the residents would spin flax and wool and make stockings and other clothes. Only one city parish and two in the Bail subscribed. By 1789 the house was full, and it was so successful that in 1796 Lincoln corporation obtained an act to reorganize the union, after which most parishes in the city joined. In 1802 another voluntary union of nineteen parishes was formed in north Lincolnshire with a house of industry on Caistor Moor, and in 1804 a further fourteen parishes joined it. A union of several rural parishes in Lincolnshire and Nottinghamshire lying east of Newark built a house of industry at Claypole in 1817 but outside these three unions each parish continued to look after its own poor.[18]

Some parishes also provided cottages for paupers and for people in employment. In the 1790s Stamford corporation erected sixteen single-room tenements in Scotgate, arranged in two rows back-to-back in an effort to provide cheap accommodation for the poor of the borough. Parish tenants were often called on to perform services for the parish, as in 1824 when the vestry of St Paul-in-the-Bail, Lincoln, required a widow to 'take in' and lodge other paupers in lieu of rent. By about 1820 there was little waste land still available for the building of parish cottages in market towns, and urban parishes then chose to pay rent to private landlords. By the early 1830s Grimsby was paying the rents of about forty houses and until the late 1830s Louth parish spent about £500 a year on the payment of rents. Some rural parishes paid the rents of people who had moved into a town such as Lincoln.[19]

During the Napoleonic wars there was a great rise in the poor rate. Between 1783–85 the total poor rates for Lincolnshire averaged £43,024 per year but the average for the three years 1813–15 was £230,191. In Horncastle the rate rose from £225 in 1780 to £1,157 15s. 0d. in 1800. In the parishes where the maintenance of the poor had been let to contractors the rapid rise in prices must have resulted in ill-treatment. In some places the official provision of the poor law was supplemented by charity. Bequests

[18] Hill, Georgian Lincoln, pp. 183, 184; LAOR 19, pp. 31, 37; LAOR 14, p. 35.
[19] J. A. Perkins, 'The Parish and the Housing of the Working Class in Lindsey, 1790–1850', LHA, 12 (1977), pp. 64, 65; RCHM. Stamford, pp. 156–57.

led to the endowment of almshouses, particularly in Stamford where they were called hospitals, and to the distribution of coal, blankets, and similar benefits. Charitable ladies followed the example of the biblical Dorcas and produced cheap rugs, clothes and blankets for sale to the poor; lying-in charities formed in Lincoln and Boston in the early nineteenth century provided linen and baby clothes at the time of childbirth.[20]

HEALTH CARE

A hospital for the sick and lame poor of the county was opened at Lincoln in 1769 and dispensaries manned by doctors who would attend the sick poor were opened in a few Lincolnshire towns after 1789. But for most people in the county medical assistance was not easy to come by and they had to rely on traditional remedies and patent medicines. In 1777 the County Hospital moved to new premises on the brow of the hill, designed by John Carr (1723–1807) of York and now the Lincoln Theological College, which could accommodate forty patients, enlarged to sixty-four by 1850 (plate IX). In 1828 the Stamford and Rutland Infirmary was opened for twenty patients as the result of a bequest by Henry Fryer. Treatment in these hospitals was free but patients had to be recommended by a subscriber and those with contagious or incurable diseases were not welcomed. The outbreaks of cholera in the 1830s and 1840s were met by the opening of temporary hospitals in barns and the like. For the mentally ill there were the workhouses, a few private asylums, and the Lincoln lunatic asylum (now the Lawn Hospital) opened in 1820.

The opening of dispensaries at Horncastle in 1789 and Boston in 1795 was later followed by other Lincolnshire towns. At first they were funded by the annual subscriptions of benevolent individuals but later more emphasis was placed on self-help and the potential patients themselves made small contributions. By 1826 there were at least two surgeons in most towns but there were hardly any physicians available outside Louth and the five boroughs. In May 1843 it was reported that 491 poor persons had been admitted as patients to the Boston general dispensary during the previous year, at a cost of only £122 14s., and there were then nine medical men attending the patients.[21]

---

[20] Brears, pp. 173, 175; *SM*, 30 August 1805, 21 January 1825, 4 January 1833, 4 October 1833.
[21] White, *Directory*, 1826; *SM*, 5 May 1843.

In Lincoln, Boston and other towns friendly societies were formed, whose members paid a monthly subscription and received benefits at times of sickness and retirement. These local societies met in public houses, spending part of their subscription on drink, and most ended in bankruptcy sooner or later. In 1819 only one remained in Lincoln and the Grimsby Royal Friendly Society was dissolved in 1822. In 1803 the presence of a friendly society with ninety-one members in Brothertoft and a school of industry employing sixty-one children in knitting stockings and making worsted meant that the parish was spending only £60 on the poor compared with £74 in 1783–85, in contrast to most parishes which showed a large increase. An act of parliament of 1828 led to the growth of national societies such as Oddfellows and Foresters with local affiliated branches or lodges. The new Poor Law encouraged the growth of friendly societies as a form of self-help, and their annual parade, church services and dinners became significant social events in their communities.[22]

RECREATION

The concentration of numbers of people in towns and the rising prosperity of the urban middle class also allowed the development of recreational facilities such as theatres, assembly rooms and pleasure gardens. Assembly rooms for social gatherings already existed in the main towns by 1760, including two in Lincoln and the Mansion House in Louth. When a new guildhall was built in Grantham in 1787, funds were provided by Lords Rutland and Brownlow to incorporate an assembly room for the town. In 1793–94 card and tea rooms were added to the Stamford assembly rooms and in 1822 the redevelopment of Boston market-place was completed by the opening of the new assembly rooms next to the town bridge. In 1760 there were small theatres in Stamford and Lincoln but by 1820 there were theatres in nearly all the main towns of the county and the 'companies of comedians' no longer had to play in granaries and other improvised settings. This success owed much to the support of the urban middle class, but the bulk of the audience was a mixed crowd from town and country and there was probably little sophistication shown in either the boxes, the pit or the gallery. Throughout this period an evening's entertainment

---

[22] Hill, *Georgian Lincoln*, pp. 59, 289; T. H. Storey, 'The Oddfellows Hall, Grimsby, and its Place in the Social Life of the Town', *LHA*, 12 (1977), p. 49; VCH, *Lincs.*, p. 354.

Figure 26   *A view of the theatre in Swinegate, Grantham in 1804. Built in 1800 and converted to a Free Methodist chapel by 1856*

would probably include a play, acrobatics of some sort, and a comic song and a farce. [23]

William Herbert took the management of the Lincoln theatre in 1750 and moved it to its present site about 1768, but the county owes more to James Augustus Whitely (d. 1781), who built the new Stamford theatre in 1766–68 and brought to Lincolnshire the Robertsons, who were associated with the Lincoln circuit for four generations. A theatre built in Gainsborough in 1772 was forced to close after the Old Hall was adapted to that use in 1787, but such competition was rare. Most Lincolnshire theatres were part of Robertson's Lincoln circuit and were visited for a few weeks each year, but Stamford was part of a midland circuit and later Joseph Smedley (1784–1863) established another company circulating from Sleaford to an area larger than Lincolnshire. Theatres were built in Grantham (fig. 26) and Boston in 1777 and in Louth by 1798.

Commercial pleasure gardens were opened in Boston and Lincoln, the Vauxhall Gardens at Skirbeck in 1815 and the Temple Gardens in Lincoln about the same time. The gardens were laid out

[23] H. H. Quilter, *Central Grantham — An Historical and Descriptive Sketch*, Grantham, 1938, p. 7; RCHM, *Stamford*, p. 50.

in pleasant walks with saloons and kiosks, of which one still remains at Lincoln on the hill-side behind the Usher Gallery, and were the scene for dances, firework displays and band concerts. In the 1820s and 1830s there were bands in several Lincolnshire towns, which joined in public processions and gave open air concerts during the summer. Horse races were held once or twice a year on commons near most towns and permanent stands were erected at the courses near Spalding, Stamford and Lincoln, though only at the latter two towns were the races really fashionable affairs. Other Georgian sports and pastimes such as bull- and bear-baiting, cock-fighting and bare-knuckle boxing were bloody and violent.

RELIGION AND MORALITY

During the reign of George III and his successors, lawlessness and violence led to the imposition of transportation and the death penalty as punishments for an increasing number of crimes. By 1800 there were 235 felonies punishable by death and even children might be hanged for sheep stealing. But at the same time there was a religious revival, reflected in the rise of Methodism in Lincolnshire and later by the Evangelical Movement in the established Church of England. By 1800 there were forty Methodist churches in Lincoln- shire and in the early decades of the nineteenth century the number increased five-fold, indicating the growth of Methodism as a strong religious force in the county. By 1826 there were eight noncon- formist chapels in Lincoln, most built within the previous thirty years. Few new Anglican churches were built in towns in this period, except for chapels of ease for prosperous parishioners of Boston and Skirbeck and the replacement of two or three of Lincoln's little parish churches. Not until the 1840s did new Anglican churches start to appear in working class areas, often dedicated to St John the Evangelist.[24]

In reaction against the spread of beershops and increasing drunkenness aggravated by the Sale of Beer Act of 1830, a move- ment arose to fight the evils of excessive drinking. Temperance societies formed in Lincoln in 1835 and Boston by 1836 set the example for other towns. Evangelical ministers of all churches often took the lead. Attempts to establish temperance hotels met with limited success but temperance halls were established in many places to provide rooms for community functions without the temptations of drink. Large scale public meetings led some people to go further and sign the pledge of total abstinence from alcohol. A

[24] Golding, *Local Government*, p. 97; Brears, pp. 117, 119.

teetotal meeting on Canwick common in August 1842 was said to have attracted a thousand people. One of the leading activists in the Boston temperance movement was William Mumford, who moved to Brixton in 1844. His daughter Catherine later married William Booth, founder of the Salvation Army.[25]

Evangelical zeal also turned against cruel sports such as cock-fighting and bull-baiting and condemned many other aspects of popular culture. Bull-baiting was made illegal in 1835 but the annual Stamford bull running was ended only in 1839 after London policemen had been sent in increasing numbers for three successive years. Changing moral attitudes among the middle class combined with easier travel to more sophisticated cities led to the decline of Lincolnshire's theatres, although melodramas and popular entertainments still drew people to tents and barns at the time of fairs and race meetings. After the Stamford theatre became a billiard club in 1871 only the Lincoln theatre remained.

By the 1840s gentlemen had formed clubs in several towns to play the more peaceful game of cricket, and archery was also in fashion, but football remained an infrequent traditional village sport. In 1835 a company erected sea-water swimming baths at Boston, on land given by the corporation.[26]

National concern at the lack of recreational space in growing towns gained expression in the reports of select committees in 1833 and 1840 and after a little while public walks were provided in Lincoln and Boston. In 1844 a rural walk was formed by public subscription along the top of the South Common and the following year trees and shrubs were planted on the haven bank opposite Skirbeck Quarter and the harbour commissioners had the path gravelled and seats provided.[27]

REFORM

It was only so far that the rising middle class could change society until they had increased their influence in parliament and government. There was dissatisfaction with the enclosed character of the municipal corporations and with the anomalies of parliamentary

[25] Hill, *Victorian Lincoln*, p. 139; Hill, *Georgian Lincoln*, p. 287; *SM*, 26 August 1836, 21 October 1836, 21 April 1837, 2 September 1842, 22 March 1844, 29 March 1844; *Lincolnshire Echo*, 24 December 1977.
[26] *SM*, 21 July 1843, 28 April 1843, 21 April 1837; Porter, *Boston 1800 to 1835*, p. 78; White, *Directory*, 1842, p. 156.
[27] A. J. Strachan and I. R. Bowler, 'The Development of Public Parks and Gardens in the City of Leicester', *East Midland Geographer*, 6 pt 6 (1976), p. 275; White, *Directory*, 1856, p. 102.

representation which allowed old decayed towns such as Grimsby to have two members while great industrial towns like Birmingham had none. But in the 1790s the excesses of the French Revolution hardened the British ruling class against any demands for change. Lincolnshire had been dominated by whig families for most of the eighteenth century, but some families such as the Custs and Chaplins remained tory and toryism started to revive in the 1790s. In 1794 Pelham and Heathcote both became supporters of Pitt's government, and Pelham was created Baron Yarborough.

Lincolnshire gentry, with Sir Joseph Banks playing a leading role, drew up contingency plans in case of a French invasion of the county. Voluntary bodies of cavalry consisting of gentlemen and yeomanry were raised and in 1796 the Long Sutton and Spalding troops of yeomanry forestalled plans made at Leake 'status' or hiring fair to burn Boston, following riots against service in the militia in Caistor and Horncastle. After this the Somerset Fencibles were quartered in the market towns of Lindsey. Petitions for parliamentary reform and retrenchment as a solution to the nation's economic problems went up from Lincolnshire to London in 1816, 1817 and 1822 and indicated continuing concern.[28]

Growing awareness of events beyond Lincolnshire was fostered by the opening of newsrooms and libraries and the launching of local newspapers, particularly in 1830 when another revolution in France brought to the surface in England the long-felt desire for reforms in church and state. By the end of the eighteenth century books were smaller and more portable and the novel had emerged as a literary form. Books were still expensive and to make them readily available book clubs and subscription libraries were established. Private subscription libraries bought selectively while commercial libraries, usually known as circulating libraries, generally placed more emphasis on entertaining literature such as novels and romances. In addition there were newsrooms which made the London and provincial newspapers more widely available. In 1786 a county newsroom was opened in Lincoln and eight years later a city newsroom was opened below hill, but no subscription library was opened in the city until 1814. Libraries had already been started in Horncastle in 1790 and Boston in 1799, a newsroom being added to the latter in 1805. The Lincoln library served the middle class and in May 1822 the New Permanent Library (referred to on p. 101) was formed in the city to serve a lower social class — tradesmen,

---

[28] *Lincolnshire Echo*, 7 September 1974; Brears, pp. 171, 183; H. Porter, *Boston 1800 to 1835*, II, Lincoln, 1942, p. 88; Stark, *Gainsborough*, p. 101.

mechanics, apprentices and villagers. The outburst of zeal for reform led to the establishment of similar libraries in Boston in November 1830 and Sleaford in 1831. Wilks and Malcolm, the two MPs for the borough, each made donations to the Boston 'library of the people' which by December 1832 had almost a thousand volumes and 397 members. The Sleaford library owed much to the liberality of Henry Handley (1799–1846), who was MP for South Lincolnshire from 1832 to 1841.[29]

Throughout the eighteenth century virtually the only newspaper published in Lincolnshire was the *Stamford Mercury*. Attempts in 1785 and 1809 to launch newspapers in Lincoln each died within a year and the first sustained local alternatives to the *Stamford Mercury* were *Drakard's Stamford News* launched in 1809 and the *Boston Gazette* which commenced in 1810. In 1828 James Amphlett founded the *Lincoln Herald* and the political agitation of 1830 led to the appearance of three more Lincolnshire newspapers which supported reform. Newspapers were expensive, so public houses took copies and placed them in their tap room. On occasions when political feelings ran high on national issues crowds flocked to the public houses to hear newspapers read aloud. The arrival of competition from the radical *Lincoln Times* pushed Amphlett over to the side of the authorities. The *Lincoln Herald* appealed for support to

those persons, who may not be prepared to see the city's authorities run down by clamour, and publicly derided, by a press exclusively in the hands of the lower classes, without any local counteractive organ — as is the case at Boston, now placed out of the pale of the law by the supreme controul of a rabble and a revolutionary journal.

Once the political agitation was past its peak there was not sufficient support for seven county newspapers and by the end of 1834 all had closed except the *Stamford Mercury*. By 1836 there had appeared in their place the tory *Lincolnshire Chronicle*, the *Lincoln Gazette* as a county Liberal paper and Amphlett's *Boston Herald*. Few other new Lincolnshire papers were launched until 1854.[30]

By 1830 tremendous pressure for reform had built up throughout the kingdom. In Grantham Sir William Manners supported reform and many public houses he owned were named blue, the radical

---

[29] Kelly and Kelly, *Books for the People*, pp. 47, 48; Hill, *Georgian Lincoln*, pp. 16, 279–80; White, *Directory*, 1826, pp. 43, 145; Thompson, *Boston*, pp. 216; 220; Porter, *Boston 1800 to 1835*, p. 80; R. J. Olney, *Lincolnshire Politics 1832–1885*, London, 1973, p. 101; *SM*, 19 November 1830, 7 December 1832, 14 December 1832.

[30] Hill, *Georgian Lincoln*, pp. 62, 229, 289, 293; Thompson, *Boston*, p. 299; T. S. Tresidder, *Nottingham Pubs*, Nottingham, 1980, p. 13.

colour, but it was in Boston that feelings between the corporation and radical reformers were most hostile; Boston corporation's ancient right to tolls on traffic crossing the town bridge was challenged in 1828 and the tolls were abolished in 1830. Hull corporation's monopoly of the ferry route to Barton was challenged by James Acland, a radical reformer, who ran a rival steamer between September and December 1831 to try and force down fares.[31]

In November 1830 the whigs formed a government committed to reform, but their first Reform Bill to extend the franchise and redistribute parliamentary seats was defeated and on 22 April 1831 William IV dissolved parliament. The ensuing election was a victory for reform and there were celebrations in Lincolnshire towns. Reform candidates won both seats in Boston and both county seats, as well as one in Stamford and another in Lincoln. Charles Tennyson won a famous victory in Stamford, being the first candidate opposed to Lord Exeter to win there since 1734. As the Reform Bill threatened to deprive Grimsby of one of its seats the whigs there stood no chance, the tories also held both Grantham seats as well as one in Lincoln and one in Stamford. In Boston the election was marked by attacks on the houses of leading tories, and attempts to arrest the culprits led to a near-riot on 13 May, with a large crowd placing a tricolour flag on the steps of the police office in the market-place. At the request of the corporation, dragoons were stationed in the town.[32]

When the second Reform Bill was rejected by the Lords on 8 October, there was great excitement throughout the kingdom; two thousand people gathered in Boston market-place on 13 October to petition for the bill, and on 18 November over three thousand people attended a county meeting in Lincoln Castle. Assured of popular support the government introduced the bill for the third time on 12 December but its rejection by the Lords on 8 May 1832 precipitated another crisis; finally the tories withdrew their opposition and the bill passed on 4 June 1832. As news of the success reached Lincolnshire there were great celebrations; church bells were rung, streets paraded with banners and music, and there was much drinking. In Spalding the tory schoolmaster was burnt in effigy and had his windows broken, and in Lincoln a few days later the duke of Wellington was burnt in effigy. In Boston William

[31] Thompson, *Boston*, p. 101; A. A. D'Orley, *The Humber Ferries*, Knaresborough, 1968, pp. 27, 28.
[32] *SM*, 6 May 1831, 13 May 1831.

Garfit ordered a large quantity of ale to be given away in the market-place but the celebrations were restrained by the presence of troops in the town. The effects of the Reform Act in Lincolnshire were not so great as in some other counties; Grimsby was deprived of one seat, two were added to the county, and the boundaries of the five parliamentary boroughs were extended. St Martin's was added to Stamford, and thereby the constituency was placed firmly in the hands of the tory marquess of Exeter.[33]

In the elections of December 1832, fought on the new boundaries, reformers won all four of the new county seats and five of the borough seats, only Grantham and Stamford being held by tories and conservatives. One of the main issues to which the reformed parliament gave its attention was the reorganization of the local government system on a more democratic and efficient basis. This was at length effected by the Poor Law Amendment Act of 1834 and the Municipal Corporations Act of 1835. The 1834 act provided for the care of the poor to be organized through new unions of parishes, administered by annually elected boards of guardians and paid officials subject to supervision by a central body. It was to be a national pattern operated by local people and, as was said about the formation of the Stamford union, 'much moral good, and great saving of expense' was expected from the change.[34] Most unions were based on a market town near their centre and those on the edge of Lincolnshire extended into other counties. The boundaries of the first few unions in the south of the county were set by assistant commissioner Henry Pilkington but most were drawn by his successor Edward Gulson. Their boundaries had to take account of the voluntary unions already existing around the houses of industry at Claypole, Lincoln and Caistor. The latter union included the towns of Grimsby and Market Rasen which otherwise might themselves have been the centres of unions. Gulson also had to guide the new guardians during their first months and allay their fears about the new system. When concern was expressed about separating an illegitimate child from its mother he declared 'our great purpose is to work out a moral improvement of the population'.

Near the centre of each union was a large workhouse for up to four hundred paupers, and the design and erection of these buildings was a great boon to architects and local builders. Bryan Browning (1773–1856) of Northorpe near Bourne and William

---

[33] *SM*, 14 October 1831, 8 June 1832.
[34] Olney, *Lincolnshire Politics*, pp. 252–55; *SM*, 3 June 1836.

Adams Nicholson (1803–53) of Lincoln each designed several in the county but the most active architect was George Gilbert Scott (1811–78), who was responsible for those at Boston, Spilsby, Horncastle and Louth; his colleague Sampson Kempthorne designed the Grantham workhouse.

As the guardians were meant to meet all the needs of the poor, the workhouse included a school and infirmary and doctors were employed as district medical officers for paupers living outside. Conditions in the workhouse were to be 'less eligible' than those outside so that the able-bodied were encouraged to remain independent, and no relief was to be given to anyone who refused to go into the workhouse. The cases of all existing paupers were reviewed by the guardians and on 21 January 1836 the Spalding guardians were mobbed and hooted when walking from the town hall to their dinner at the White Hart.[35]

Opposition to the arrival of the new Poor Law was strongest in the Gainsborough area, where good management had left little scope for further economies. Local clergy considered making weekly collections in their churches to supplement the relief which could be given by the guardians. A crowd gathered at West Butterwick in June 1837, 'rattling old pans, blowing beasts' horns and making other discordant noises', to meet the packet bring the first relieving officer from Gainsborough to the Isle of Axholme. Finding that he had landed at Ferry the frustrated crowd attacked two constables who were present, and the Gainsborough cavalry were called out to restore order. At the end of July a bye-election for a guardian generated much heat at Gainsborough and the partly-built workhouse was destroyed. In September 1837 many people 'anxious for the public good' still had misgivings about the new system and it needed persistent directives from London to enforce the new regulations. At Gainsborough out-relief cost £70 per week, but at Louth it was £197 because the guardians were said still to 'adhere to old practices'. But in general costs declined. Most unions managed to cut expenditure by about half in their first year of operation, as in Bourne from £8,506 per annum to £4,256 in 1838 and in Caistor from £10,439 to £5,793. In 1834 the cost of the Poor Law in Lincolnshire as a whole had been 10s. 2d. per head of population; by 1837 it was down to 7s.[36]

[35] SM, 15 January 1836, 29 January 1836.
[36] SM, 12 May 1837, 16 June 1837; J. D. Birkbeck, A History of Bourne, Bourne, 2nd edn 1976, p. 160.

I

Private records kept by the surveyor of highways for Tetford show that money received from the lime kilns, herbage on the roads and the rent of parish property was used to relieve distress and keep people out of the union. In June 1837 General Johnson of Witham-on-the-Hill formed a local institution to relieve distress and so 'soften down the asperities of the new Poor Law'. There was a rapid and continuous decline in both the provision of parish cottages and the payment of cottage rents by parishes, as auditors gradually disallowed such expenditure in the accounts.[37]

The reform parliament did not try to make major changes in the system of turnpike trusts, although they did relieve the trusts of the financial burden of renewing their act every twenty-one years by introducing an annual Turnpike Acts Continuance Act from 1834. Trusts only needed to obtain a new act if they wished to make significant changes in their powers and duties.

While the Royal Commission on the Poor Law was preparing its report, another Royal Commission was appointed to investigate the affairs of the boroughs, most of which were tory-dominated. The whig-dominated commission was scathing in its criticism of the old system, under which citizens had no control over the corporations which used corporate and charity property for the political and financial advantage of their members. The corporations were responsible for the administration of income from certain properties bequeathed for charitable purposes, but it had often been merged with their own income from other sources and so was vulnerable to abuse. Boston corporation used income from the erection lands, their main charity property, for corporate purposes and their guildhall was really charity property. Despite this and other abuses the Boston charity property still produced the large income of £2,137 11s. 0d. in 1837.[38]

Thomas Fydell had died in 1812 at the height of his influence, but in 1835 the commissioners inquiring into the municipal corporations chose his career as an example of what might happen. As an alderman he helped to select the freemen who voted him to parliament and the councillors who elected him as deputy recorder — at a small salary; he sat as the recorder to try cases with a jury whom, if he happened to be mayor, he had selected; while he had also helped to choose the chief constable, whose delight it was to write scurrilous political squibs for Mr Fydell's party and to

[37] Brears, p. 183; SM, 9 June 1837; Perkins, 'Parish and Housing of the Working Class', pp. 66–67.
[38] Thomson, Boston, pp. 275–76.

summon for libel those who wrote squibs just as scurrilous against it. Before an election there was nearly always a great recruiting of new freemen to swell the tory vote, while the distribution of charities notoriously displayed political bias. The corporations were not elected; once one party had gained control it was difficult to unseat it. In May 1832 there were five vacancies on Boston corporation and five reformers offered themselves but were rejected by the corporation. By 1835 two political opponents had got on to Boston council, but only by concealing their true colours. Dissatisfaction with the corporation meant that their power to maintain law and order was undermined, as citizens declined to act as special constables and the police were seen as the servants of one political party.[39]

The 1835 Municipal Corporations Act laid the foundation for them to become democratic local administrations, exercising powers conferred by the central government. Councillors would be elected by ratepayers for a three-year term, and would themselves elect aldermen, up to one quarter of the council, to serve for six years. The act imposed a standard constitution in place of the individuality conferred by the ancient charters. Boston, Lincoln, Louth and Stamford each had eighteen councillors and six aldermen while the smaller boroughs of Grantham and Grimsby both had twelve councillors and four aldermen. In Louth the warden and six assistants had been formed originally to manage the grammar school and had never had the full privileges of a municipal corporation. They received special consideration in the 1835 act and were allowed to continue as governors of the grammar school in parallel to the new corporation, which took over their municipal powers and other property held by the old corporation. Stamford municipal borough absorbed St Martin's and Lincoln absorbed the Bail and Close on top of the hill, although the four rural parishes south of the city were excluded. Similarly Grantham lost its old jurisdiction over the soke. The Municipal Corporations Act of 1835 also took local charities out of the control of the corporations and established new boards of charity trustees in each town, appointed for life by the lord chancellor.[40]

In most places the introduction of democratic elections resulted in an almost complete change of membership of the corporations

[39] A. M. Cook, *Boston (Botolph's Town)*, Boston, 2nd edn 1948, pp. 106–7; *SM*, 30 March 1832, 9 June 1832.
[40] White, *Directory*, 1856, pp. 61, 882; Hill, *Victorian Lincoln*, p. 40; A. R. Bowen and C. P. Willard, *The Story of Grantham and its Countryside*, Newark, 1949, p. 36.

when the first elections were held in December 1835. In Lincoln reformers, whigs and radicals captured every seat and only four members of the old corporation were re-elected. Similarly only four members of the old Grimsby corporation were re-elected, and eleven of the sixteen members were Methodists. The break with old traditions was in many places symbolized by the refusal to use gowns, maces and other marks of office and by the sale of civic plate. Prices were depressed as many other reformed corporations were doing the same, but Lincoln's plate was sold for £240 and Boston's for £583. In recent years both towns have recovered some of the pieces for their historic associations. The proclamation of the accession of Queen Victoria in 1837 was a drab affair in many towns, not reflecting the popular enthusiasm for the new sovereign.[41]

The only significant function given to the corporations was control of the police, exercised by the watch committee, which in Boston and Lincoln took over from the old watching commissioners. In Stamford, Grantham and Louth the new police force was established from scratch. In Gainsborough, which was not a borough, the commissioners retained their police powers until the Lincolnshire constabulary was formed. In May 1837 Crowland sought to emulate the boroughs and establish a police and night watch, recruitng a policeman from the metropolitan force. Grimsby was slow to carry out its police duties, appointing twelve part-time constables in 1838 but no full-time force until 1846 when construction had started on the railways and the new dock. The old system of election of borough justices by the municipality was also ended. In Boston the members of the corporation were also the harbour trust and ex-officio paving and lighting commissioners.[42]

---

[41] Hill, *Victorian Lincoln*, p. 39; Gillett, *Grimsby*, p. 212.
[42] M. Pointer and M. G. Knapp, *Bygone Grantham*, II, Grantham, 1977, p. 2; *SM*, 13 January 1837, 22 January 1836, 26 May 1837.

PART III
THE RAILWAY AGE
1845–1914

CHAPTER 5

THE ARRIVAL OF RAILWAYS

RAILWAYS, said a correspondent of the *Stamford Mercury* in 1848, represented 'the annihilation of time and space'. The railway was fast and cheap, for people and for goods; and this, of all the inventions of the Industrial Revolution, had perhaps the most direct and visible effects upon all walks of society. The opening of the Liverpool and Manchester Railway in 1830 brought together the elements developed over the previous century, and ushered in the great age of railways. Within five years of its resoundingly successful debut, there were 338 miles of railway open to the public. Rural Lincolnshire, however, had to wait to feel the benefits. Most of the early proposals were for railways not to the county, but through it, in the form of rival trunk lines from London to the north. But in the event the first lines built in Lincolnshire were comparatively local ones, aimed at Lincoln itself and the ports of Boston and Grimsby, and provided only a devious route to the north. The county's economy meant that its railway map, like its turnpike one, remained thin compared to more industrial districts, and there were too few rival companies to turn Lincolnshire into the promoters' battleground that some areas became. Nor was construction difficult: on the flatlands it was easy, and only the Wolds and the limestone uplands presented obstacles to the engineers. Within four years of the first railway opening in the county, a full third of the final mileage was complete, and the outline of the system was laid.[1]

Two local names stand out. Henry Handley (1797–1846) of Culverthorpe campaigned not only for political reform but also for agricultural improvement and the greater use of steam-power. He encouraged the use of steam on farms, supported a company running steamships from Boston to London and fought to get railways that would serve the needs of Lincolnshire. Another Kesteven gentleman who took a leading part in railway affairs was

---

[1] *SM*, 27 October 1848; Dow, *Great Central*, I, p. 18.

George Hussey Packe (1796–1874) of Caythorpe, whose father became one of the first directors of the Leicester and Swannington Railway in July 1830.[2]

EARLY SCHEMES

Tramways had served local industrial needs for many years before 1830, and one had been built in 1813–15 to supply Belvoir Castle with coal from the Grantham canal. Long-distance, main-line railways were a different matter. As early as 1821 the visionary William James had surveyed a route from London to Cambridge and suggested its extension to Lincoln, but this county had less industry and inhabitants than other targets for the early railway promoters. A survey of 1827 by John and George Rennie of a line from Cambridge via Lincoln to York and a suggestion in 1831 for a railway from Sheffield to Grimsby as the eastern end of a Liverpool to Grimsby line only served to indicate the route of later proposals. Lincolnshire lacked coal and the main traffic it offered railway promoters was its agricultural produce, grain which was moved by water and livestock which travelled on their own feet.[3]

People outside Lincolnshire who proposed railways through the county usually had one of three possible objectives in mind. Many surveyors saw the long stretch of flat country across the fens, through the Lincoln gap and around the head of the Humber as the ideal route from London to York and the north. Other proposed lines came from inland cities such as Birmingham and Sheffield to existing or potential ports on the Lincolnshire coast. Thirdly from the 1840s there appeared schemes to cross the county diagonally and link East Anglia to the midlands and northern England. Some schemes in all three categories sought to use the Lincoln gap and during the nineteenth century the county town had perhaps more railway proposals than any other town in the kingdom.

A project launched by Nicholas Wilcox Cundy in 1833 for a 'Grand Northern Railway' from London to York via Cambridge and Lincoln, with various branches to Norwich, Nottingham and other towns, was the first of several schemes promoted in the mid 1830s. Cundy's proposal was facing oblivion until it received the attention of Henry Handley. With Cundy's concurrence he had the

---

[2] J. Haining and C. Tyler, *Ploughing by Steam*, Hemel Hempstead, 1970, p. 48; J. Varley, *The Parts of Kesteven — Studies in Law and Local Government*, Sleaford, 1974, p. 91; *SM*, 8 July 1830.

[3] C. Hadfield and A. W. Skempton, *William Jessop, Engineer*, Newton Abbot, 1979, p. 172; Honeybone, *Grantham*, p. 58; Ruddock and Pearson, pp. 43, 56; Dow, *Great Central*, I, p. 36; White and Tye, *Grimsby and Cleethorpes*, p. 7.

route re-surveyed and slightly modified in 1835 by James Walker, engineer of the recently completed Leeds and Selby railway, and then formed a new Northern and Eastern company. Early in 1835, before Walker's proposed route through Cambridge, Peterborough and Lincoln had been published, Joseph Gibbs announced a similar 'Great Northern Railway'. By this time a railway from London to Birmingham had already been approved and George Stephenson was planning further extensions north to Derby, Leeds, York and beyond. In 1836 parliament considered bills for these various proposals and was persuaded by Stephenson and George Hudson, a York draper, that the line to the north via Derby would be quite sufficient, so Handley's Northern and Eastern was authorized only from London to Cambridge and Gibbs's Great Northern was rejected completely. Parliament approved a line from Manchester to Sheffield and the MCR to connect Nottingham with other towns but schemes to link Boston to London and Nottingham fell by the way. The approved lines were built during the following years but few new schemes were put forward.[4]

Opposition to new schemes was so great that even a Blisworth to Peterborough branch proposed by the LBR in 1843 was only carried in the house of lords by one vote. The line from London was opened to Birmingham in 1838, to Nottingham via Derby in 1839, and to Leicester, Leeds, York and Hull in 1840. By the latter date railways circled round Lincolnshire but came no nearer than Nottingham or Hull. The railways from London to Cambridge and from Manchester to Sheffield took much longer to build, although the final section of one from Manchester to Leeds was opened in 1841.[5]

Lincolnshire lacked the benefit of railways, but the coaching trade of Stamford and Grantham started to suffer from the railway competition on the route to the north. Coach timetables were adapted to make connections with the nearest train services. In 1838 the *Railway* coach started a service from Lincoln to a station on the LBR near Northampton and four years later the *Sliding Scale* light four-inside coach started running 'under the patronage of the NMR company' between Norwich and the Masborough station via Boston, Sleaford and Lincoln. Other coaches ran from New Holland to Masborough and from Boston to stations near Chesterfield and

[4] E. G. Barnes, *The Rise of the Midland Railway 1844–74*, London, 1966, pp. 57, 58; Grinling, *Great Northern*, pp. 2, 3; Ruddock and Pearson, pp. 43, 89; names of MCR and other lines are listed in full in Appendix III below, pp. 262–63.
[5] Grinling, *Great Northern*, pp. 4, 8.

Leicester. The LBR branch reached Peterborough in 1845 and on the same day a new coach service was inaugurated between Louth and Peterborough station. Lincoln stage-coaches ran to Wansford where that railway crossed the Great North Road. Goods wagons also adapted their routes to take advantage of the developing railway system: when the first railway entered Lincolnshire, Pickford and Co. established an office at the Lincoln station and premises in Louth and Grimsby. Long-distance wagons eventually disappeared from the roads but local carriers became, even more numerous in the second half of the century.[6]

RAILWAY MANIA

As the economy recovered in the late summer of 1843 sober city financiers started to invest in new railway schemes and their lead was followed with astonishing enthusiasm by the investing public. A London committee employed Sir John Rennie and Mr Gravatt to survey a Direct Northern line between London and York, but local landowners and recently established companies in adjacent counties also launched several projects for Lincolnshire railways in the spring of 1844. One of the first was for a Wakefield and Lincoln railway, engineered by William Cubitt; this scheme was later extended to Boston and for much of its length was to be built on the banks of the Fossdyke and the Witham navigation.[7]

A committee of Lincolnshire landowners headed by Charles Chaplin (1786–1859) of Blankney and including Henry Handley, G. H. Packe and Lord Worsley employed a reluctant James Walker to re-survey his earlier proposal and they issued a prospectus for a Cambridge and York railway on 22 February 1844; the ECR already had authority for a line to Cambridge. The earl of Yarborough owned much land in north-east Lincolnshire and his son Lord Worsley (1809–62) dominated railway developments in the north of the county. Worsley and the three other county members of parliament were more involved in railway schemes than most of their borough colleagues, with the exceptions of Sir James Duke (1792–1873) and William Rickford Collett who sat for Boston and Lincoln respectively. Colonel Charles de Laet Waldo-Sibthorp (1783–1855), the other Lincoln member, was an implacable enemy of all railways and said he would vote for no railroad save one that would take ministers to hell.[8]

[6] Ruddock and Pearson, p. 37; *SM*, 29 April 1842, 11 June 1844, 5 February 1847.
[7] Barnes, *Rise of the Midland Railway*, p. 64; Ruddock and Pearson, p. 43.
[8] Grinling, *Great Northern*, p. 9; Hill, *Victorian Lincoln*, pp. 22, 30.

The Cambridge and York scheme immediately aroused the opposition of the ECR and three companies which on 10 May were to amalgamate as the MR, with George Hudson 'the railway king' as their chairman. They responded by proposing branches to Lincoln from several directions, including Nottingham. Branches to Lincoln and Gainsborough were also proposed by Michael Ellison of Sheffield and others connected with the SAMR.[9]

In April two other groups joined the contest for the London to York route; Major William Amsinck's London committee proposed a Direct Northern railway through Peterborough, Doddington (near Lincoln) and Gainsborough, and Edmund Denison (1787–1874) of Doncaster gave preliminary notice of a Great Northern railway, a version of Joseph Gibbs's nine-year-old scheme revised to go further west through Stamford, Grantham, Newark, Gainsborough and Doncaster. Denison had originally been called Edmund Beckett and his elder brother Sir John Beckett lived at Somerby Park near Gainsborough; their other brothers included the Revd George Beckett, some-time vicar of Gainsborough. As an MP during the 1830s Sir John (1775–1847) had chaired parliamentary committees examining several railway bills and in 1844 he was one of the first to invite Hudson's NMR to extend to Gainsborough.[10]

The Direct Northern and Great Northern schemes prompted the original Cambridge and York group to have Walker survey an extension of their line through Peterborough to London and they issued a new prospectus on 3 May for a London and York railway. A fortnight later Chaplin, Packe and others met Denison and Francis Mowatt and decided to unite their efforts. William Astell, MP for Bedfordshire, became chairman of the new London and York committee with Denison and Mowatt as vice-chairmen. The six directors from Lincolnshire were Packe, three county members of parliament (Trollope, Turnor and Christopher), Viscount Alford, son of Lord Brownlow and the Hon. Alexander Leslie-Melville. Denison quickly emerged as leader of this group and Packe became his principal Lincolnshire confederate. Melville (1800–81), brother of the earl of Leven and Melville, represented Smith, Ellison and Co., the principal Lincolnshire bankers, and later also became treasurer of Lord Worsley's GGSJR. The Direct Northern stayed out of Denison's group and the ECR and MR

[9] Barnes, *Rise of the Midland Railway*, p. 38; Grinling, *Great Northern*, pp. 11, 13.
[10] Grinling, *Great Northern*, pp. 10, 11, 13; White, *Directory*, 1856, p. 189; R. J. Olney, *Lincolnshire Politics 1832–1885*, London, 1973; p. 109.

extended their own proposals for branches across the county including a line from Syston (near Leicester) to join an authorized ECR branch at Peterborough. The most urgent issue for Denison's group was whether their main line should follow Walker's 'fens' line via Peterborough, Sleaford, Lincoln and Gainsborough or Gibbs's 'towns' line via Stamford and Grantham. The fens line would be cheaper to construct but the towns line would have more traffic, and on 22 August 1844 the directors announced that their line would go via Stamford, Grantham, Gainsborough and Doncaster with branches to Lincoln and Newark. Earl Fitzwilliam objected to the main line avoiding his town of Peterborough, even though it was smaller than Stamford, and by the time the scheme went to parliament the towns line had been modified to include Peterborough, Newark and Retford. [11]

The choice of the towns line (shown in fig. 27) led Henry Handley and Cambridge supporters of the original scheme to defect from the London and York group. With the support of Earl Fitzwilliam they adopted a Cambridge and Lincoln scheme already surveyed by James Meadows Rendel (1799–1856) for a line via Peterborough and along the Car Dyke with branches to Stamford, Spalding, Sleaford and Boston. Rendel declined to be their engineer because of the 'multiplicity and importance of his professional engagements', which shortly included the new Grimsby dock. [12] The position was filled by George Watson Buck, engineer of a proposed Ely and Bedford railway in which General Birch Reynardson, one of Handley's few Lincolnshire supporters, was also involved. George Hudson encouraged Handley's party as a further harassment to Denison but Chaplin, Packe and other Lincolnshire landowners stayed loyal to the London and York. Further disadvantages of the new group were that Handley was in declining health for some time before his death in 1846 and the survey they had adopted only went as far north as Lincoln. To overcome this latter difficulty a committee headed by Earl Fitzwilliam employed George Leather and Son of Leeds to survey a 'Lincoln, York and Leeds Direct and Independent Railway' through the Isle of Axholme as an extension of the Cambridge and Lincoln line, but the prospectus did not appear until December 1844.

On 30 August Captain Law's Wakefield and Boston scheme had united with Denison's group and William Cubitt, the London and

---

[11] Grinling, *Great Northern*, pp. 15, 16; Barnes, *Rise of the Midland Railway*, p. 38.
[12] *SM*, 4 October 1844.

York's new engineer, combined that scheme with a proposed branch from Peterborough to Boston as a Lincolnshire loop line, which would leave the towns line at Peterborough and pass through Boston and Lincoln to rejoin it at Bawtry. Together with branches to Wakefield, Sheffield, Bedford and Stamford the proposals of the London and York amounted to 327½ miles of route, a far longer system than any company then controlled, and Cubitt estimated the cost at £6½ million. [13]

Schemes were also afoot in north Lincolnshire. In August 1844 the SAMR agreed to unite with the proposed SLJR from Sheffield to Gainsborough and Lincoln and in October they proposed a GGSJR running from Gainsborough to Grimsby. The provisional committee included Lord Yarborough and Lord Worsley together with John Parker, Michael Ellison and other directors of the SAMR and the SLJR. A meeting in Grimsby on 6 November chose a route via Brigg with branches to the ferry at New Holland and from Brigg to Market Rasen. With the support of the Grimsby Haven company, of which Lord Worsley was chairman, a new Grimsby Docks company was proposed to improve the port at an estimated cost of £320,000. [14]

Railway companies needed statutory powers for many purposes such as the compulsory purchase of land and the right to hold up road traffic at level crossings. Plans and details of proposed railways had to be deposited by 30 November for consideration in the next parliamentary session and 224 bills were deposited in 1844. The Lincolnshire schemes included the GGSJR, three north–south routes proposed by different committees, and three branches proposed by the MR. A board of trade committee examined all railway schemes and submitted recommendations to parliament on their relative merits. Their report on the group of schemes for the north-south route appeared on 11 March 1845 and favoured the Cambridge and Lincoln line as continued northwards by the Direct Northern, in preference to the London and York scheme. The Direct Northern promoters had on the previous day indicated to the committee that they would agree to combine with the Cambridge and Lincoln and build only the northern end of their line. Parliament usually accepted the board's advice, so Handley and his friends were delighted at the recommendation. But the London and York bill had already passed its second reading in the Commons

[13] *SM*, 30 August 1844; Grinling, *Great Northern*, p. 25.
[14] Dow, *Great Central*, I, pp. 46, 85, 86, 95.

and on 12 March its promoters declared their intention to continue.[15]

The decision of the board of trade produced a variety of reactions
in Lincolnshire, from satisfaction among Gainsborough merchants
who favoured the Direct Northern line to protests in Boston and
dissatisfaction in Grantham. In Lincoln feeling between the rival
factions was strong: a city meeting endorsed the Cambridge and
Lincoln scheme but ended in disorder. A great meeting in the castle
yard which had attracted about eight thousand people from all over
the county was indecisive but was eventually declared in favour of
the London and York. With these indications of local support the
London and York not only continued to press its deposited scheme
but also decided in conjunction with the GGSJR to promote an ELR
from Grimsby to Boston with a board including Denison, Packe,
Michael Ellison and Charles Tennyson d'Eyncourt. In March the
GGSJR had also launched a scheme for a fifteen-mile extension
from Market Rasen 'to join the line of railway which may be
sanctioned from Lincoln to London'.[16]

The parliamentary examination of the various north-south
schemes was protracted and all bills in this group were deferred
until the following session. Proceedings in other committees
moved more smoothly; on 30 June 1845 acts were passed for the
GGSJR and the MR's branches from Nottingham to Lincoln and
Syston to Peterborough. Bells were rung in Stamford, which by
then had an omnibus to Sibson station on the LBR's Peterborough
branch opened on 2 June. The Grimsby Docks act was passed on
8 August and public rejoicings were held in that borough. The
company took over the assets of the old Haven company and
resolved to amalgamate with the GGSJR, only Charles Tennyson
d'Eyncourt voting against.[17]

NEW HOLLAND FERRIES

In January 1845 a group of GGSJR directors and six other people
had bought the New Holland and old Barrow ferries, including the
jetty, Yarborough Arms and other land and property at New
Holland for £10,000. They considered that they had purchased in
their own right, not on behalf of the GGSJR, and in October 1845

[15] Grinling, *Great Northern*, pp. 30, 31, 33.
[16] *SM*, 28 March 1845, 25 April 1845; Ruddock and Pearson, p. 77; Dow, *Great
Central*, I, p. 93.
[17] Grinling, *Great Northern*, pp. 42, 44; R. S. Lambert, *The Railway King — A
Study of George Hudson and the Business Morals of his Times*, London, 1934, p. 149;
Dow, *Great Central*, I, pp. 87, 97.

sold them to the company for £21,000: they had made a profit of £11,000 on an outlay of £10,000 in less than nine months. The disgrace of George Hudson in 1849 prompted inquiries in other companies and exposure of the Humber ferries deal led to the resignation of Michael Ellison in June 1849, his place on the board being taken by Samuel Morton Peto.[18]

A PLETHORA OF SCHEMES

During 1845, while parliament was considering the previous year's proposals, many more railway schemes came out. Speculation in railway stocks and shares reached hysterical proportions and practical schemes had to contend with a mass of dubious and even dishonest projects. Public interest was so great that in June W. G. Wagstaffe opened shop as a dealer in railway shares in Westgate, Grantham and in the autumn several brokers opened offices in Lincoln; in November a stock exchange was opened in the city in a room annexed to the city assembly rooms. As the mania swept the country not only did new schemes appear but considerable extensions were proposed by operational railway companies and by the promoters of railway schemes launched in 1844. The situation was one of constant change as promoters responded to the new schemes that appeared week by week during the summer and autumn of 1845. Some were promoted to meet the genuine needs of commerce but many were pure speculation by financiers looking for gaps in the railway map of England. It eventually reached such proportions that a local humorist placed an advertisement in the *Stamford Mercury* of 7 November for a 'Bridge-End, Burton Pedwardine, Scredington, Three Queens, and Midland Junction Railway, with a branch to Rauceby and Byard's Leap'; the claims for many other projected railways were often as ridiculous as those in this advertisement allegedly inserted by Messrs Bubble and Squeak of Scredington and Timothy Teazer of Burton Pedwardine![19]

In southern Lincolnshire several schemes extended westwards from the LDR at Kings Lynn, while in the north many proposed to run east from the MR at Lincoln to serve the towns of Lindsey. Many other schemes were also planned to connect with these and other approved railways such as the WPGR. In September representatives of the GGSJR, the SLJR and the SAMR agreed to amalgamate their three undertakings as the MSLR. The GGSJR

[18] A. A. D'Orley, *The Humber Ferries*, Knaresborough, 1968, pp. 37, 39; Dow, *Great Central*, I, p. 142.
[19] *SM*, 5 October 1845, 7 November 1845, 14 November 1845.

was already expecting to absorb the Grimsby Docks company, and they agreed to include the ELR if it concurred. For the next session the GGSJR sought several further lines in Lincolnshire, including a branch from New Holland to Barton-on-Humber, and the SLJR's Lincoln branch, rejected by parliament in the previous session, was revived as the independent SLER.[20]

One of the main new Lincolnshire schemes to appear in 1845 was the ANBEJR, which was to extend from Boston westwards via Grantham and Nottingham to join a proposed transpennine railway at Ambergate in Derbyshire. In direct competition was a Grand Union railway from Nottingham to Lynn, to which were soon added an extension to Ambergate and a branch to Boston; both schemes enjoyed considerable support in Boston. Other schemes put forward at this time varied from grandiose projects such as the Lincolnshire and Eastern Junction (from Selby to Cambridge via Brigg and Horncastle) to the East Coast Railway promoted by William Skelton of Sutton Bridge to connect Lynn and Boston with a branch to Spalding. Altogether over eight hundred railway bills were deposited in 1845 but by then panic was setting in as first calls were being made on shares in many of the schemes. The new Lincoln stock exchange had only two or three deals a day; everyone wanted to sell and none to buy.[21]

The London and York and other bills were carried over from the previous session and George Hudson, who was now also chairman of the ECR, pursued his opposition even more vigorously. But as the need for a direct trunk line had been proved he tried more seriously to provide this himself. The promoters of the Cambridge and Lincoln line agreed to join the ECR but an invitation to the London and York was vigorously rejected. The Direct Northern group remained independent until May 1846 when they united with the London and York to form the GNR. The abandonment of some projects and amalgamation with similar schemes was in response to the depression which followed the mania; there was not enough money to build all the authorized lines.[22]

New lines authorized in 1846 included the SLJR and the SLER which amalgamated with their partners to form the MSLR in 1847. Hudson's pressure on the London and York was in the end of no avail and on 28 June 1846 it obtained its act as the GNR. Henry

[20] Dow, *Great Central*, 1, pp. 75, 77, 98; Ruddock and Pearson, p. 145.
[21] N. R. Wright, *The Railways of Boston*, Boston, 1971, p. 14; *SM*, 25 April 1845, 12 May 1845, 30 May 1845.
[22] Lambert, *The Railway King*, pp. 160, 162; Ruddock and Pearson, p. 46.

Handley died on the following day, but his dream of a main railway line through the centre of the county was to be achieved thirty-six years later as the GNGEJR. Handley's admirers contributed over £1,000 for the erection of the large monument which still stands in South Street, Sleaford. [23]

The GNR obtained the act for its main line and the Lincolnshire loop line but lost several branches and most of its allied lines except the ELR, which it leased in 1847. The ANBEJR also obtained its act, much to the pleasure of its Boston supporters, who regarded it as the line of most potential benefit to the town. Hudson's wish to add it to his system was defeated and instead a working agreement with the GNR was reached in 1852. Denison was elected chairman of the GNR in 1847 and Packe succeeded him as deputy chairman until 1864 when he became chairman in his turn. Packe was also a director of the ELR and other companies in which the GNR was concerned. The only other Lincolnshire directors of the GNR were Richard Ellison and Charles Chaplin, the latter in place of the Revd Humphrey Waldo-Sibthorp who was named in the act. [24]

CONSTRUCTION

In the autumn of 1845 there was not a single mile of railway in Lincolnshire but four years later there were about 220 miles of route open and a further fifty under construction, most of them double track. These railways were made by pick and shovel, with very little mechanical assistance. To undertake this a considerable workforce was needed; although some would be local labourers, the skilled labouring would fall to navvies who moved from job to job, often following a good employer such as S. M. Peto. Most lines across Lincolnshire were relatively easy to construct and there would perhaps be a high proportion of local labour.

The navvies earned considerably more than an agricultural labourer and spent almost all of it on food and drink, for theirs was hard physical labour. Night after night, according to the shocked *Stamford Mercury*, Kirton-in-Lindsey presented a scene of intemperance and uproar caused by the railway navvies and a few local troublemakers: the inhabitants were said to be 'kept in a constant state of terror and alarm' by this riotous conduct. When the Blisworth to Peterborough line was approaching completion and

---

[23] Lambert, op. cit., p. 185; Olney, *Lincolnshire Politics*, p. 154; White, *Directory*, 1856, p. 433.
[24] Grinling, *Great Northern*, p. 56; J. Wrottesley, *The Great Northern Railway*, London, 1979, pp. 26, 243.

K

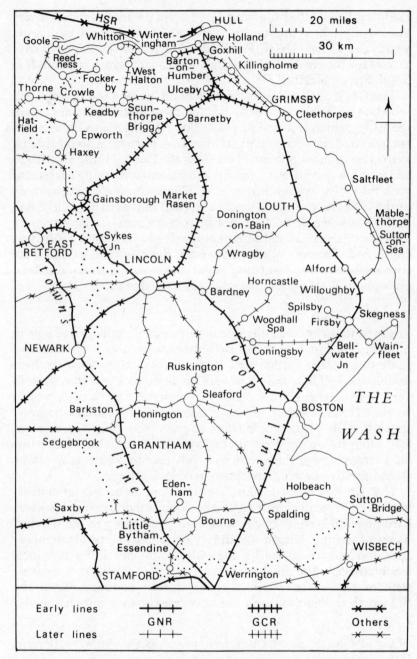

Figure 27   *Railways in Lincolnshire in 1914*

Early lines: railways open by 31 December 1850; *later lines*: railways open
by 31 December 1914

navvies were leaving the area south of Stamford a correspondent told the *Mercury* that they left

bills unpaid in all the villages where they could obtain credit with tradespeople or those who let lodgings; the losses sustained are in many cases very severe. And not only does the district suffer in a pecuniary view from the visit of these freebooters, but the fellows have taken many women from the neighbourhood, and in some instances the wives of decent men and the mothers of families, who have been induced to rob their husbands and abscond.[25]

On the credit side local people stood to gain by the sale of timber, food and beer to the contractors. Iron had to be imported but bricks could be made near sites such as Kirton tunnel or Deeping St James next to the loop line. In the short term many small local firms benefited by the demand for railway equipment. Smith's shipyard in Gainsborough installed a steam saw-bench to meet the railways' demand for timber.

Early in July 1845 surveyors appeared in Lincoln and Stamford and construction of the Lincoln line started in October. Hudson promised completion within a year, and the thirty-three mile line was opened for regular service on 4 August 1846. The Syston and Peterborough line took longer to construct and the two end sections were opened first. Until the middle part was opened the Stamford to Peterborough section was operated by the ECR, whose own line from Ely to Peterborough had been opened in 1847. The contract for the GGSJR's main line from Grimsby to Gainsborough and the New Holland branch was let in August 1845, and the contract for the Market Rasen to Lincoln extension a year later. Lord Yarborough accepted shares in payment for the land crossed by this railway and so became the third largest shareholder and eventually first chairman of the MSLR.[26]

During the mania many people of small means had put their names down for shares, hoping to sell and make a quick profit, but as the market collapsed in 1846 and 1847 they found great difficulty in meeting the calls made upon them for capital to finance construction. As shareholders defaulted, some new companies collapsed and authorized lines were never built. The ANBEJR was burdened with liabilities in respect of canals; in the event it managed to construct only its central section between Grantham and Nottingham, abandoning its eastern and western sections to the chagrin

[25] *SM*, 28 March 1845, 7 November 1845.
[26] *SM*, 15 August 1845, 22 August 1845; Ruddock and Pearson, pp. 107, 108, 193; N. C. Birch, *Stamford — An Industrial History*, Lincoln, 1972, p. 33; Dow, *Great Central*, I, pp. 84, 87, 92.

of its Boston supporters. Work on the MSLR was slowed down so much that it lost the advantage of being authorized one year before the GNR. Construction did start on the other authorized lines in Lincolnshire, even if it proceeded only slowly. The GNR awarded the contract for their line between London and Peterborough in November 1846, but north of Peterborough the towns line was deferred. The company decided to proceed first with the loop line between Peterborough and Gainsborough. Contracts were also issued for the ELR, the MSLR branch from Barnetby to Market Rasen, and the New Holland pier and associated works. In July 1847 Charles Kirk of Sleaford undertook the contract to build stations and level crossing houses on the MSLR between New Holland, Grimsby and Lincoln for £36,000. During the following decades Kirk and Parry were to undertake several contracts for the GNR.[27]

OPENINGS

On 1 March 1848 the GNR and the MSLR opened their first sections simultaneously, nineteen months after the MR's Lincoln branch, to provide a through service between Louth and the New Holland ferry. The initial service was provided jointly by the two companies and figure 28 shows the first train passing Grimsby church. Trains ran right along the 1,500 feet long New Holland pier designed by John Fowler (1817–98) for passengers to catch the iron steam ferry-boats acquired by the MSLR. Early in 1849 the company installed a floating pontoon at the end of the pier to make transfer easier between railway and steamer. Trains continued to use the New Holland pier until the Humber bridge was opened on 24 June 1981. The growth of New Holland and its railway connections soon put an end to other ferries to Hull though the Barton–Hessle ferry survived throughout the 1850s. Steam packets continued to run between Hull and Gainsborough until the present century, and sailing packets ran from Hull to Barton and other places on the Lincolnshire coast until about 1950.[28]

Later in 1848 a further portion of the ELR was opened from Louth to Firsby and at about the same time the first section of the GNR's main line was also in use, namely the five miles from

[27] Lambert, *The Railway King*, p. 221; Grinling, *Great Northern*, pp. 63, 108; Dow, *Great Central*, I, pp. 112, 113; Wrottesley, *Great Northern Railway*, pp. 99, 127–28, 165.
[28] Grinling, *Great Northern*, p. 3; Dow, *Great Central*, I, p. 172; D'Orley, *Humber Ferries*, p. 48; the dates of opening of all railways in Lincolnshire are given in Appendix III.

Figure 28   *The first train between Louth and New Holland, passing St James's church, Grimsby*

Doncaster to Askern junction. Soon the final section of the ELR was opened to Boston and then the fifty-eight miles of the loop line between Lincoln and Werrington (near Peterborough), giving the GNR one hundred miles of railway operating in Lincolnshire. From Werrington to Peterborough trains ran on MR tracks and from Peterborough there were two rail routes to London, by the ECR and the LNWR. The opening of the GNR caused little excitement in Lincoln, which had grown used to the MR, but in Boston there was great enthusiasm and celebrations. At this time the MSLR had only sixteen miles of route open in Lincolnshire but by the end of the year their services extended beyond Ulceby to Brigg and Lincoln, where they crossed the High Street to enter the MR station. In 1849 further sections were opened in the north-west of the county, to give through routes from Lincolnshire to Leeds and to Liverpool. The company then had only the Leverton branch and the Grimsby dock to complete. On 18 April 1849 Prince Albert travelled by train via Lincoln to lay the foundation stone of the dock, returning via Boston.[29]

By the autumn of 1849 lines were opened between Lincoln and Doncaster and the GNR started developing a coal trade between

[29] Grinling, *Great Northern*, p. 79; Dow, *Great Central*, I, pp. 122, 123, 127.

south Yorkshire and Lincolnshire. A year later work started on the towns line in the vicinity of Grantham, tunnelling through the Kesteven uplands on what, at £25,000 per mile, was the most expensive stretch of the whole GNR. This included the 1,352 yard long Stoke tunnel between the Glen and Witham valleys and Peascliffe tunnel to avoid the vicinity of Belton House.[30]

By the end of 1849 all of the lines in Lincolnshire authorized in 1845 and 1846 were in operation, with the exception of the towns line, the Leverton branch, the ANBEJR (parts of which were under construction) and an independent Stamford–Wisbech line, which had been abandoned. Work was also going ahead on the great dock at Grimsby. The ANBEJR was only able to build the central part of its line between Grantham and Nottingham and was absorbed by the GNR, whose towns line between Peterborough and Retford was opened in 1852; the expresses were then transferred from the loop to the main line.[31]

CONSEQUENCES FOR TRAVEL

Once the railways were open, the immediate effect was to provide a means of transport more reliable than the waterways, able to carry greater quantities than road vehicles, and faster than either. For passengers they were cheaper, faster and, in the first class, more comfortable than coaches. Every day there was at least one 'parliamentary train' which stopped at every station and had facilities for third-class passengers. Stage-coaches could not compete and only survived as feeders, bringing to the stations passengers from villages and towns like Sleaford which lacked railways of their own. Coachmen and guards, recently admired for their dash, became redundant: the inns in Stamford and Grantham were badly hit by the end of long-distance coaching. The income of toll-gates furthest from towns also fell, but it rose at gates on the edges of towns that had stations. This occurred at both ends of the Alford–Boston turnpike road after the ELR opened and the Lincoln–Peterborough road was similarly affected by the opening of the loop line. Following the opening of the MSLR, takings at most gates on the Barton–Lincoln road fell greatly except at Brigg where at one gate they actually increased.[32]

---

[30] Ruddock and Pearson, p. 49; Grinling, *Great Northern*, pp. 80, 83, 85, 86, 89, 90; Honeybone, *Grantham*, p. 58; A. Rogers, *A History of Lincolnshire*, Henley-on-Thames, 1970, p. 81.
[31] Grinling, *Great Northern*, p. 117.
[32] *SM*, 4 August 1848, 3 August 1849.

Patterns of travel changed as railways came closer to Lincoln-shire; coaches and other road users took new routes in order to reach the nearest railway station. In 1842 it was reported that many sheep from Boston were driven seventy miles and travelled the remaining fifty to London by railway, saving four or five days in time, and the small additional charge was less than the value of sheep which would have been lost on the road. Cattle pens were established at many country stations as well as in the towns to carry livestock to London and take this important traffic off the roads. In 1849 takings at the Witham Common bar on the Great North Road were only £151 compared with £1,010 in 1834 and near Grantham the Spittlegate Hill bar on the same road took only £771 compared with £1,355 in 1834. Although traffic on the Great North Road had declined, the takings at other gates around Grantham suggested an increase in traffic between places east of the town and the railheads of Nottingham and Melton Mowbray, followed by a decline after the loop line was opened. In 1850 it was said of Grantham that 'no town in England has suffered more by railways'.[33]

The opening of the railway between Stamford and Leicester was followed by an increase in traffic on roads from places like Bourne and a further decline on the Great North Road and on the road to Rutland, which was now served by the railway. In April 1850 the lessee of the Newstead toll-bar complained of the 'immense' loss he had sustained in consequence of the Uffington railway station being used as a coal depot. In October 1852 the trustees of the roads around Stamford were told that revenue on the Grantham road had fallen considerably and they reduced the tolls on all bars by one third with effect from 1 February 1853.[34]

Proprietors of navigations such as the Fossdyke and the Gran-tham canal did well by selling or leasing their undertakings to railway companies, and when the Great Northern act was passed in 1846 the bells of St Peter-at-Arches in Lincoln were rung in celebration by the owners of the navigation whose future income was thus assured. But the future of those working on the water-ways was less secure. Passenger traffic on the waterways continued for some decades: even on the Witham, though the GNR intro-duced a fourth-class fare of 1s. 3d. for the journey between Lincoln and Boston, it finally succumbed only in 1863. The fate of the ports was decided by the railway companies. The construction of a dock at Grimsby turned that old port into a significant town while the

---

[33] Wright, *Railways of Boston*, p. 1; *SM*, 16 November 1849, 24 May 1850.
[34] *SM*, 14 April 1850, 8 October 1852.

coastal traffic of Boston and Gainsborough was greatly reduced by railway competition. The GNR was carrying the agricultural produce which had previously gone by water either to London or Yorkshire, taking some into their Skirbeck Quarter granary direct from barges in the Redstone Gowt drain.[35]

The opening of railways affected not only road and water traffic but over the next hundred years was to lead to changes in commerce, industry and society. Raw materials, finished goods and passengers could move about much more easily than in the days of canal and turnpike, and most of the changes described in the second half of this volume are consequences of the arrival of the railways. Even if time and space had not been annihilated they had certainly shrunk.

[35] Ruddock and Pearson, p. 87.

CHAPTER 6

ENGINEERING FIRMS

E VERY self-respecting Victorian market town had a foundry, to supply the often humble needs of local agriculture and industry. Not many of them expanded their market much outside the immediate area. Lincolnshire, however, while possessing its normal quota of such iron works, was quite exceptional in the number of them which made the grade to national and indeed worldwide renown. Some, like those in Boston, made their names known throughout England, but having flowered early, wilted early. The real successes were concentrated in the west, at Lincoln, Grantham and Gainsborough, and rose to prominence after 1845. The coming of the railways gave them cheaper coal and iron and improved access to markets throughout Britain and overseas. But their initial success was founded on the mechanical revolution of agriculture, in which Lincolnshire was in the forefront: the farms adopted the new machinery, the engineering firms produced and disseminated it throughout the world. The secret of their continued success, through later depressions and altered demands in agriculture, was diversification into different realms of engineering. Not only an astonishing number of actual machines, but a bewildering variety of machine types was produced. It was big business, with the annual output of machines and the number of employees both counted in thousands — an industry on a scale hitherto quite unknown in Lincolnshire.

The development of agricultural engineering was encouraged by shows such as those held annually by the Royal Agricultural Society of England, in whose formation in 1838 Henry Handley had been concerned and of which he became president in 1841. Several of the Lincolnshire engineers became life members of the society, and Clayton and Shuttleworth of the Stamp End iron works in Lincoln advertised extensively in its journal. The initial success of Lincolnshire engineering firms was based on the production of thrashing machines and steam engines for agriculture, though they also had other lines. During the first half of the century the introduction of thrashing machines had been violently resisted by agricultural labourers, who saw them as a threat to their main winter employment. But after 1850 the rural population was not growing as fast as it had been in the first half of the century and the railways made available to Lincolnshire firms cheaper coal and iron and new markets for their heavy products. Not only was Lincolnshire and the United Kingdom open to these firms but so were new grain areas being developed on distant continents.[1]

THE PORTABLE THRASHING MACHINE AND ENGINE

Britain led the world in the use of steam in agriculture and it has been estimated that by 1851 there were already eight thousand portable engines at work on British farms, but it still took several years for the use of steam to become widespread. Tuxford's steam-driven thrashing machine had been demonstrated at a local show in 1842 but at the Royal Show at York in 1848 most of the forty-eight thrashers on show were hand- or horse-powered. However, by 1852 there were nine firms demonstrating steam-powered moveable thrashing machines at the Royal Show at Lewes including Clayton's, who took the prize, Tuxford's and Hornsby's of Grantham. The next year at Gloucester twelve firms entered and three Lincolnshire firms took the top prizes for this type of machine, Clayton's winning in the category for fixed thrashing machines. By 1854, when the show was held at Lincoln, the portable thrasher had reached the essential form it was to retain until after the First World War. Mechanical details were improved in the following years but little change was made to the basic concept illustrated in figure 29. Lincolnshire firms produced a great many thrashing sets, consisting of elevators and portable or traction engines as well as the thrasher and perhaps a binder.[2]

Howden and Tuxford in Boston and Clayton and Shuttleworth in Lincoln had all produced portable steam engines by 1845 and within five years their example had been followed by A. Y. Barrett of Horncastle and Richard Hornsby (1790–1864) of Grantham. Barrett left the county within a short while but Hornsby's became one of the greatest firms in Lincolnshire. Hornsby produced his first portable engine in 1849 and it was an immediate success.

[1] J. Haining and C. Tyler, *Ploughing by Steam*, Hemel Hempstead, 1970, p. 101; R. J. Olney, *Lincolnshire Politics 1832–1885*, London, 1973, p. 114; N. J. L. Lyons, 'Some Notes on the Advertisements of Lincolnshire Firms in the Journal of the Royal Agricultural Society, 1853–1883', *LIA*, 4 no. 3 (1969), p. 42.
[2] H. Bonnett, *Saga of the Steam Plough*, London, 1965, pp. 45, 48; W. Tritton, 'The Origin of the Thrashing Machine', *Lincs. Mag.*, 2 (1934–36), pp. 56, 57.

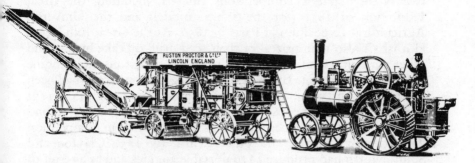

Figure 29 *A thrashing set made by Ruston, Procter and Co. of Lincoln,*
comprising a traction engine, thrashing machine and elevator

Figure 30 *A view of the great Stamp End iron works of Clayton and*
Shuttleworth, beside the river Witham at Lincoln in 1869

During the next eight years it won twenty-one first prizes out of twenty-three public competitions entered, including the Great Exhibition of 1851 (for the 8 h.p. model) and the Universal Agricultural Exposition at Paris in 1856. At the Great Exhibition Hornsby's also won prizes for their seed drill, oil cake bruiser and other agricultural machines, and from 1851 their portable engine was a major product. By 1854 the Spittlegate iron works had been extended to thirty-four furnaces and fourteen steam engines were in production simultaneously. At the Great Exhibition the second prize for portable engines was taken by Tuxford's in competition with Garrett, Burrell and other firms. By 1851 Clayton and Shuttleworth had produced 126 portable engines and as a result of their prominent place in the Great Exhibition they produced a further 209 engines that year.[3]

Up to 1850 the Lincolnshire firms had been producing portable engines only in small numbers, dozens rather than hundreds, but production greatly increased during the 1850s. Clayton and Shuttleworth claimed that by 1857 they had made 2,400 portables, of which five hundred were sold in 1856 alone. Five years later they were turning out fifteen per week, and *The Engineer* described the Stamp End works as the greatest manufactory in the world, employing no less than 940 men.[4]

OVERSEAS MARKETS

In 1848 Clayton and Shuttleworth had been proud to announce that their portable engine was used in other English counties as well as in Lincolnshire. Within ten years their horizons were much greater and other firms were eagerly following them into the wider world. Once thrashing sets had reached their standard design there was a constant search for new markets and Lincolnshire mechanics helped to build one of the greatest industrial empires ever seen. One of the first overseas markets for their thrashing sets was in Russia and Austro-Hungary, the great granary of Europe. In the museum of agriculture in Budapest is an early Clayton engine, no. 310, which was sold to Joseph Fehrer of Hungary in 1851 and worked continuously until 1900. In 1856 the *Stamford Mercury* 'noted that large

[3] R. H. Clark, *Steam Engine Builders of Lincolnshire*, Norwich, 1955, p. 3; M. Pointer, *Hornsby's of Grantham 1815–1918*, Grantham, 1976, pp. 6, 10; Honeybone, *Grantham*, p. 113; Haining and Tyler, *Ploughing by Steam*, p. 72; Lincolnshire Library, 'Industry II'.

[4] Lyons, 'Advertisements of Lincolnshire Firms in JRAS', p. 36; W. H. Hughes, *A Century of Traction Engines*, Newton Abbot, 1968, p. 73.

quantities of Clayton products were seen passing through Berlin on their way to Vienna for Hungarian grandees and landowners'.[5]

Richard Hornsby and new Lincoln firms of Ruston, Procter and Co. and William Foster were quick to follow Clayton and Shuttleworth into Europe. Hornsby exported his self-binding harvester as well as thrashing machines, and his portable engine won prizes at exhibitions in St Petersburg and Gothenburg. Clayton and Shuttleworth had addresses in both Vienna and Budapest by 1858 and moved into Russia after the Crimean War. Most of their portable engines made in 1864 were said to be bound for Russia, Austria and Hungary. In 1883 Joseph Shuttleworth's brother John was living in Vienna, where the firm's branch works had 1500 employees, but in 1911 they sold their branches in eastern Europe to a large Austrian syndicate. Their factory in the eastern suburbs of Pesth continued in business under the Hafer Schranz Clayton Shuttleworth label until at least 1949. William Foster opened a branch works and repair depot in Budapest, and his engines won prizes at exhibitions in Moscow in 1864, Hungary in 1869 and Vienna in 1873. In the latter years his Hungarian works built several torpedo boats for the Danube but because of the financial difficulties of the 1870s this branch was sold to a local syndicate in 1877. Robert Robey of Lincoln and Ruston, Procter and Co. also had branches in Budapest and other eastern European cities in the late nineteenth century.[6]

Other European markets for Lincolnshire products included France, where one of Tuxford's portable engines drove the machinery of the Paris Exhibition of 1855, but they also exported to markets outside Europe. By 1855 there was said to be a considerable foreign and colonial demand for Tuxford's products, and in 1857 Richard Hornsby employed five hundred men and was sending engines not only to Austria, Sweden and France but also to more distant markets in South America, Australia and New Zealand. That year Tuxford's exported traction engines to the West Indies, and in 1861 to Australia. Three years later Robert Robey won medals in Santiago. Thrashing sets were also exported to Canada, the USA and Egypt, and Joseph Ruston organized agencies in India, Japan, Chile, Argentina, USA, Russia, Hungary and elsewhere.[7]

[5] Hill, *Victorian Lincoln*, p. 122; Bonnett, *Saga of the Steam Plough*, p. 45.

[6] Honeybone, *Grantham*, p. 113; B. Newman, *One hundred years of good company*, Lincoln, 1957, p. 65; Hill, *Victorian Lincoln*, p. 122; Hughes, *Century of Traction Engines*, p. 73; Lincolnshire Library, 'Industry II', pp. 21, 148; *Lincolnshire Echo*, 3 October 1976; Lyons, 'Advertisements of Lincolnshire Firms in JRAS', p. 36.

[7] Thompson, *Boston*, p. 348; Pointer, *Hornsby's of Grantham*, p. 13; Hill, *Victorian Lincoln*, pp. 120, 122; Newman, *One hundred years of good company*, p. 14.

In many of these areas coal and timber were very scarce, whereas the straw left after thrashing had little or no value. The Head and Schemioth straw-burning system introduced at the Vienna Exhibition of 1873 proved a godsend for ploughing and thrashing, and the Lincolnshire firms offered engines designed to burn whatever local fuel was available. Marshall's of Gainsborough sent portable engines to the Andes and the hinterland of China and supplied the first steam-driven portable engine for oil-well drilling in Iraq.[8]

LINCOLNSHIRE FIRMS

William Tuxford was joined by his sons and the firm continued to experiment and develop new ideas for several years, producing many novel engines. In 1855 their wide range of products also included iron bridges and powerful pile-driving machinery. That year they purchased land to extend their works, but the firm did not expand as much as Clayton's, Hornsby's or Ruston's; in the 1880s it succumbed to the agricultural depression. Howden's foundry declined even more quickly. It was continued by his son until 1859 when he withdrew and left it in the hands of his partners William Wilkinson and Henry Wright who in 1861 employed fifty men and twenty boys. In 1862 they divided the premises between them and a year later Wilkinson moved to a foundry in Poole (Dorset), with Stephen Lewin, a Boston timber merchant, as sleeping partner. Lewin became more actively involved and in 1868 took over the Poole foundry, where he produced agricultural implements and a number of steam locomotives. Wright continued the Boston foundry on a reduced scale until about 1880.[9]

Before the railways arrived in the late 1840s, Boston's engineering firms had been foremost in Lincolnshire but by the 1890s none could compare with those in the west of the county. This decline may have been related to the general loss of economic vitality in the town, but Marshall's of Gainsborough grew in spite of the decline of that port. Another factor was perhaps the lack of railway sidings direct into the Boston works, since the haven lay between Tuxford's and the main line, and the extra cost of carrying raw materials into eastern Lincolnshire.

Clayton and Shuttleworth quickly grew into the principal engineering firm in the county, helped in 1848 by a bank guarantee from the steam millers, Coupland, Keyworth and Seely. At that

---

[8] Hughes, *A Century of Traction Engines*, p. 133; H. W. Brace, *Gainsborough, some Notes on its History*, Gainsborough, 1965, p. 87.

[9] Clark, *Steam Engine Builders*, p. xv; Thompson, *Boston*, p. 348.

date Clayton's employed a hundred men and the following year they began to exhibit at agricultural shows, taking the first of many prizes at Norwich. They were prominent at the 1851 Great Exhibition and by 1854 employed 520 men and eighty boys, whose average earnings were about £1 a week. In the centre of their Stamp End iron works, shown in figure 30, was a navigable strip of water connecting to the Witham and a little later a siding was laid into their works from the MSLR. Many of the buildings still standing today were erected in the 1860s, including the office block near the entrance. The thrashing machine and wood-working business was mainly east of the basin while the foundry and engine works were on the newly drained land on the west. By 1861 the firm had nine hundred employees, more than any other Lincolnshire firm at that time, and this had risen to 2,300 in 1885. By 1890 Clayton's total output of portable engines amounted to 26,000 plus 24,000 thrashing machines. The Stamp End iron works was well placed between the river and the railway; most of the city's engineering works were in this eastern part of the Lincoln gap, lying alongside the railways. The only firm to leave this area was Foster and Co., whose original Wellington works was cut off from the railway.[10]

In the 1850s and 1860s the established iron works of Smith and Ashby in Stamford, James Hart in Brigg and William Marshall and Sons in Gainsborough also started to produce portable steam engines, and new iron works were set up in Lincoln by Robert Robey, William Foster and Michael Penistan. By about 1875 the city had become the main centre of engineering in the county.

On 1 January 1857 the dynamic Joseph Ruston (1835–97) joined the partnership of Procter and Burton in Lincoln. He rapidly transformed their small business into the great Sheaf iron works (he had been apprenticed in Sheffield) and bought out his more timid partners, though the firm continued to trade as Ruston, Procter and Co. until 1918. Ruston's skills were commercial rather than those of an innovative engineer, and he soon followed Clayton and Hornsby into the eastern European market. By 1870 Ruston had increased the size of his workforce from twenty-five to seven hundred, which was a similar number to Tuxford's and Marshall's and was exceeded in Lincolnshire only by Clayton's and Hornsby's. In 1876 Ruston purchased the freehold of his site from the corporation and within thirty years his firm had expanded on to

[10] *Lincolnshire Echo*, 22 November 1977; Hill, *Victorian Lincoln*, p. 122; G. Measom, *Official Illustrated Guide to the Great Northern Railway*, London, 2nd edn 1861.

two other large sites in the city. When Joseph died in 1897 his firm had produced more than twenty thousand steam engines, most of them portables or traction, and nearly eleven thousand thrashing machines.[11]

In the 1850s Robert Robey from Nottingham and William Foster (c. 1816–76) from Manchester also established new iron works in this part of Lincoln, Foster's developing from his business as a merchant and miller. Foster produced his first portable engine at the Wellington iron works in 1858. Michael Penistan of Lincoln also progressed from the manufacture of horse-driven thrashing machines to steam engines, but it proved his ruin and the foundry in St Rumbold's Lane off Broadgate was acquired by William Rainsforth and Son about 1870. Rainsforth already had a fleet of keels and he started to produce agricultural machinery. Other Lincoln firms included the Lindum Plough works founded by John Cooke in 1851 and Penny and Porter of Broadgate. Harrison's Malleable iron works near St Mark's church was founded in 1874; thirty years later it amalgamated with the Hykeham Foundry Co. and moved to a rail-side site a little way out of the city. The extent of Lincoln's engineering industry allowed some firms to specialize; Edward Clarke started to produce cranks for other firms in 1859 and James Dawson made belting for power transmission after 1872. William Singleton developed from rope-making into the production of oil cloth and waterproof covers which brought him business from the railway companies and engineering firms.[12]

In Grantham William Hempstead started producing agricultural implements in 1852, and twenty years later a whole tribe of Hempsteads had separate firms, which amalgamated and became the Phoenix iron works on Dysart Road, making 7 or 8 h.p. steam engines of their own from 1877; but in December 1879 they went into liquidation.[13]

William Marshall (1812–61) purchased a small iron works at Gainsborough in 1848; as well as servicing the local oil and flour mills he also produced thrashing machines. On his early death the business passed to his two sons James (1836–1922) and Henry (1841–1906), who controlled the firm until the twentieth century

[11] Hill, *Victorian Lincoln*, p. 124; Newman, *One hundred years of good company*, p. 27.
[12] Hill, *Victorian Lincoln*, pp. 119, 120; Tritton, 'Origin of the Thrashing Machine', p. 57; Lincolnshire Library, 'Industry II', pp. 21, 93; L. Elvin, *Lincoln as it Was*, III, Nelson, 1979, p. 33; *Lincolnshire Echo*, 19 January 1977, 22 November 1977.
[13] Honeybone, *Grantham*, p. 113; *Lincolnshire Chronicle*, 5 December 1879.

and made it one of Lincolnshire's largest enterprises, completely dominating the economy of Gainsborough. William had moved to a site in front of the railway station in 1856; during the rest of the century the works extended southwards alongside the railway, with workers' housing filling the space between the railway and the old town on the river bank as shown in figure 22. Between 1885 and 1904 the number of employees rose from about 1,500 to 3,600 and the works then covered about twenty-eight acres. [14]

Small engineering firms developed in Grimsby to meet the needs of the expanding fishing industry, and other Lincolnshire towns also had small iron works but none grew to the scale found in Lincoln, Grantham and Gainsborough. The marquess of Exeter provided a site for Grant's iron works in Stamford but it did not last long: the entrance archway erected in 1845 still survives, though moved a short distance in 1937.

STEAM PLOUGHING

As early as 1829, Henry Handley had offered a prize of one hundred guineas for a satisfactory method of ploughing by steam power and during the next twenty-five years there were many experiments with different systems. Direct traction, a machine moving itself across a field and pulling a plough behind it, never really succeeded on the soft damp soils of Great Britain. The weight of the engine and the experimental state of self-moving engines led to the development of cable ploughing with an engine on the edge of a field hauling the plough on a long cable, the other end of which was attached either to another engine or to anchors. [15]

The flat fields and heavy clays of eastern England were particularly suitable for steam ploughing and in the early 1850s Lord Willoughby de Eresby (1782–1865) contributed greatly by his interest and money towards its development (fig. 31). His engines were made for him at the railway works in Swindon by his close friend Daniel Gooch, locomotive superintendent of the GWR, although one may have been made by Hornsby's. By 1852 his lordship had a stable of four iron horses which were used for a wide range of duties on the estate, two being leased to tenants for ploughing. In 1851 his first engine and a two-furrow plough had

[14] Brace, *Gainsborough, Notes on its History*, p. 81; I. S. Beckwith, *The Industrial Archaeology of Gainsborough*, Gainsborough, 1968; I. S. Beckwith, 'Religion in a Working Men's Parish 1843–1893', *LHA*, 5 (1970), p. 30.

[15] Haining and Tyler, *Ploughing by Steam*, p. 48; Bonnett, *Saga of the Steam Plough*, pp. 21, 24; idem, *History in Camera — Farming with Steam*, Princes Risborough, 1974, p. 14.

L

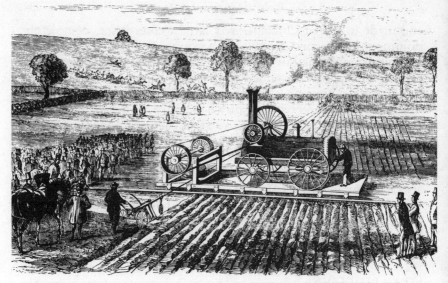

Figure 31   *Ploughing by steam. A demonstration by Lord Willoughby de Eresby at Grimsthorpe in 1850 was reported in the* Illustrated London News

Figure 32   *Traction-engine made by Tuxford and Sons of Boston with Boydell wheels, as exhibited at the Smithfield show in 1857*

been displayed at the Great Exhibition and in 1854 through *The Times* he invited gentlemen to visit Grimsthorpe by appointment to see his system in operation and freely to take notes and drawings. Lord Willoughby then used his engines to establish the Edenham and Little Bytham Railway to connect Grimsthorpe Castle to the GNR's towns line.[16]

In an attempt to overcome some problems of direct traction James Boydell produced a detailed specification in 1854 for wheels to be fitted with shoes round the rim, designed to form a continuous track as the vehicle moved along. After 1855 several firms produced self-moving engines with Boydell wheels and on three days in July 1857 there were well-publicized demonstrations in Lincolnshire of a Burrell-Boydell hauling different makes of plough. Many implement makers were present as well as spectators from Cuba, Russia, Germany and Sweden. Tuxford's was the first Lincolnshire firm to produce a self-moving engine with Boydell wheels (fig. 32). They exported several to Cuba and the West Indies in 1857, for ploughing and haulage on sugar plantations. They were three-wheeled vehicles, with a steersman at the front and a stoker at the rear: Clayton and Shuttleworth made and exported a similar vehicle to Odessa in May 1858. Boydell's wheels gave considerable pulling power to any engine to which they were fitted but the shoes and guides were easily broken on hard stony roads and most firms had abandoned the system by 1860.[17]

The production of steam ploughing equipment on a commercial basis was finally achieved by John Fowler (1826–64), who from 1856 had sets manufactured by Clayton and Shuttleworth and other firms before he opened his own works in Leeds in 1862. In the early 1860s Robey's produced a few ploughing engines for a system patented by W. Savory and Son of Gloucester but this did not prove popular. By 1871 the novelty and excitement of steam cultivating exhibits at the Royal Shows had worn off; they were established. Steam ploughing sets were produced for over fifty years and many were used in Lincolnshire, but none were manufactured on a regular basis by firms in this county, even though Marshall's tried to break into the market about 1880. Tuxford and Sons also made a few traction engines which were employed on roundabout ploughing using manilla ropes. The sets were usually owned by contractors rather than by farmers, because of the cost involved and the

---

[16] Bonnett, *Farming with Steam*, p. 12; idem, *Saga of the Steam Plough*, pp. 27, 28, 30; *Illustrated London News*, 12 June 1852.

[17] Hughes, *A Century of Traction Engines*, pp. 37, 41; Clark, *Steam Engine Builders*, pp. 120, 121; P. A. Wright, *Traction Engines*, London, 1959, p. 13.

limited and specialized work. One of the largest contractors in the kingdom was Ward and Dale of Sleaford, which was formed in the 1870s and reached its peak about 1918. They had twenty-four double engine sets, of which one is now preserved in the Museum of Lincolnshire Life; in 1914 they harrowed 386 acres, ploughed 9,521 acres and dragged 54,842 acres. [18]

THE SELF-MOVING ENGINE

The thrashing machines and portable steam engines being exported from Lincolnshire each needed several horses to pull them; there would be great benefit to agriculture if machines could move themselves and also haul thrashing machines, elevators and other items. Tuxford's, Clayton's and Robey's were actively involved in the development of self-moving steam engines for use on roads and fields, although individual designs also came from Foster's, Hornsby's and two small firms. The main subjects of experiment were the transmission of power to the driving wheels and the steering. Power could be transmitted to the rear wheels by chains, gears or cranks and in several experiments steering was done by a driver at the front with a horizontal wheel to turn the single front wheel. Boydell's patent design was not a success but the idea of the self-moving or traction engine was pursued. Clayton and Shuttleworth made one to the design of Thomas Aveling of Rochester in 1859 and they and Tuxford's continued to experiment and improve throughout the 1860s. Robey and Foster had each produced their first traction engine by 1861 and at the Great Exhibition of the following year entries included engines by Robey and the short-lived Lincoln firm of Taplin and Co. Under the Locomotive Act of 1861 agricultural users of traction engines were exempted from paying road tolls but they were still subject to the Red Flag Act. Hornsby's of Grantham started producing traction engines in 1863, under Bonnall and Astbury patents, but apparently only a few were made. Richardson and Darley of Kirton-in-Lindsey also produced some during the 1860s. [19]

By 1866 the wheels of Clayton and Shuttleworth engines were made of wrought iron instead of cast iron and were close to the design which later became nearly universal for traction engines.

---

[18] Bonnett, *Saga of the Steam Plough*, pp. 34, 49, 71, 116; Hughes, op. cit., pp. 34, 89; Haining and Tyler, *Ploughing by Steam*, pp. 92, 93, 95, 180, 237; Bonnett, *Farming with Steam*, p. 16.
[19] Clark, *Steam Engine Builders*, pp. 12, 53, 83, 85, 111–13; Hughes, op. cit., pp. 74, 79, 80; Bonnett, op. cit., p. 29.

R. W. Thomson of Edinburgh patented solid rubber tyres for large vehicles and road engines in 1867, and as Tennant's of Leith were unable to supply the whole market, Robey's of Lincoln also started to produce engines on Thomson's principles. The two rear driving wheels were shod with Thomson's patent rubber tyres protected by steel tread plates, and the single front steerage wheel was iron-shod. In December 1870 one of Robey's steamers hauled an omnibus with forty-five passengers along Canwick Road and up Lindum Hill, which it climbed at 4 to 5 m.p.h., but the Red Flag Act prevented them reaching their full potential on English roads and they were not a success in agriculture.[20]

By 1870 most of the main features of the ultimate traction engine had already appeared even if they were not yet in common use, and during the next decade other firms entered the growing traction engine business. Ashby, Jeffrey and Luke of Stamford exhibited a somewhat unsuccessful engine in 1871 and Marshall's and Ruston's each made their first traction engine in 1876, entering the markets developed by pioneers such as Clayton's and Robey's. Hornsby's had produced very few engines of their unusual 1863 design but in 1880 they exhibited a traction engine of more orthodox layout and this became one of their best-known products. Similarly Marshall's produced a great many traction engines after they had improved the design in 1881, but Ruston had correctly anticipated later conventions and his design needed no drastic alteration.[21]

DIVERSIFICATION

The agricultural depression in the final quarter of the century greatly reduced the market for agricultural machinery on which the Lincolnshire engineering firms had been founded. Their economic success could no longer be based on thrashing machines and portable engines. Tuxford's of Boston followed Howden's and Hempstead's into oblivion in 1887 and Foster's sold their Hungarian branch, but most firms survived by diversifying into other lines. Some firms continued to produce agricultural equipment until the 1930s, and indeed the export trade in thrashing sets reached its peak in the years before 1914, but other firms moved away from agriculture and steam engines.

Several Lincolnshire firms, but particularly Robey and Co., went into the market for mining machinery such as winding engines and pit-head towers. A Robey Undertype steam engine drove the

---

[20] Hughes, op. cit., pp. 95, 100, 104; Clark, op. cit., p. 87.
[21] Hughes, op. cit., pp. 99, 131; Clark, op. cit., pp. 54, 62, 65, 101.

dynamo for the first electric light in Cleethorpes in 1882, and thereafter the firm introduced from the USA the first Edison dynamos and coupled them to their high-speed steam engines for electric power-station work. In conjunction with the patentee, Mr Dunbar, Ruston's developed steam excavators to replace the hard pick-and-shovel work of large civil engineering projects. They sold their first steam shovel in August 1875 and it was made almost entirely of wrought iron instead of the cast iron and timber used in earlier models by other manufacturers. They were used in the construction of the Albert dock in London in 1875–80 and on the construction of the Manchester Ship Canal in 1887 (fig. 33).[22]

During the agricultural depression Joseph Ruston's skill at searching out new markets was of inestimable value and his firm surpassed in size Clayton and Shuttleworth and all other Lincolnshire firms. When Ruston, Procter and Co. became a limited company in 1889, their most important products included not only steam engines and boilers but also electric lighting machines, centrifugal pumps and sugar mills. Marshall's of Gainsborough also developed other lines and by 1904 their products included tea-processing machinery and gold-dredging plant. Through William Jackson, a tea planter from Assam, Marshall's had started to produce machinery for the tea plantations of India in the early 1870s, and in 1884 Jackson and Marshall's together produced the world's first mechanical hot-air dryer.[23]

The success of the Lincoln firms in overcoming the agricultural depression led to the extension of their premises and the development of a new industrial area south-west of the city centre, on the banks of the upper Witham with sidings from the MR. About 1885 Ruston's established their saw mills, wood works and boiler works in the Spike Island area. Foster's also established premises for making thrashing machines in the same vicinity, and when rebuilt after a serious fire in 1898 the whole Wellington works was moved to the new site.[24]

STEAM ON THE ROADS AFTER 1880

Most turnpike trusts came to an end in the 1870s and after 1880 the use of steam traction by haulage contractors grew rapidly even

[22] Clark, op. cit., pp. 58, 95, 125; Hill, *Victorian Lincoln*, p. 120; Newman, *One hundred years of good company*, p. 16; *Lincolnshire Echo*, 2 August 1975.
[23] Newman, op. cit., p. 23; E. M. Hewitt, 'Agricultural Implement Makers', in VCH, *Lincs.*, p. 395; Beckwith, *Industrial Archaeology of Gainsborough*, p. 4; Brace, *Gainsborough, Notes on its History*, p. 84.
[24] Lincolnshire Libraries, 'Industry II'.

though their use on the roads was restricted by statute until 1896. The period 1890 to 1930 was the hey-day of steam road traction; not until the latter date could internal combustion engines compete with steam in undertaking real hard work. From the 1890s until 1914 there was a great increase in the export of British traction engines, steam rollers and road locomotives. During this time steam rollers were produced by Clayton and Shuttleworth, Ruston's, Marshall's and Robey's (plate XII). The Locomotive Act of 1878 had done away with the notorious red flag requirement but imposed speed limits of 4 m.p.h. in the country and 2 m.p.h. in towns. An act in 1896 allowed lighter mechanically propelled vehicles to travel at up to 14 m.p.h. and the Heavy Motor Car Act of 1903 permitted steam tractors not exceeding five tons in weight to travel at 5 m.p.h. This led most makers to introduce a tractor within that limit and light steam tractors started to appear in increasing numbers. They were essentially miniature road loco-motives, designed principally for continuous haulage work, and mounted on springs to reduce jar and vibration on roads, with compound cylinders for economy and belly tanks for longer jour-neys without replenishment. Foster's, Ruston's, Marshall's and Robey's all-produced five-ton tractors and Clayton's went on to develop their famous steam wagon, with a high-speed engine mounted on top of a small locomotive-type boiler at the front and a long lorry body behind the cab.[25]

The first Clayton and Shuttleworth steam wagon was sent from the works on 14 August 1912; a five-tonner running on steel tyres and supplied to A. Thompson Alford of Aberdeen. By 1913 they had produced forty, mostly of the five-ton size, and hundreds more followed from the Abbey works on the north side of the Witham near Stamp End. Robey's and Foster's also produced steam wagons and on several occasions the latter firm fitted self-moving road engines with Diplock's patent wheel or Pedrail, a revised version of Boydell's earlier design. Foster's and Marshall's produced show-men's engines, with dynamos and decorative trimmings, to operate huge fairground rides such as galloping horses, dragons or cock-erels and move them from one fair to another.[26]

[25] Wright, *Traction Engines*, pp. 27, 56–57; Hughes, *A Century of Traction Engines*, pp. 155, 175, 197, 214, 249, 250; Clark, *Steam Engine Builders*, p. 19.
[26] N. G. Robson, *Some Notes on the Steam Wagons of Clayton and Shuttleworth Ltd, Lincoln*, Newcastle upon Tyne, 1948; Clark, op. cit., pp. 34, 77, 97, 132; Hughes, op. cit., p. 212; Wright, op. cit., p. 27.

Figure 33   *A Ruston-Dunbar steam excavator or 'navvy', made by Ruston, Proctor and Co. of Lincoln in 1880*

Figure 34   *A Hornsby-Akroyd portable oil engine of 1893, predecessor of the modern 'diesel' engine, developed by R. Hornsby and Sons of the Spittlegate iron works, Grantham*

OIL ENGINES

While some firms were developing steam road vehicles others moved out of steam altogether. Hornsby's cut wages in order to survive the agricultural depression and suffered strikes in 1886 and 1890, but as a result of intelligent management appointments the company moved into its period of greatest prosperity. The firm produced gold-mining equipment for South Africa and their generating machinery produced the electricity to light the Kremlin in Moscow at the coronation of the Tsar, but their greatest success arose from the development of the heavy oil engine, now usually known as the diesel engine. As early as 1860 Etienne Lenoir had produced the first commercial gas engine, powered by the internal combustion of gas, and Ruston's and other firms had produced such engines for industrial use in towns. A version of the gas engine as improved by N. A. Otto was later to be adapted by Daimler and Benz to burn petrol or 'light mineral oil' but the development of the so-called 'diesel' engine burning heavy oil was largely achieved by Herbert Akroyd Stuart and Hornsby and Sons of Grantham. During the 1870s and 1880s several engineers were trying to develop a successful heavy oil engine and in particular Herbert Akroyd Stuart (b. 1864) and Dr Rudolph Diesel (1858–1913) independently developed improvements to the oil engine. The modern heavy oil engine is closer to the working principles of Akroyd Stuart than those of Diesel but it is the latter whose name is applied to this type of engine.[27]

Akroyd Stuart was the first to develop a commercially successful oil engine, producing a few for sale at his little works in Bletchley in 1890, but he had no capital or experience to undertake large-scale production. He offered the manufacturing rights to most of the leading builders of gas engines of the day, but they all refused it; Richard Hornsby and Sons offered to make the engine on a royalty basis. Akroyd Stuart accepted their offer and Hornsby's started manufacture in 1891, putting fixed and portable versions of the Hornsby-Akroyd patent oil engine shown in figure 34 on sale even before Diesel had taken out his first patent. Twenty firms entered oil engines in trials held by the Royal Agricultural Society in 1894 and Hornsby's won first prizes for both fixed and portable engines. By the time Diesel produced his first experimental machine in 1897 Hornsby's were selling theirs all over the world, the Grantham engineers having further developed the original Akroyd design. In

[27] Honeybone, *Grantham*, p. 115; Newman, *One hundred years of good company*, pp. 33, 71, 72; L. T. C. Rolt, *Victorian Engineering*, London, 1970, p. 272.

1893 the right to manufacture the Hornsby-Akroyd engine in the
USA was sold to the De La Vergne Company of New York and
those were the first commercially successful heavy oil engines to be
built in the United States. [28]

After the appointment of David Roberts as works manager in
1895 the energies of Hornsby and Sons were increasingly directed
into the development of the oil engine, and in the years up to 1914
they were the most important makers of oil engines in the world. In
1905 the firm employed two thousand workers and supported
about one third of the population of Grantham. At the start of this
century Hornsby's decided to concentrate on the production of
internal combustion engines: the production of steam engines,
thrashing machines and other agricultural machinery was run
down and in 1906 their boiler business was sold. Under the same
policy they amalgamated in 1905 with J. E. H. Andrew and Co. of
Stockport, who produced a successful range of gas engines. [29]

Hornsby's oil engines were used on farms and in quarries, saw
mills and refrigeration plants. They also generated electricity for
factories, hospitals, schools, hotels and early cinemas. In 1902 one
provided the power for Marconi's first radio transmission across
the Atlantic and by 1905 four thousand were generating electricity
in country houses such as those of Lord Rothschild, Viscount
Curzon and Rudyard Kipling. In 1897 Hornsby's sold one oil
tractor but this was ahead of its time. In 1908 they were the only
firm to enter for a £1,000 prize offered by the British War Office for
a road tractor and their oil-powered machine exceeded the conditions sufficiently to earn a bonus of £180. [30]

As patents expired other firms began to make oil engines but
Hornsby's had a good start and they continued to flourish until
1914. The Stamford firm of Blackstone and Co. entered the oil
engine market in 1896–97 with an engine that could also run on
town gas; after 1897 Ruston, Procter and Co., under the management of Johann August Bornemann (b. 1854), successfully changed
its emphasis from steam to oil. Marshall's were also early in the field
with an oil-engined tractor but other firms like Clarke's crank
works in Lincoln found entrance into the oil-engine business a
dangerous gamble. [31]

[28] Newman, op. cit., pp. 73, 74; Pointer, *Hornsby's of Grantham*, p. 33.
[29] Newman, op. cit., p. 75; Honeybone, *Grantham*, p. 115; Pointer, op. cit.,
p. 27.
[30] Newman, op. cit., pp. 80, 81, 86; Pointer, op. cit., pp. 24, 27.
[31] Newman, op. cit., pp. 34, 43, 76, 258; N. C. Birch, *Stamford — An Industrial
History*, Lincoln, 1972, p. 7; Bonnett, *Saga of the Steam Plough*, p. 120.

CATERPILLAR TRACK

Hornsby's foresight in developing the heavy oil engine appeared again a decade later when David Roberts developed a chain-tracked tractor. The idea of a vehicle riding on an endless chain looped over the wheels was not new, but Roberts's patents covered the first practical introduction of such a system. Hornsby's fitted tracks to oil traction engines and to a 40 h.p. Rochet-Schneider motor car, which were tested and modified and demonstrated to the military at Aldershot several times up to 1908. The tracked vehicles gave an impressive performance, hauling loads over boggy ground and loose sand and pulling a dummy gun up a slippery clay incline of one in two. It was at these trials at Aldershot that the nickname 'caterpillar' was given to the chain-track tractor. In both Britain and America the press gave enthusiastic coverage and Hornsby's made a short film, one of the first produced for commercial purposes, showing their machines going through their paces. Military attachés of embassies and legations in London were invited to a special exhibition and showing of the film at the Empire music hall, Leicester Square. But mechanized transport was distasteful to cavalrymen and the project was not pursued.[32]

Not only was chain track rejected by the military but the anticipated demand from the developers of foreign and colonial territories also failed to materialize. Only one order was received, and that was for the caterpillar tractor shown in plate XIV to haul coal from an isolated mine in Alaska to Dawson City in the Yukon forty miles away. A steam tractor was required, so Hornsby's produced the tracked vehicle to which Foster's of Lincoln fitted a steam engine and boiler. This unique vehicle weighed forty tons and did good service in Canada, where its neglected chassis and track still remain.[33]

The chain track idea was a commercial failure and Hornsby's sold the American and Canadian patent rights for a mere £4,000 to the Holt Manufacturing Co. of New York (now the Caterpillar Tractor Co.). Holt's persevered with their experiments and six years later when Winston Churchill pressed for the development of 'small armoured shelters, holding men and machine guns, mounted on caterpillar tracks', specimen Holt tractors had to be imported. Foster's of Lincoln were contracted to develop the first British 'tanks' and William Tritton their managing director borrowed from Grantham the original drawings of the Roberts chain-track

[32] Newman, op. cit., pp. 86, 88; Pointer, *Hornsby's of Grantham*, p. 30.
[33] Newman, op. cit., pp. 89, 91; Clark, *Steam Engine Builders*, p. 34.

system, to which Foster's had fitted the boiler for the Yukon tractor. Tritton's part in the development of the tank is often acknowledged but Roberts receives less recognition.[34]

ZENITH OF THRASHING MACHINE PRODUCTION

Despite the diversification into other lines the manufacture of thrashing sets remained important, nearly all of them being sent for export in this later period. These sets included maize shellers and huskers as well as thrashing machines and portable or traction engines. The trade reached its zenith between 1906 and 1912 when about seven thousand sets were exported each year. There were then six makers in the county; Clayton's, Marshall's, Ruston's, Robey's, Foster's and Hornsby's, and together their sales amounted to perhaps 4,500 sets per annum for about £1½ million. Only about one hundred sets per year were sold on the home market and the remainder carried the names of the great Lincolnshire firms to eastern Europe, South America and the far reaches of the British Empire. In South America most traction engines and thrashing sets were made either by Clayton and Shuttleworth or Ruston, Procter and Co. In fifty-five years Ruston's grew from a shed with twenty-five men and boys to three large plants covering fifty-two acres and employing 5,200 men in the city, one of the largest establishments of its kind in the kingdom. By 1911 the sales of this firm alone totalled at least 42,800 steam, oil and gas engines, 36,880 boilers, 24,000 thrashing machines, 5,200 centifugal pumps and six hundred excavators: average annual output then exceeded six thousand of these items.[35]

When the Royal Show was held in Lincoln in 1907 two triumphal arches over the streets carried representations of a thrashing machine and a portable engine to symbolize Lincoln's wealth. Nathaniel Clayton and Joseph Shuttleworth's son Alfred (1843–1925) each left an estate of over a million pounds when they died. These two families had at various times five houses in the city, but Hartsholme Hall, Eastcliff House and Eastgate House have all been demolished. Joseph Shuttleworth purchased an estate at Old Warden in Bedfordshire and in 1881 was high sheriff of that county, while Nathaniel Clayton held the same office in Lincolnshire. When Ruston's business was formed into a limited company in 1889 he was paid £465,000 for it, and became chairman of the new

---

[34] Newman, op. cit., pp. 90, 92; Pointer, *Hornsby's of Grantham*, p. 31.
[35] Tritton, 'Origin of the Thrashing Machine', p. 59; Newman, op. cit., pp. 35, 42.

board. Ruston subscribed generously to local Congregational churches while Clayton and the Shuttleworths contributed to the erection of St Swithin's and All Saints churches.[36]

Engineering firms like theirs dominated the economies of Lincoln, Grantham and Gainsborough in Edwardian times, and supported a large part of the urban population of the county. The iron works of 1845 had mostly been small family concerns where the master knew every man by name, but as the number of employees and workshops increased the overseers needed horses to carry them on their rounds. By 1914 Clayton's various premises covered about thirty acres and Ruston's over fifty acres. Work in the foundries was hard and hot: men's work, though in 1912 Ruston's started to employ women to make the sand cores. It was dirty work and an old hand at Ruston's later recalled that 'in 1900 the factory, like all others, was filthy, with inches of litter on the floor. If you had to kneel down, your trousers stank. And the sanitary arrangements — the less said the better — a hole and a long pole'. Though most of the owners' houses have gone many of their industrial buildings still remain either empty or in use by other firms and are an eloquent reminder of the size of Lincolnshire's engineering industry on the eve of the First World War.[37]

[36] Newman, op. cit., pp. 23, 28.
[37] Hill, *Victorian Lincoln*, p. 122; Newman, op. cit., p. 39.

CHAPTER 7

THE IRONSTONE DISTRICTS

THE boom in agricultural machinery generated industry on a scale new to the county. It was followed quite shortly by another boom and another industry, heavier still, which gave birth to a large town on a site previously occupied by five insignificant townships. If the engineering firms had made their physical mark only on a few existing towns, Scunthorpe, its blast furnaces, steel mills and ironstone quarries altered the face and the society of the north-west corner of Lincolnshire. Fortunately, perhaps, iron working spread no further; ironstone quarried in the south of the county was taken elsewhere for smelting, and most of rural Lincolnshire avoided the fate of the South Wales valleys and parts of Staffordshire.

Since the middle of the nineteenth century the bulk of British iron ore supplies have come to be derived from the deposits in the Lias and the Oolites which outcrop in a broad strip from Lincolnshire down to Dorset and north to the mouth of the Tees. In Lincolnshire they outcrop near the cliffs which extend along the western boundary of the county and the beds slope gently south-eastwards beneath newer geological formations. In north Lincolnshire the Frodingham ironstone occurs in the Lower Lias but in the southern portion of the county it thins out to an insignificant band of limestone. In south Lincolnshire and Leicestershire a valuable iron ore is found in the Marlstone Rock bed, which forms the upper portion of the Middle Lias and outcrops as a cliff along the eastern side of the vale of Belvoir. East of this is the even more striking escarpment where the Lower Oolites outcrop, passing through Grantham and Lincoln, and containing the ironstone of the Northampton Sand bed.[1]

Iron ore was known and worked by the Romans in the Frodingham and Colsterworth areas and in south-west Lincolnshire it

[1] H. B. Hewlett, *The Quarries — Ironstone, Limestone and Sand*, Stanton, 1935, reprinted Market Overton, 1979, pp. 9, 11.

was also smelted in the Middle Ages. The industry declined in this county as stern laws were enforced to suppress the destruction of timber by charcoal burners and iron could be produced more economically elsewhere. Eventually even the presence of ironstone, as such, was forgotten in Lincolnshire.[2]

With the arrival of the railway age, demand for iron vastly increased and new deposits of iron ore were urgently sought to supplement the existing supplies from the coalfields. In 1846 exploitation of the Liassic ore in the Cleveland area started and in 1851 attention was drawn to the occurrence of workable stone in Northamptonshire. In the same year a paper in the Royal Agricultural Society's journal noted that the yellowish soil in the High and Low Risby areas of north-west Lincolnshire was impregnated with iron. The quantity and suitability of this Frodingham ore for smelting was not appreciated and the stone was used for road mending, building and, being rich in lime, was burned for agricultural use.[3]

Charles Winn (1795–1874) of Nostell Priory near Wakefield owned over two thousand acres in Appleby, Scunthorpe, Frodingham and Brumby, where he was also lord of the manor. The latter three townships were in Frodingham parish and as figure 35 shows they extended in narrow bands from Bottesford Beck, across the sandy warren, escarpment and low riverside moors to the Trent. The fourth township in Frodingham was Crosby, which was dominated by the Sheffield family of Normanby Park, and to the south was Ashby township in Bottesford parish. These five townships, excluding their western moors, were in 1919 to be united as the town now called Scunthorpe, but in 1861 their combined population was only 1,423, of whom 503 lived in Ashby. In contrast the nearby market town of Winterton had 1,780 inhabitants and there were 983 in Burton Stather. East of the villages were warrens for the breeding of rabbits, but beneath this sandy covering was the bed of ironstone which sloped away eastwards, with an ever-increasing thickness of overburden, until it disappeared beneath the escarpment of Lincoln Cliff on the east side of Bottesford Beck. In 1832 the commons east of Scunthorpe had been awarded to Charles Winn.[4]

[2] Ibid., p. 12.
[3] Ibid.; Holm, p. 1.
[4] D. C. D. Pocock, 'Land Ownership and Urban Growth in Scunthorpe', East Midland Geographer, 33–34 (1970), p. 52; Walshaw and Behrendt, p. 2.

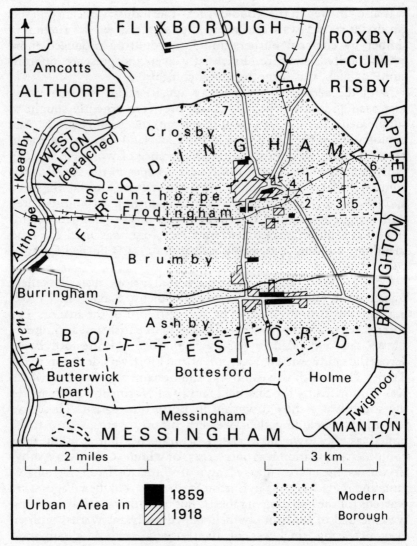

Figure 35   *Scunthorpe ironstone district, 1860–1914*

1. Trent iron works
2. Frodingham iron (and steel) works
3. North Lincolnshire iron works
4. Lindsey iron works
5. Redbourn Hill iron works
6. Appleby iron works
7. Lysaght's iron and steel works

I and II *Eighteenth-century transport*: above, *turnpike toll-house at Hallington on Louth-to-Horncastle road which was turnpiked in 1770 — notice recesses for toll-boards either side of the corner door*; below, *narrow boats moored at Harlaxton wharf on the Grantham canal, midway through the Harlaxton cutting — compare the scales on the wharf with those in figure 10 on page 62.*

IV *John Grundy, Jnr (1719–83), engineer of Spalding. He was perhaps the first engineer to be trained for his profession, and was a pioneer in the construction of waterways, dams, docks and other works.*

III *The reconstruction of Packhouse quay in Boston allowed the Corporation to erect the London warehouse and express their municipal pride by the architectural embellishments — built 1817, demolished c.1950.*

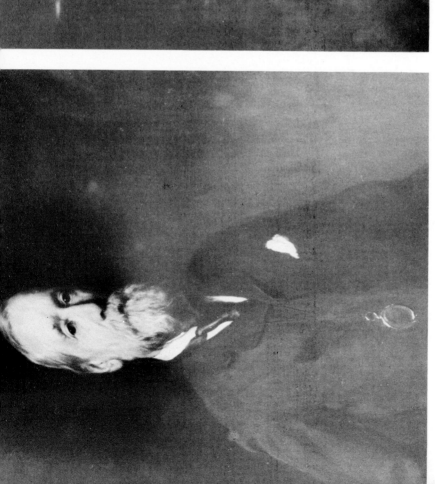

V and VI Founders of Lincolnshire's greatest nineteenth-century engineering concern: left, Joseph Shuttleworth (1819–83); right, his brother-in-law Nathaniel Clayton, Jnr (1811–90). Their Stamp End iron works at Lincoln is shown in figure 30 on page 139.

VII *John Daulton's view of Boston haven half a mile below the town, in August 1822. Features of the bank include (left to right) distant views of Boston Stump (the tower of St Botolph's church and Hussey Tower. On the bank itself are the four-sailed Gallows mill, Maud Foster sluice eight sailed Tuxford's mill, cottages, Neptune inn with bathing huts on the river's edge, and S Nicholas' church, Skirbeck. Traffic on the river in this picture includes the steam packet Commerce of Trade, a brig being hauled downstream by a tug boat and a gang of men on the bank, and several shrimp boats returning from sea.*

VIII *A resort of the railway age — a 1902 photograph of the pier opened at Skegness in 1881; t landward end has since been altered out of all recognition and much of the seaward end w destroyed by a storm in January 1978.*

Sarah · Claxworth May 13 1797
Tell Me ye knowing and diſcerning few
Where I may Find a Friend both firm and tr[ue]
Who dare ſtand by me when in deep diſtreſs
And then his love and friendſhip moſt expreſs

Lincoln Hoſpital

IX *The County Hospital founded in 1769 at Lincoln was managed and supported by local gentry and served by a rota of local doctors. This sampler of 1797 shows the building designed by John Carr of York and occupied by the hospital from 1777 until 1878.*

X *Construction of the Trent iron works' first blast furnace in rural north-west Lincolnshire in 1864 led to the creation of the new town of Scunthorpe, which within fifty years had become one of the largest in the county.*

XI and XII *The large scale of late-Victorian industry: above, Sleaford maltings built for Bass, Ratcliff and Gretton Ltd between 1899 and 1905; below, a line of steam-rollers in the erecting shops of Ruston, Procter and Co. Ltd at Lincoln.*

XIII and XIV *Products of Lincolnshire engineers*: above, *two Lincolnshire-made automobiles, on the left by Richardson of Saxilby (CT 77A) and on the right a Rose-National made at Gainsborough (R 135)*; below, *the unique Yukon tractor for which the caterpillar track was made by Hornsby's of Grantham and the boiler by Foster's of Lincoln in 1910.*

XV and XVI *Contrasts in housing*: left, *houses for middle-class families in South Square, Boston, with between them the narrow entrance to White Cross Lane, down which was, right, this row of small working-class cottages. A similar relationship between different classes of housing was to be found in most towns in the eighteenth and nineteenth centuries.*

MODERN IRON-WORKING STARTS IN SCUNTHORPE

By 1856 Charles Winn's son Rowland (1820–93) was residing at Appleby Hall, the family's local seat, and in 1859 he had some of the ironstone analysed. When the results were favourable he sought ironmasters prepared to buy the ore and became the driving force behind the development of the iron industry on his family's Lincolnshire estate. Rowland Winn succeeded in selling small amounts of ore to several ironmasters and by November 1859 he had persuaded William and George Dawes, ironmasters of Barnsley, to lease land at Low Santon and Scunthorpe for ironstone mining. The Dawes were then smelting the clay-band ironstones from the coal measures in their district and the Frodingham ironstone had two advantages, cheapness and a high lime content. By 1861 a mineral lease for a smaller area had also been granted to Samuel Beale and Co. of the Parkgate works in Rotherham.[5]

The Dawes brothers began working the ore in July 1860 and transported it to their iron works at Elsecar, Milton and Denby Dale. It was at first carried in horse-drawn carts from Scunthorpe to the Trent at Chatterton's wharf, but in June they had invited tenders for a four and a half mile long railway to be built on Winn's land from the foot of the cliff to Gunness wharf. Later an incline was installed to enable full wagons coming down the hill to haul empty ones up. Across the Trent was the entrance to the Stainforth and Keadby canal and in September 1859 the SYR company, owners of the canal, opened an extension of their railway to Keadby. The directors of the SYR immediately gave thought to bridging the Trent and obtaining access to Winn's ore field. This would suit George Dawes, who was considering the erection of blast furnaces in the area, either on the banks of the Trent or on the Ancholme or at Scunthorpe, and would need improved transport to bring in coal. Rowland Winn and his brother Edmund John favoured these schemes and also wanted the SYR to extend westwards into other parts of the Barnsley coalfield.[6]

The MSLR was also interested in linking south Yorkshire to the new ironstone area. In October 1860 the directors received a report from John Hedley on the ironstone in north Lincolnshire. He told them that there were three beds: an upper bed 'too lean in iron' to be worked, a second, or Kirton bed, about four feet thick, and a lower

[5] Holm, pp. 1, 2; Walshaw and Behrendt, p. 36.
[6] Holm, p. 2; Henthorn, ed., *Trent, Ancholme and Grimsby Railway*, pp. xv, xvii, xviii; Ambler, ed., *Workers and Community*, p. 17; D. L. Franks, *South Yorkshire Railway*, Leeds, 1971, pp. 29, 43; Walshaw and Behrendt, p. 36; the names of all railways are shown in full in Appendix III, pp. 262–63.

M

bed at Scunthorpe eight to nine feet thick and about forty yards below the Kirton bed. The Kirton bed was extensive, but with a high percentage of 'silicious matter' only 22 or 23 per cent of inferior iron would be yielded and it was not thought there would be a demand for this ore. The third bed under Winn's property included easily worked deposits from which would come about five million tons of good ore. When the outcrop was exhausted there were still ten square miles where ore could be obtained at a depth of fifty yards from the surface, and at the depth of one hundred yards, over ten square miles 'there is an unlimited supply of this bed'. The yield of iron from this area would be 35 per cent. Hedley's judgement of the Kirton bed was borne out by events. In November 1859 Roseby and Oxley had leased land close to the railway at Kirton-in-Lindsey and started excavating for ironstone but in 1864 the works were abandoned as uneconomic. Agreement was reached between the MSLR, the SYR and Rowland Winn in November 1860 to share the cost of constructing a railway from Scunthorpe to Barnetby where it would join the MSLR. This was to be known as the TAGR and was to purchase the existing line owned by Dawes and Winn. The SYR also agreed to build a railway two and five-eighths of a mile long to cross the Trent and join their line near Keadby to the Dawes-Winn line near Gunness. On 27 February 1861 agreement was reached for the MSLR to lease the SYR and this came into full effect in 1864; the MSLR also absorbed the TAGR on 12 July 1882 having operated it since 1866.[7]

Acts for the TAGR and the South Yorkshire (Keadby extension) were both passed on 22 July 1861. Apart from concern in Gainsborough at the danger which the bridge would cause to river traffic, which led to alterations in the bridge design, there was very little opposition to Winn's scheme. Both railways took longer to build than expected and cost considerably more than the estimate. Keadby bridge was first crossed by a train on 1 July 1864 but it was not until 14 April 1866 that official permission was received to open this short railway and unite Scunthorpe to south Yorkshire. Work on the TAGR had started by 28 September 1861 when the first board meeting was held at Doncaster. By 27 February 1862 four miles of line between the Trent and Scunthorpe, including the section laid in 1860, had been working for some time and in October 1862 the bridge over the Ancholme was completed, but there was some delay before the whole line was opened on

[7] Henthorn, ed., *Trent, Ancholme and Grimsby Railway*, pp. x–xii, xxv–xxvii; Dow, *Great Central*, II, p. 33.

1 October 1866 as part of the MSLR system. Between Keadby bridge and Trent Cliff the railway was carried by the Scotter Road viaduct of eighty-five arches, which during 1911 was partly filled in to form an embankment. The estimate for the TAGR had been £120,000 but the eventual cost was £265,848 7s. 9d.[8]

IRON WORKS

In 1862 the Dawes brothers leased from Winn a site beside the railway route across Scunthorpe warren and the following year started construction of the Trent iron works (plate X). The first of the three furnaces was blown in on 20 January 1864 and they were charged with ore obtained close to the works. While the railway was still under construction another iron works was established in the parish. Joseph Cliff, Snr (1806–79) was a Leeds brickmaker with interests in a colliery, and these supplied the bricks and coal for the four furnaces of his Frodingham iron works, but he had no previous experience of iron smelting and employed a Mr Reviller from Stockton-on-Tees to build the works and continue as their first manager. The first furnace was blown in during May 1865 and in 1866 the owner's second son Joseph Cliff, Jnr (1841–1914) moved to Frodingham and was manager of the works until 1904. His wife was a member of the Kitson family of Leeds, who supplied several steam engines and the works' first two locomotives. Cliff's works were in Frodingham township, where the railway crossed the Brigg road, but were only half a mile from Scunthorpe village. He built two furnaces first, with an inclined hoist worked by water ballast tanks. By 1871 another two furnaces had been built, together with a vertical tower which replaced the inclined hoist, and Cliff then employed 150 men and six boys.[9]

The example of these Yorkshire entrepreneurs was followed by Daniel Adamson and other Lancashire partners, whose North Lincolnshire Iron Company blew in their first furnace during April 1866. It was situated on Frodingham warren half a mile east of the earlier works and was served by a branch from the TAGR. In 1872 their second furnace was blown in and two more followed in 1875. The firm became a limited company in 1872 with a share capital of £150,000. By the late 1860s the development of the ironstone district was proceeding under its own momentum and in 1868

---

[8] Henthorn, ed., *Trent, Ancholme and Grimsby Railway*, pp. xlvii, xlviii, liii, lv; Leleux, *East Midlands Railways*, p. 224.

[9] Holm, p. 2; Walshaw and Behrendt, pp. 37, 38, 40, 128, 130, 131; Ambler, ed., *Workers and Community*, p. 19.

Rowland Winn became a Conservative member of parliament for north Lincolnshire. He served as a lord of the treasury in Disraeli's 1874–80 administration, but he was defeated in 1881 and four years later was raised to the peerage as Baron St Oswald. He had come into the estate in 1874 when his father died and he moved to Nostell Priory near Wakefield, the family's main seat; Appleby Hall then became the home of his mother.[10]

During the 1870s the existing companies built more furnaces in the Frodingham district and three new works were established. Two furnaces at the Lindsey works built by the new Lincolnshire Iron Smelting Co. in Scunthorpe began work in November 1873 but ran into financial difficulties, were purchased by the Redbourn Hill Iron and Coal Co. in February 1883 and after lying derelict for several years were dismantled in 1905. The Redbourn Hill company's own works in Frodingham had two furnaces at work by 1875. The sixth and last iron works to be established on Winn's Lincolnshire estate in the nineteenth century belonged to the Appleby Iron Co.; the first of their two furnaces in Appleby parish was blown in by December 1876. By 1871 the companies had built seven furnaces in Lincolnshire, but only four were then in blast, using 106,000 tons of ore and 84,000 tons of coal to produce 30,122 tons of pig iron. Nine years later the number of furnaces had increased to twenty-one, of which fifteen were in blast, and they produced six times as much iron; 790,819 tons of ore and 481,807 tons of coal made 207,704 tons of pig iron. The water supply for the works came from Santon in Appleby parish, where there was a pumping house with steam donkey engines, and was sent in pipes along Dawes Lane.[11]

QUARRIES

The Trent and Frodingham works each obtained their ore from land leased from Winn, their first quarries being adjacent to the furnace sites. Their leases also required them to sink mines at Appleby on top of the Lincoln Cliff, and the Frodingham Iron Co. sank two shafts between 1870 and 1875, of which the north shaft reached Frodingham ironstone at a depth of 293 feet 2 inches. This shaft and some galleries were lined with brickwork but by 1881 it had apparently been decided to abandon the mine and its buildings. Underground mining was much more expensive than the open-cast

---

[10] Walshaw and Behrendt, pp. 35, 130; Henthorn, ed., *Trent, Ancholme and Grimsby Railway*, p. xiv.
[11] Holm, pp. 5, 13; Walshaw and Behrendt, pp. 35, 42, 102.

methods possible on Scunthorpe and Frodingham warrens and drainage was also a problem in the underground mines. [12]

The later iron companies established in the district were supplied by Rowland Winn from his own open-cast mines, although after trials by the Frodingham Iron Co. in 1871 most of the works used a mixture of local ironstone and silicious Northampton Sand ore, suitable beds of which were found near Lincoln. Winn also granted mineral leases to some companies which did not erect furnaces in the district, including the Parkgate Co. of Rotherham, the York-shire Iron Co. of East Ardsley and the Staveley Coal and Iron Co. of Chesterfield. The works were all located where the TAGR crossed Scunthorpe and Frodingham warrens and as the first open-cast mines were worked out the excavations spread north and south across the warrens of Crosby, Brumby, Ashby and adjoining villages. [13]

In the early days all the work in the open-cast mines was done by hand. The overburden of sand and soil was first 'stripped' or 'barred' by 'sanders' and then wheeled in barrows across a trestle precariously high in the air to be dumped in a part of the pit already worked. In 1875 the sanders were paid 4s. a day. A moveable railway in the pit bottom ran parallel to the face and when a strip of overburden nine feet wide had been removed then the ironstone was loaded into wagons, drilling and blasting being needed to loosen the lower levels. The ore was graded by its depth from the surface and placed in different wagons under the scrutiny of inspectors appointed by the ironmasters to reject any unsuitable ore. This was a cause of considerable friction between Winn and the companies he supplied. In the early days only the top ten to twelve feet was taken, leaving the poorer stone below untouched. [14]

Removing the overburden and then the ore was hard manual labour. Nearly all the men working in these quarries came from agriculture and there was probably movement between the two occupations on a seasonal as well as a long-term basis. It was noted by a divisional inspector of mines in 1912 that 'you may have a perfectly good quarryman working three weeks or a month in a quarry, and another time he is a farm labourer or working on some other work altogether'. Demand for agricultural labour increased at harvest, and in iron it might fall when furnaces in Scunthorpe or elsewhere were being repaired or replaced. At the time of the 1861

[12] Holm, p. 2; M. J. G. Upton, 'The Appleby Ironstone Mine', LIA, 6 no. 4 (1971), p. 68.
[13] Holm, pp. 2, 3, 6; Walshaw and Behrendt, p. 35.
[14] Holm, pp. 6, 7.

census twenty-four men living in this district were described as miners, eighteen in Scunthorpe and others in Crosby and Ashby. Three-quarters of them had been born in Lincolnshire.[15]

WORKING CONDITIONS IN THE IRON WORKS

All of the furnaces were hand-charged, the coal and ironstone being raised to a high level in large iron barrows, which were then wheeled along catwalks to the top of each furnace and the contents tipped in. At first the Trent works used raw coal, but by 1869 they were using a mixture of coal and coke, Durham coke being preferred for the furnaces because it was of better quality than that made from Yorkshire coal. The Frodingham ironstone had a high lime content which made it self-fluxing, but this was not fully appreciated at first and extra lime was often added unnecessarily. Several explosions occurred at the Frodingham and North Lincolnshire works, which used closed-topped furnaces, and this led to a preference for open-topped furnaces in the area until smelting techniques best suited to the variable properties of the Frodingham ore had been devised. The hand-loading methods used in the mines allowed size and quality to be dealt with there and consequently the ore could be charged in the furnaces in its raw state without being pre-treated, although in the early days ore was calcined at Gunness before being shipped to Yorkshire.[16]

Until 1890 the works in Frodingham parish were producing only pig iron, the molten metal being run from the taphole into pig beds moulded in sand in front of the furnaces. After cooling the pigs were loaded into wagons by pig iron carriers, who in 1875 were paid 2½d. for each ton loaded. Slag was run off into cast-iron moulds placed on flat-topped bogies, which in the cramped sidings at the foot of the furnaces were often shunted by horses. When the slag had solidified sufficiently the mould was lifted clear and the slag removed to the slag bank, where it was tipped and broken up. It appears that many of the skilled posts such as furnacemen in the iron works were filled by men who already had experience of iron manufacture in established iron producing areas such as Tipton and South Wales, and some had moved about the country before finally reaching Scunthorpe.[17]

In contrast the bulk of the unskilled workforce, as in the mines, was drawn from the agricultural workers of the surrounding area

---

[15] Ambler, ed., *Workers and Community*, pp. 23, 25.
[16] Holm, pp. 6, 8.
[17] Holm, pp. 6, 9; Ambler, ed., *Workers and Community*, pp. 12, 14, 18.

and many families still had strong links with the land. As the country entered the agricultural depression even more land workers looked to Scunthorpe for a new type of job and some came from a considerable distance. Men coming to work on ironstone in the early days may well have had a three-sided seasonal working arrangement, in which they changed between the iron works, ironstone excavation and farm work as relative demand fluctuated. It appears that the first union at Frodingham was a branch of the Lincolnshire Labourers League, an agricultural union.[18]

THE BIRTH OF URBAN SCUNTHORPE

Up to 1859 the population of the villages in Frodingham parish had depended for their livelihood on agriculture and had increased at about the same rate as other rural communities in north-west Lincolnshire. As the ironstone industry started to develop houses were built for miners and furnace workers and shops were opened. In 1919 the five townships with an interest in iron were to be united, but before then they lacked a single civic identity and there was great disparity in their rates of growth. In the mid 1860s Rowland Winn built six streets of houses at New Frodingham on the edge of the ironstone beds for workers attracted to the area and by 1871 108 new houses had been built in Frodingham township. The streets at New Frodingham were more spaciously laid out than most industrial housing of the period and space was left for shops along the main street, named Rowland Road. In 1867 Winn erected a school for 120 children at New Frodingham, enlarged in 1875, 1884 and 1900 to provide eventually for a thousand children, and in 1871 he built a 'town hall' on Rowland Road to hold four hundred people with a reading room and library 'for the comfort and mental improvement of the workpeople employed in the mines and iron works of the parish'. He also provided allotments and a cricket ground for the workmen.[19]

Before the ironstone was developed the only school in Frodingham was a small one at Crosby for twenty children, whereas National schools had been built in many neighbouring villages in the 1840s and 1850s. Winterton had a Wesleyan day school as well as a National school. None of Winn's land in New Frodingham was available for sale but in Scunthorpe village half a mile to the north were numerous owners of closes, paddocks and vacant land eager

[18] Ambler, ed., *Workers and Community*, pp. 18, 22, 27.
[19] Walshaw and Behrendt, pp. 1, 3; Ambler, ed., *Workers and Community*, pp. 12, 26; Holm, p. 3; White, *Directory*, 1872, p. 455; *Kelly's Directory*, 1913, p. 201.

to build houses for the influx of workers and to release sites fronting the main street to small shopkeepers and tradesmen. During the 1860s and 1870s the population of Frodingham grew rapidly as workers moved into Winn's development but it rose even faster in Scunthorpe. In June 1866 a sale of building land in Scunthorpe 'presented an animated appearance' and 'attracted a number of speculators' though not all the lots reached their reserve price. It was reported in 1867 that in response to the considerable increase in the population of the area new houses and shops were rapidly springing up at Scunthorpe and at the time of the 1871 census there were ninety houses being built in this township. [20]

Winn's proposed shopping area at New Frodingham never materialized and the land was eventually used for housing, shopkeepers preferring freehold sites in Scunthorpe to the leasehold sites Winn was offering. In Scunthorpe itself very little development was on land owned by Winn, the first streets being built on land sold by the Revd John Posthumous Parkinson of East Ravendale. By 1872 Miss Sussanah Langton had opened a private school in Scunthorpe but there was no National school in the township until 1886 when one was built by public subscription. The population also rose in Ashby, though not to the same extent as in Frodingham or Scunthorpe, and by 1871 nearly a fifth of its working population was engaged in either ironstone mining or iron manufacture. Its inhabitants had multiplied during the early nineteenth century; by 1871 there were perhaps more labourers than the farmers needed, creating a pool of surplus unskilled labour to be mopped up by developments in the ironstone field. Ashby was a long way from the railway and the early iron quarries and works, but there were many freeholders in the township so building was steady and continuous. Many of the small shopkeepers in Ashby commenced similar businesses in Scunthorpe, as did some from Messingham, Winterton and Brigg. [21]

In the 1860s local boards of health were established in small towns such as Brigg and Winterton and in the rural parishes of Broughton and Roxby-cum-Risby adjoining Frodingham; none were set up in the ironstone district for a further quarter of a century. Winn provided the public school, town hall and other

---

[20] Walshaw and Behrendt, pp. 2, 3; Ambler, ed., *Workers and Community*, pp. 11, 12, 19.
[21] Holm, p. 4; Pocock, 'Land Ownership and Urban Growth in Scunthorpe', p. 57; Ambler, ed., *Workers and Community*, pp. 22, 23; Walshaw and Behrendt, p. 3.

facilities at New Frodingham for the whole parish and the Frodingham Iron Company's gas works also supplied the public streets and later some houses in the town, but many public services in the ironstone district were not supplied until the twentieth century. During the 1860s the combined population of the five townships rose by a thousand and in the next decade more than doubled to 5,758, but all this growth was in Scunthorpe, Frodingham and Ashby. Crosby was owned by the Sheffield family of nearby Normanby Hall, who did not release land for building until after 1901. Similarly Brumby was owned by Earl Beauchamp, who before 1914 released only twenty acres on the Frodingham boundary for the erection of a few streets which became New Brumby.[22]

OTHER MINES IN NORTH LINCOLNSHIRE

Frodingham and Appleby parishes had the only blast furnaces in Lincolnshire but there were ironstone mines and quarries elsewhere in the county. Hopes of exploiting ironstone found at several Cliff villages between Lincoln and Frodingham were raised in 1865; an act was then obtained for a railway along the Cliff foot, but they were dashed in 1868 when the act was repealed. In 1861 it was said that Lord Yarborough, whose estate extended to Appleby, had leased land for iron working and in 1873 the MSLR built the quarter mile long Santon branch to an ironstone field on his land at Appleby. In September 1860 the MSLR rejected proposals for a branch railway to Caistor in connection with ironstone finds, but in November 1867 they started building one to Claxby, south of Caistor, where Frith and Co. opened an underground mine the following year. The bed of ore was about six feet six inches thick and was worked on the traditional pillar-and-stall method driven into the escarpment east of the Ancholme valley. A cable-operated incline ran between the mine and the head of the mineral railway. The mine was taken over by the West Yorkshire Iron and Coal Co. of Leeds in 1873 when production reached a peak of 70,000 tons, but it then declined rapidly and the mine was closed in 1885.[23]

Fifteen terraced cottages and a detached villa residence for the manager were built near the Claxby mine between 1870 and 1872

---

[22] Walshaw and Behrendt, pp. 1, 48.
[23] Henthorn, ed., *Trent, Ancholme and Grimsby Railway*, pp. xi, xii, xiv; Dow, *Great Central*, II, p. 33; E. Audin and others, *Aspects of Life and Work in Nettleton in the Nineteenth Century*, Nettleton, 1980, p. 11; White, *Directory*, 1872, p. 477; I. J. Brown, 'Gazetteer of Ironstone Mines in the East Midlands', *LIA*, 6 nos 2 and 3 (1971), p. 43; J. Leverington and N. C. Birch, 'Claxby Ironstone Mines', *LIA*, 3 no. 2 (1968), p. 9.

and one house had its front room converted into a shop for the little community. Some miners lived in the adjacent village of Nettleton and others walked three or four miles every day from Market Rasen or Caistor. Of the thirty-four miners living in Nettleton in 1871 seven were born in the parish, fifteen elsewhere in Lincolnshire and six in Yorkshire. The Claxby mine was 'notoriously dangerous' and in May 1872 it was said that scarcely a month passed without a serious accident. In 1869 a friendly society had been formed at Caistor, the Snowdrop Lodge of the Free Gardeners, and in July 1872 it was said that most of its members were ironstone miners.[24]

Ironstone mining at Greetwell on the eastern edge of Lincoln was started about 1873 by the Mid-Lincolnshire Ironstone Company. Their underground workings extracted ore from the Northampton Sand bed and continued in operation until 1939. The same type of ironstone was worked at a small mine opened about 1874 at Coleby six miles south of the city. The Frodingham Iron Co. obtained its first supplies of Northampton ore from the Lincoln mines but as they became exhausted it looked further south, in 1909 they made unsuccessful trials at Leadenham but later found a satisfactory supply at Colsterworth.[25]

MINES IN SOUTH-WEST LINCOLNSHIRE

The value of the ironstone in the Marlstone rock bed in east Leicestershire had been recognized in 1874; this was eagerly exploited after the Holwell iron works had been built outside Melton Mowbray in 1878–81. It appears that the first ironstone mines in south-west Lincolnshire were developed on Hussey Packe's property at Caythorpe by the West Yorkshire Iron and Coal Co. in the late 1870s. By 1882 they had been joined by other firms and Caythorpe was being extensively worked, with open-cast mines on each side of the GNR's Honington to Lincoln line. For a time John George Carr managed the West Yorkshire company's mines at both Claxby and Caythorpe, and he then continued as manager at Caythorpe until about 1910–12. From 1883 to 1897 the Stanton Iron Works Co. of Ilkeston also worked a small quarry south of Caythorpe. One quarry in this parish, managed by Walter Burke, was still operating on the eve of the First World War.[26]

More extensive quarries in the Marlstone rock were developed by the Stanton company at Woolsthorpe and Denton, east of

[24] Brown, op. cit., p. 43; Leverington and Birch, op. cit., p. 12; Audin, op. cit., pp. 11, 38, 39, 43.

[25] Brown, op. cit., p. 46; Walshaw and Behrendt, p. 28.

[26] Hewlett, *The Quarries — Ironstone, Limestone and Sand*, pp. 14, 23.

Belvoir Castle. Trial pits were sunk about 1879 and in 1883 the company leased land from the duke of Rutland and Sir W. E. Welby-Gregory. That year the GNR opened the northern portion of the Woolsthorpe branch railway and from there the Stanton company laid an incline up to the workings. On 3 August 1883 the first trainload of stone was taken to the GNR's main Grantham–Nottingham line by the contractor's locomotive. In 1885 the Woolsthorpe branch was continued into Harston parish and in 1886–87 the ironstone was opened out between the terminus and the Harston to Denton road. Later the ore south of that road was quarried, both faces being pushed westward, and a tramway between the two quarries was laid under the road. The workings later spread further in Harston, Denton and Knipton. They continued in use until after the First World War but all have now ceased, and the only visible reminder is the low level of the fields on the site of the former quarries. From 1901 to 1921 the Stanton company also had a quarry at Honington, served by a short branch from the GNR's Grantham to Boston line.[27]

In 1885 the Northampton Sand bed on the Leicestershire–Lincolnshire boundary was also proved as a source of ironstone and the opening of the railway between Saxby and Bourne in 1894 provided the necessary outlet. That year the Holwell Iron Co. of Melton Mowbray obtained a lease of the ironstone, limestone and sand under the greater part of the earl of Dysart's estate, extending almost to Colsterworth on the north and the Great North Road on the east. In 1895 the company was quarrying Lincolnshire limestone beside the railway in South Witham for their furnaces, and in 1907 began another limestone quarry one mile further east, next to South Witham station. At the beginning of 1898 the Holwell company constructed a mineral railway northwards from the Saxby line at South Witham and began to work the ironstone north of the Sewstern to Gunby road. The ironstone in this bed is a material distinctly softer and less massive than the ore of the Marlstone rock bed. From their first gullet they excavated eastwards and in 1908 opened a second pit working westwards from the same gullet. In 1910 they started calcining the ore on the site. These two quarries met all the company's requirements until the war.[28]

STEEL-MAKING

The making of cast steel was a laborious and costly small-scale process, in comparison with the production of wrought or cast

[27] Ibid., pp. 21–23.
[28] Ibid., pp. 14, 25, 40; Leleux, *East Midlands Railways*, p. 198.

iron, until the second half of the nineteenth century when Henry Bessemer patented his converter and the alternative open-hearth system was also developed. In 1888 the Cliff brothers decided to build a steel works next to their Frodingham iron works, using the open-hearth system for which the local ore was more suitable. The establishment of the steel works was entrusted to Maximilian Mannaberg (1857–1929), an Austrian who in 1884 had been invited to Glasgow by P. C. Gilchrist to establish a steel works and who had recently visited India to advise the British government on the possibility of steel-making there. [29]

The Frodingham steel works was one of the first to adapt the Gilchrist-Thomas process to the Siemens open-hearth process. They first built two open-hearth steel furnaces, a cogging mill and a billet stand. Two large wrought-iron frame buildings, obtained second hand from the Antwerp Exhibition, served as a melting shop five hundred feet long and a mill building four hundred feet long. The original furnaces were hand charged with materials brought by railway to the Brigg Road side of the building. The first steel furnace was tapped on 21 March 1890 and the company changed its name to the Frodingham Iron and Steel Co. Their original target was to produce four hundred tons of steel a week but as the number of furnaces steadily increased weekly output reached 670 tons in 1895 and 1,473 tons in 1900, when they had seven furnaces in operation. [30]

In 1901 Joseph Cliff and Max Mannaberg visited Philadelphia, where the first furnaces for continuous operation had been built two years earlier, and on their return preparations were made for a hundred-ton furnace of this type, the first to be installed in Europe. The melting shop was lengthened, the two original steel furnaces were demolished and new furnaces constructed. Benjamin Talbot, patentee of the process, spent much time at Frodingham but the construction and commissioning of the furnace was supervised by Isaac Mainwaring, who had considerable experience in the working of the original 75–ton furnace at Pencoyd, Philadelphia. In 1902 the Talbot furnace produced 23,379 tons compared with 71,490 tons from the rest of the shop and in 1906 and 1912 two more Talbot furnaces were installed. In 1904 the firm became a limited company and Max Mannaberg succeeded Joseph Cliff as managing director. [31]

[29] Walshaw and Behrendt, pp. 48, 63, 133.
[30] Ibid., pp. 64, 66–68, 128, 132.
[31] Ibid., pp. 69, 70, 128.

LATER MINES AND IRON WORKS IN NORTH LINCOLNSHIRE

By the turn of the century ironstone was being excavated north and south of the original mines in Frodingham; the Staveley Coal and Iron Co. had been mining part of Crosby warren since the early 1880s. After 1900 the mining operations in Crosby became more extensive and Sir Berkeley Sheffield and others promoted a light railway running north from Frodingham to the Humber bank at Winteringham. This NLLR was to be worked by the MSLR, by then known as the GCR, who saw it as a defence against an invasion of north Lincolnshire by the LYR. To this end they persuaded the NLLR in 1905 to obtain an act to extend its line along the Humber bank from Barton to Alkborough, though only the Winteringham to Whitton section was ever built. The first six miles of the NLLR from Frodingham station northwards were opened in May 1906 and the remaining two and half miles to Winteringham and a further half mile to the haven were both opened on 15 July 1907. At the haven a small wharf was built, with two chutes for handling slag and coal, and a weekly ferry service to Hull was introduced. The two and a half mile Whitton branch was opened on 1 December 1910 and the Scunthorpe trains ran to a pier where the Hull–Gainsborough packet steamer called three times a week, but in 1912 the service consisted of just two trains each day, both third class only.[32]

Most processes in the ironstone mines were manual until the twentieth century but in 1885 Lord St Oswald introduced grab cranes. His first cranes were made by Priestman Brothers of Hull and they were followed by other machines of much greater radius and capacity made by Wilson's of Sandhills, Liverpool. The Frodingham Iron and Steel Co. installed their first Wilson crane in the Ashby Ville pit about 1903. Changes in blast furnace technique meant that selective mining was no longer necessary and the full depth of the ore could be used. This allowed greater use of machinery in the mines and ore left in previous workings could now be extracted. In 1905 Lord St Oswald introduced a dredger-type excavator to remove the overburden more efficiently, and in 1912 his mine began using a steam shovel to load the ore. By 1917 Lord St Oswald's mines were supplying one twelfth of the nation's total output of iron ore and he was the largest single producer in the kingdom.[33]

---

[32] Dow, *Great Central*, III, pp. 113, 114, 249.
[33] Holm, pp. 7, 8, 14; Walshaw and Behrendt, pp. 14, 18.

There were some changes in the Scunthorpe works in the years before 1914. The Dawes brothers went bankrupt in 1887 and after passing through the hands of a Leeds solicitor their Trent works was acquired in 1907 by John Brown and Co. of Sheffield. After the turn of the century John Lysaght Limited established a new iron and steel works to supply steel for processing at their Newport plant. The Normanby Park works one and a half miles north of Scunthorpe was opened in 1912 and its blast furnaces, coke ovens, steel furnaces and rolling mills generated extra freight traffic on the adjacent NLLR; a goods station near the works was opened on 1 August 1912. About 1910 differences between Lord St Oswald and the Appleby Iron Co. led to the prospect of their lease not being renewed; as a result of the coal strike of 1912 the works closed and the firm went into liquidation. The Frodingham company, in conjunction with the Steel Company of Scotland, then took the lease on more favourable terms and started to produce steel plates. The first of the Appleby blast furnaces were restarted in 1912 but the results of neglect delayed a return to full production.[34]

GROWTH OF URBAN SCUNTHORPE

Most of the iron works were on Frodingham warren and the school and town hall built by Lord St Oswald were in that township, but the bulk of the new workers lived in Scunthorpe and most shops were located there. Frodingham became inhabited by senior managers living in large detached houses and a wide social gulf opened up between the two communities. The population of Frodingham township reached 1,300 in 1881 but then stayed at about that size until the end of the century, subsequently rising to about 1,750 by 1911. In all five townships the original villages were west of the warrens and, except for a few houses adjacent to four of the ironworks, new housing was also located well clear of the ironstone bed. By the 1880s the streets of Scunthorpe had reached the northern and southern boundaries of the township, which were less than half a mile apart, and it could only expand westwards until Sir Berkeley Sheffield released the adjacent part of Crosby for residential development two decades later. Ashby also grew because of the ironstone but its inhabitants had to walk about two miles through rural Brumby to reach the iron works and Ashby remained a distinct community. The population of Ashby doubled in the

[34] Dudley, *Scunthorpe and Frodingham*, p. 142; *An Industrial Island: A History of Scunthorpe*, ed. R. E. Armstrong, Scunthorpe, 1981, p. 38; Holm, p. 10; Dow, *Great Central*, III, p. 249; Walshaw and Behrendt, p. 102.

1870s, from 669 to 1,462, but it then grew more slowly until the next century when the mining of the southern extremity of the ironstone caused it to rise from 1,843 in 1901 to 3,237 in 1911. In 1879 a school board was established there but none were established in Frodingham or Scunthorpe because of the adequacy of their existing school provision. After the Lindsey County Council became the education authority in 1902 large new schools were provided in most urban parts of the ironstone district. [35]

As their population increased so Scunthorpe and Ashby became also the commercial centres of the ironstone district. By 1905 there were 173 shops listed in Scunthorpe and thirty-seven in Ashby compared with five and nine listed in 1861, whereas few extra shops had been built in Brumby, Crosby or Frodingham. As the communities grew the shops extended westward along Scunthorpe High Street, taking over some of the early houses. Similarly nonconformist chapels were built and rebuilt as the community grew, but the established church was slower to act. Even before 1860 there had been three Methodist churches in Frodingham parish and two in Ashby township. The Wesleyan chapels in Scunthorpe and Ashby were soon rebuilt, the Primitive Methodists erected one in Scunthorpe and in 1877 the Lincolnshire Congregational Union formed a limited company to build Milton Hall in Scunthorpe for entertainment and worship, with seating for four hundred. In August 1888 the Salvation Army opened a mission in Scunthorpe. From 1863 the vicar of Bottesford used a small school at Ashby for Sunday worship but it was 1880 before the Anglican church in Frodingham established missions in Scunthorpe and Crosby, largely at the instigation of Mrs J. H. Dawes. St Hugh's Mission in Scunthorpe soon moved into a prefabricated iron room at the top of Dawes Lane, which had previously been used in Appleby. [36]

Scunthorpe's status in the ironstone district was belatedly acknowledged in the 1890s. On 23 August 1889 Scunthorpe and Crosby became a separate ecclesiastical district, distinct from Frodingham and Brumby, and in 1890 a local board of health was created for Scunthorpe township. In the latter year Lord St Oswald enlarged the Scunthorpe National school; he also paid over £20,000 for the erection of the church of St John the Evangelist in Scunthorpe, a stone church in the Perpendicular style opened in 1891. In

---

[35] Pocock, 'Land Ownership and Urban Growth in Scunthorpe', pp. 52, 53.
[36] Ibid., pp. 58, 59; Dudley, *Scunthorpe and Frodingham*, pp. 157, 161, 165; *Lincolnshire Chronicle*, 9 November 1977.

the twentieth century more churches and chapels were opened in the areas of new development in Ashby, Crosby and western Scunthorpe and for long the public houses of Scunthorpe were outnumbered by places of worship. Winn's town hall at New Frodingham was some distance from the centre of population at Scunthorpe and in 1886 the upper part was converted into a cottage hospital with three beds. In October 1897 a large working men's constitutional club was opened by the earl of Yarborough in Station Road, Scunthorpe and the facilities included a reading room. Within a few years the cottage hospital extended into the former reading room and library at the old town hall. By 1899 an operating theatre and a new ward for twelve patients had been built but in 1912 the staff was still only one matron and one nurse. During that year the hospital cared for fifty-eight inpatients and 305 outpatients. It was supported by voluntary subscriptions and remained in use until 1920.[37]

The growth of Scunthorpe eclipsed Winterton, which had previously been the nearest market town. In the 1840s and 1850s, new buildings in Winterton included two schools, a temperance hall, police station and gas works but after 1861 its population gradually declined. A police station was erected at Scunthorpe and when rebuilt in 1901 it replaced Winterton as the centre of the petty sessional division. Scunthorpe also gained a cattle market and Winterton's fairs were transferred to the new town.

CIVIC AFFAIRS

The skilled technical managers of the works living in Frodingham formed something of an educated elite and tended to look down on the shopkeepers and tradesmen who took the lead in Scunthorpe. The coldness between the two communities was indicated in 1884 when they established separate burial boards and cemeteries. Ten years later the local board of health at Scunthorpe was replaced by an Urban District Council and at the request of Frodingham and Brumby a separate UDC was formed for their two townships. Scunthorpe UDC took over its burial board in 1895 and sought to develop other facilities, but their relations with Frodingham and the distance to Ashby prevented any joint provision of services for several years. Proposals that the two urban districts might have a common water supply fell through in 1897 because of Scunthorpe's insistence on having a majority on any joint board. It would be

---

[37] Dudley, *Scunthorpe and Frodingham*, p. 159, 181; A. Marson, 'Fifty Years Ago', *Appleby Frodingham News*, 16 no. 2 (1963), p. 42.

more economic to provide a single water supply, sewage scheme, public lighting system, isolation hospital and administrative staff but Frodingham ratepayers were unwilling to be dominated by their larger neighbour. The two communities were both dependent on iron and more than half of Scunthorpe's workforce were employed in the iron works of Frodingham but in civic affairs their interests diverged; Frodingham had much lower rates than Scunthorpe owing to a lack of urban facilities and the high rateable value of the three iron works.[38]

In 1903 Scunthorpe made its first approach to Lindsey County Council for the amalgamation of the ironstone district but this was immediately resisted by Frodingham. One of their councillors considered that 'in no single thing where Frodingham had joined with Scunthorpe had good feeling existed, and one might just as well try to unite Sweden and Norway'. The solicitor of Scunthorpe UDC declared that 'we . . . have nothing whatever to do with Frodingham . . . and there is no reason to suppose that those Frodingham people would wish for one moment to have their [water] supply shared with the people of Scunthorpe'. Frodingham's resistance was supported by the major landowners and in January 1904 the county council decided against amalgamation. Later that year Frodingham dismissed Dr Behrendt who since 1894 had been medical officer for both authorities, considering that it was 'unwise to have the same medical officer . . . as the interests of the districts have now become so antagonistic'.[39]

Scunthorpe UDC developed more services than did its smaller but richer neighbour. The town outgrew the gas supply available from the Frodingham Works and after opposing an attempt to form a private gas company the Scunthorpe UDC obtained an act in 1899 to provide gas and water themselves. They declined an offer of the Frodingham company's gas works and their own works on the far side of their district were completed in May 1901. They obtained power to supply gas to Crosby in 1910 and Ashby in 1913 but only in 1914 were they able to include Brumby and Frodingham. Water supply was more of a problem and Scunthorpe needed another act in 1903 in order to establish a reservoir on Sawcliff Hill; the works were completed in 1907 and also supplied Winterton, but a further act to improve the supply was needed in 1912. In 1908 Brumby and Frodingham UDC completed separate waterworks for their own

---

[38] Dudley, *Scunthorpe and Frodingham*, p. 169; D. C. D. Pocock, 'Scunthorpe and Frodingham — Early Struggles in Civic History', *Appleby Frodingham News*, 16 no. 1 (1963), pp. 33, 35.
[39] Pocock, op. cit., pp. 34, 36.

district, drawing from a well in Appleby parish. When water was available Scunthorpe installed fire hydrants and purchased a horse-drawn fire engine and hose. In 1907 Sir Berkeley Sheffield gave a steam fire engine of the latest design, with uniforms and equipment, and in 1909 the UDC opened a new fire station to accommodate it in Cole Street.[40]

Other Edwardian improvements were the erection of free libraries in Scunthorpe and Ashby, with the help of Andrew Carnegie, and the opening of a museum in Scunthorpe in 1909 to reflect the wealth of archaeological material being revealed by the ironstone mining. Scunthorpe UDC also erected a covered market, which was opened by Lord St Oswald in 1906. By 1900 the Frodingham Iron and Steel Co. had a small steam-driven dynamo providing electric light for their works and in 1901 they erected larger equipment to provide power as well; by 1913 this was also supplying electricity to Frodingham township. When Sir Berkeley Sheffield started releasing building land after 1901, there was a rapid march of bricks and mortar over the fields of Crosby; between 1901 and 1911 the population increased from 364 to 3,339, exceeding Ashby, Frodingham or Brumby. In 1906 a small cemetery was provided by Crosby parish council, who now found themselves facing urban problems, and in 1909 they formed a joint board with Scunthorpe to provide sewage works on Risby warren, which were opened in 1914.[41]

In 1909 negotiations had started for Crosby to unite with Scunthorpe, but they dragged on and in 1912 Crosby parish council applied unilaterally for urban status. This was unsuccessful, but in 1913 Crosby and Scunthorpe were joined by Ashby in seeking amalgamation. In 1914 the Brumby and Frodingham UDC briefly considered joining the project but then turned against it. It was only developments during the First World War which eventually led to their amalgamation in 1919. By 1911 the population of the five townships was 19,678, only a little less than Boston, Grantham or Gainsborough and twice the size of Louth or Stamford. In the space of fifty years, the ironstone district had changed from a group of small villages into one of the main urban centres of Lincolnshire, yet its local administration was still divided between at least six distinct authorities.[42]

[40] Dudley, *Scunthorpe and Frodingham*, pp. 171, 173.
[41] Dudley, *Scunthorpe and Frodingham*, pp. 172, 173; Walshaw and Behrendt, p. 80.
[42] Pocock, 'Scunthorpe and Frodingham — Early Struggles in Civic History', p. 36.

CHAPTER 8

RAILWAYS AND THE COAST

B Y 1850 the basic railway network of Lincolnshire was complete and the main towns were connected to the national system. The rest of the story is the filling-in of the pattern: for twenty years the emphasis lay more on direct routes and on branches to market towns, but from 1870 the dominant theme was better access to the east coast and the development of the seaside resorts. Hand in hand with the railway came two major changes elsewhere in the transport scene: waterways decayed, and ports, on the whole, developed. Grimsby, as a successful port, was made by the railway, and its fishing fleet was built up to become second in the whole kingdom only to Yarmouth's. At the very end of the period, Immingham was created, also by the railway, as Grimsby's deepwater dock, to become the present-day giant among Humber ports. Gainsborough's history was the reverse, for the railway did it nothing but permanent harm, while Boston likewise declined until it achieved its own dock, and seaborne trade revived. As everywhere else, the weakest went to the wall, and the railway was often the deciding factor.

The MSLR, renamed the GCR in 1897, developed Grimsby docks and the TAGR was built in the 1860s, but most railway developments before 1890 were extensions to the GNR system in the south and centre of the county. A few lines were promoted by the GNR itself, mainly to prevent the GER entering Lincolnshire, but most of the new lines were comparatively small schemes, proposed by local landowners and businessmen who raised the capital for the initial creation of the line. The GNR usually leased and operated them with its own rolling stock and motive power. In many cases the local company was later purchased and absorbed into the GNR in the same way as the MSLR took over the TAGR. By this process the GNR and MSLR remained the principal railway operators in Lincolnshire until 1923. The MR and the GER were joint owners with the GNR of two other lines in the county and the MR had stations of its own at Stamford, Lincoln and a few villages on the Nottingham line, but the only other incursion into Lincolnshire was the Edwardian light railway in the Isle of Axholme. The small scale of this latter enterprise only serves to emphasize the dominance of the two main companies.[1]

Railways replaced waterways as a factor in the economy of urban Lincolnshire. They developed Grimsby at the expense of Boston and Gainsborough, decimated the coaching traffic of Stamford and Grantham but facilitated the development of engineering firms in Lincoln, Grantham and Gainsborough. The great Horncastle horse fair was eclipsed by Lincoln, which had better railway links for the use of dealers, customers and horses alike. Similarly the number of sheep penned at Boston May fair declined as more were sold at weekly markets. Commerce in corn and barley led to the opening of a Corn Exchange in Lincoln in 1847 and during the 1850s others were built by private enterprise in at least a dozen Lincolnshire towns. Such halls were also used for other purposes such as dances and auctions, and set the precedent for later general purpose public halls in most towns.[2]

GRIMSBY DOCKS

The only Lincolnshire town which grew substantially because of a railway company's activities was Grimsby. When the MSLR entered Grimsby the stimulus of the dock opened in 1800 was wearing off and the population was in decline, but during the reign of Victoria the little old market town was to be swamped by the great fishing town that covered its fields and marshes with bricks and mortar and spilled over into Clee parish. The heart of this new town was at the entrance to the Royal Dock, near the junction of Cleethorpe Road and Freeman Street.

The old town of Grimsby was nearly a mile inland from the Humber and after 1800 streets for a projected new town had been laid out alongside the dock to the Humber bank. Beyond the bank were extensive mud flats on each side of the harbour entrance and the railway company reclaimed 138 acres of the eastern flats as the site for their new dock shown in figure 21. James M. Rendel was the engineer in charge of the dock works with Adam Smith of Brigg as the resident engineer. Rendel's plans were of quite a different order

[1] Dow, *Great Central*, II, p. 297; R. E. Pearson, 'Railways in relation to Resort Development in East Lincolnshire', *East Midland Geographer*, 29 (1968), p. 284; names of all railways are shown in full in Appendix III.

[2] *Lincolnshire Echo*, 26 August 1974; H. Porter, *Boston 1800 to 1835 continued to 1868*, Lincoln, 1943, p. 61; Honeybone, *Grantham*; C. Tallens, 'Lincoln Fairs and Markets in Georgian and Victorian Times', *LIA*, 4 no. 2 (1969), p. 25.

of magnitude to the old dock. Work started in the spring of 1846 on the coffer dam which was to exclude the tide from the dock site. On the west was a wharf extending 2,431 feet into the Humber from the old lock entrance while three-quarters of a mile to the east was an embankment extending out towards the same point. Between the outer ends of the wharf and the embankment was the immense coffer dam, thirty-two feet wide at the base and using ten thousand piles. The construction of these sea defences was completed by the end of 1848 and work then started on the construction of the dock basin and the entrance locks. Prince Albert laid the foundation stone on 18 April 1849 and the contractors completed the work within three years. The largest lock was 70 by 300 feet, with a smaller one for barges built alongside, 200 by 45 feet. This was the first major dock to use hydraulic machinery, produced by Sir Wm Armstrong and Co., to work the lock gates, cranes and other machinery; central to this system was the great campanile or dock tower, which symbolized the modernity of the works and the success of Grimsby. This three hundred feet high tower, with water at the top, was built between the two locks on a foundation of sand and stands to this day as the most distinctive landmark of Grimsby. The dock covered fifteen acres, with in addition a shallower five-acre timber pond. A banquet was held on the floor of the larger lock pit on 18 March 1852; water was admitted to the dock four days later and it was opened for traffic from 27 May. A branch railway from Grimsby Town station to the dock was opened in 1853. Queen Victoria and Prince Albert visited Grimsby in the royal yacht on 14 October 1854 and consented to the name Royal Dock.[3]

The importing of construction materials while the dock and the railways were being built increased traffic through Grimsby and there was consequently a slight depression when the dock was completed, but gradually traffic built up in the following years. The tonnage of shipping using the Royal Dock increased from 118,000 in the second half of 1855 to 162,000 in the second half of 1856. When the dock first opened some Hull merchants transferred to Grimsby but soon returned to the larger port, which had more facilities for a mercantile community. The MSLR had to develop traffic themselves. From 1852 steamships sailed weekly from Grimsby to northern Europe and in 1856 the MSLR formed their own steamship company, the Anglo-French, with Lord Yarborough as chairman, to export Yorkshire coal to France. The first

[3] Dow, *Great Central*, I, pp. 142, 173, 175; White and Tye, *Grimsby and Cleethorpes*, pp. 7–9.

coal traffic had passed through Grimsby in 1853 and two coal drops were built at the landward end of the dock, the first in 1856 and the second shortly after. Total traffic in coal from Grimsby rose from 46,000 tons in 1856 to 363,000 tons in 1875 and 1,744,000 tons in 1911.[4]

Other traffic through the dock also increased, mainly with north European ports. Coal, cotton goods and textile machinery were exported, reflecting Grimsby's links with Manchester, and timber and oil cake were imported. As early as 1853 Clayton and Shuttleworth were exporting thrashing machines through Grimsby, but most agricultural machinery went through Hull, which had more quay space. By 1865 Grimsby ranked as the fifth port of the kingdom, exporting just over £4 million of British goods in that year. By then the MSLR had spent over £1 million on Grimsby docks, including a graving dock, coal hoists, and a separate Fish Dock.[5]

There were fishermen at Cleethorpes and other places round the Lincolnshire coast but none in Grimsby when the railway arrived. It is thought that the first fishing smack to land at Grimsby was the *Prince of Wurtemburg* from Barking in 1850, but to encourage the traffic the GNR gave a bonus to James Howard and Co. to bring their fleet of thirteen smacks from Manningtree. In April 1854 the MSLR sponsored the formation of the Grimsby Deep Sea Fising Co. and by the end of the year the GNR and MR were also involved. In 1856 fourteen smacks moved to Grimsby from London and Brixham. At first smacks used both the Royal Dock and the Old Dock but a separate six-acre Fish Dock was built in 1855–57, complete with a floating pontoon on which a fish market was held. Most of the early smacks caught cod by line fishing and few were trawlers.[6]

The presence of the railway to London attracted the first smacks to Grimsby but the construction of the Fish Dock enabled the industry to grow. In 1852 about five hundred tons of fish was dispatched by rail from Grimsby and this had risen to 3,400 tons in 1857, but eight years later 10,360 tons were carried. While fish was a luxury reserved for the London market the GNR had the bulk of the traffic, but as demand grew in the industrial north the MSLR began

[4] Gillett, *Grimsby*, p. 222; White and Tye, *Grimsby and Cleethorpes*, p. 9.

[5] Gillett, *Grimsby*, pp. 225, 226; White and Tye, *Grimsby and Cleethorpes*, pp. 9, 10, 12.

[6] White and Tye, *Grimsby and Cleethorpes*, p. 10; Dow, *Great Central*, I, p. 176; Gillett, *Grimsby*, p. 230.

to get a good share of the trade. In a few decades Grimsby became the largest community in Lincolnshire and the leading fishing port in the kingdom. In March 1857 regular imports of ice from Norway started and in 1863 the Great Grimsby Ice Co. was founded. Other towns were also supplied with Norwegian ice and imports grew to 40,000 tons a year.[7]

DECLINE OF OTHER PORTS

Gainsborough served the east midlands, but Boston and most other Lincolnshire ports had mainly been *entrepôts* for the county and were effectively replaced by railway stations throughout Lincolnshire. Most people in Gainsborough got their living from the river trade and as railways linked the midlands to other parts of the kingdom so the population of Gainsborough declined during the 1850s from 7,261 to 6,320. As recently as 1840 Gainsborough had achieved official recognition as a separate customs port and ships no longer had to receive clearance from the Hull customs, but already the port was at the end of its most important period. The move to obtain such recognition had been stimulated by booming river trade in 1837 and 1839, when stone, lime and timber needed for the construction of railway stations, tunnels and bridges had been carried inland on the Trent. Construction of the MSLR and GNR at Gainsborough in the late 1840s delayed the decline in customs and excise duties received at Gainsborough. They fell only from £73,231 in 1844 to £61,412 in 1848 but both railways at Gainsborough were opened in 1849 and by 1854 the duties had fallen dramatically to £13,224. In the period 1847 to 1855 the trade of the Trent as a whole fell by 54 per cent and the support given to Gainsborough traffic by railway activity in the late 1840s made the subsequent decline even greater.[8]

After 1851 the remaining trade of the port declined slowly for twenty years or more. Between 1871 and 1879 the customs and excise duties fell from £11,142 to £2,438. In 1861 the Gainsborough shipping interest was still sufficiently vociferous to complain that the proposed Keadby bridge would obstruct river traffic, but George Gamble, formerly a merchant and now a railway director, declared that the introduction of the railway system generally had led to Gainsborough's decline since 1849. The growth of Marshall's Britannia iron works gave the town new life, but the traffic of the

[7] Gillett, loc. cit.; Dow, loc. cit.; White and Tye, loc. cit.
[8] I. S. Beckwith, *The History of Transport and Travel in Gainsborough*, Gainsborough, 1971, pp. 25–27.

port continued to fall until after the First World War and the independence from Hull granted in 1840 was revoked in 1881.[9]

The port of Boston was also adversely affected by the opening of railways north to Grimsby and south to London. Boston's trade was mostly coasting (in 1850 1,060 coasters visited the port compared with only thirty-four foreign vessels) and was largely in competition with the railway to London. The port of Boston also included Spalding, which had about one seventh of the port's trade. The traffic in grain had declined since 1811 when nearly 400,000 quarters had left the port but in 1840 it still totalled over 140,000 quarters. The railway took most of this cereal trade, opening six stations in the sparsely populated fens north of Boston and erecting a large granary on the bank of the Redstone Gowt drain at Boston to intercept grain barges from the west. There were also country stations north and south of Spalding and at Surfleet, where there was an interchange between the railway and traffic on the river Glen. In 1850 the amount of grain shipped from the port was 89,000 quarters from Boston and 25,398 quarters from Spalding but by 1854 the railway had reduced this to 53,406 quarters from Boston and 2,210 quarters from Spalding. Between 1850 and 1854 the number of vessels belonging to the port of Boston fell from 179 to 152 with a consequent reduction in the number of men employed from 580 to 495, and in 1853 the harbour at Boston was described as giving 'an odd impression of bustle, and sluggishness, and decay, and a remnant of wholesome life'. The dues collected from vessels navigating the Welland between Spalding and the Wash fell from £6,000 in 1846 to less than £1,000 in 1865, but a few vessels continued to visit Spalding until the twentieth century.[10]

Boston, in contrast to Grimsby, lacked a convenient east-west railway link and dock facilities, and several early railway schemes had proposed to link the port of Boston with the midlands. Even the original plans of the London and York railway included a short branch to the haven bank in Skirbeck Quarter, but the GNR did not build this branch and had no other plans for the development of the port. The eventual revival was to be a local achievement. The GNR's own proposal for a line between Boston and Grantham had been rejected by parliament in 1847 and the unfortunate ANBEJR,

[9] Beckwith, op. cit., pp. 27, 28; Henthorn, ed., *Trent, Ancholme and Grimsby Railway*, p. xxxix; I. S. Beckwith, 'The River Trade of Gainsborough 1500–1850', *LHA*, 5 (1970), p. 10.
[10] M. J. T. Lewis and N. R. Wright, *Boston as a Port*, Lincoln, 1974, pp. 10, 12; Thompson, *Boston*, pp. 350–52; Boyes and Russell, *Canals*, p. 252; N. R. Wright, *Spalding — An Industrial History*, Lincoln, 1973, p. 39.

to which Boston's hopes were pinned, gave up its larger plans after opening its central section between Nottingham and Grantham in 1850.[11]

Herbert Ingram and John Rawson had both represented Boston on the ANBEJR board and they became directors of a new company formed in 1852 to link Grantham and Boston direct and build docks at the southern end of the town. The BMCR obtained its act in 1853 but their single-track line took over five years to build. Traffic on the Grantham to Nottingham line increased fourfold after the line was opened to Boston and in 1875 a cut-off was opened from Sedgebrook to Barkston so that coal from Nottinghamshire could gain access to Boston without going through Grantham. Boston now had the desired railway line but the company failed to build either the proposed docks or a branch authorized in 1860 alongside the haven. For the next twenty years the shipping interests considered that the hope for the port was a railway or tramway to Freiston Shore with a pier extending out into Boston Deeps. Many vessels already anchored in the Wash and transferred their cargo to smaller boats to be taken up the rivers to Boston or Spalding. The first scheme was proposed by the BMCR in 1862 but came to nothing; no other schemes were put forward until the early 1870s.[12]

RAILWAYS AND WATERWAYS IN MID CENTURY

During the 1850s and 1860s some other gaps in the county's railway network were filled and several short branch lines were opened to small Lincolnshire towns. These included railways from Stamford to Essendine and from Horncastle to the loop line at Kirkstead. One of the few lines which the GNR refused to operate was the four mile long ELBR which Lord Willoughby de Eresby built from Grimsthorpe to the towns line at Little Bytham. It had two small locomotives, several steep gradients and a speed limit of 15 m.p.h. The passenger services on the line started in 1857 but were intermittent after 1866 and were withdrawn in 1871; the subsequent horse-drawn goods service ended in the early 1880s.[13]

The opening of railways took longer to affect the waterways of Lincolnshire than to affect the ports. Some of the waterways lost all their traffic within twenty or thirty years of railways arriving but

[11] N. R. Wright, *The Railways of Boston*, Boston, 1971, pp. 9, 37.

[12] Ibid., pp. 39, 40; Leleux, *East Midlands Railways*, pp. 197–98.

[13] N. C. Birch, *Stamford — An Industrial History*, Lincoln, 1972, p. 34; Leleux, *East Midlands Railways*, pp. 198, 199; J. D. Birkbeck, *A History of Bourne*, Bourne, 2nd edn 1976, p. 95.

others were still used by commercial traffic until after the First World War. Four Lincolnshire waterways were taken over by the GNR, either directly or indirectly, and despite neglect these navigations survived longer than the independent waterways. The Stainforth and Keadby canal fell into the hands of the MSLR via the SYR and similarly survived. The ANBEJR tried unsuccessfully to go back on its agreement to lease both the Nottingham and Grantham canals but both were transferred a few months before the company was leased by the GNR in 1855. Takings on the Grantham canal had reached a maximum of £13,079 in 1841 but in 1873 it was complained that wide boats could not use it for lack of dredging and by 1905 the takings were down to a mere £242, when only 18,802 tons of manure, roadstone, plaster, coal and other traffic was carried: this canal was formally abandoned in 1936. [14]

The ELR purchased the Chaplin lease of the Louth navigation and the GNR operated the waterway until the lease expired in 1876. The navigation then reverted to the commissioners, who received a satisfactory income from toll lettings until after the turn of the century. The peak of £1,417 was received in 1887, but after 1900 there was a fairly rapid decline until 1916 when traffic virtually ceased. The navigation was formally closed in 1924. [15]

The GNR itself directly leased the Witham and Fossdyke navigations and built much of its loop line on their banks. The stations were located close to the main packet landing places and there was direct competition between the trains and the packet boats. The GNR introduced fourth-class fares of ½d. a mile in 1850 and by 1863 the last of the packet boats had finished. The competition also reduced freight traffic on the river, the amount of coal passing through the Grand Sluice at Boston falling from 19,535 tons in 1847 to 3,780 in 1854. The total tonnage on the Witham fell from 276,154 in 1848 to 85,134 in 1868 and a mere 18,548 in 1904. Despite this the company had to maintain the river for navigation as well as drainage and in 1871 they had to deepen Bardney lock. The Fossdyke continued to carry more traffic than the Witham, amounting to 75,881 tons in 1904, of which 60,342 was consigned to Lincoln. The Trent had suffered like many navigations but the enthusiastic efforts of the Trent Navigation Co. and Nottingham corporation from the 1880s led to a revival of the trade and improvements to the river. The Ancholme was maintained

[14] C. Hadfield, *The Canals of the East Midlands*, Newton Abbot, 2nd edn 1970, pp. 63, 195, 196, 200; J. Wrottesley, *The Great Northern Railway*, London, 1979, p. 90.
[15] Boyes and Russell, *Canals*, pp. 309, 310.

primarily for drainage but also enjoyed a slight commercial revival at the end of the century. In 1846–48 the tolls had raised £3,020 p.a. but fell to £1,482 in 1849 and £949 in 1850. By the late 1850s they were at about £700 p.a., but after 1890 they started to rise and averaged about £1,000. In 1879 the Ancholme Packet Co. was formed to run daily services between Brigg and South Ferriby in connection with the Hull steamers and in 1891 the Goole and Hull Steam Packet Co. introduced a steam service on the navigation.[16]

The other waterways closed several years before the end of the century. The Caistor canal was never a success and its fate was sealed when the MSLR opened a station halfway between Caistor and the basin at Moortown. The opening of the ELBR apparently affected traffic on the Bourne Eau as in 1857 it was said that boats only 'occasionally' navigated from the town. The Welland navigation between Stamford and Deeping was also quick to suffer. All traffic ended in 1863 and by 1868 Stamford corporation had sold off what parts they could. The Horncastle and Sleaford navigations lasted a little longer because of the delay in building railways to the towns they served. Indeed for a while they benefited by conveying goods between their towns and Dogdyke station on the loop line. It was said that in 1852 the GNR paid £1,677 in dues to the Horncastle navigation. After the Horncastle railway opened there was a dramatic fall in the navigation company's dividend and traffic was described as 'trifling' in 1874: the last recorded cargoes were carried in May 1878. Revenue on the Sleaford navigation similarly fell in the 1860s and 1870s, after the railway arrived, and notice of closure was given at the final AGM in May 1881.[17]

Market boats on the navigable drains north and west of Boston were not in direct competition with the railways and continued sailing to Bargate bridge and the Black Sluice in Boston until the arrival of motor buses in the early twentieth century. Similar packet boats survived on the Humber and the lower Trent, carrying people to the markets at Hull.

JOINT LINES

Two unsuccessful schemes of the 1840s had been for lines from Leicestershire to Norfolk and from Cambridgeshire to Yorkshire. The GNR strenuously opposed other companies seeking to enter its territory and although these two strategic routes were eventually

[16] Ibid., pp. 200, 266, 267, 299; C. J. Page, *History of the Ancholme Navigation*, Lincoln, 1969, pp. 10, 11.
[17] Boyes and Russell, *Canals*, pp. 241, 252, 275, 279, 287.

created, the GNR held them back until the 1880s and then had half
ownership of them. The line from Leicestershire to Norfolk was
developed in a piecemeal way by small companies. The first section
from Spalding to Holbeach was opened in 1858 and by 1866 there
was a continuous line from King's Lynn to Bourne and so through
to the midlands via Stamford. That year the companies on the
Bourne–Lynn route amalgamated as the MER and gained running
powers over a new line from Sutton Bridge to Peterborough via
Wisbech. In 1888 a western extension from Bourne to join the MR
at Saxby was authorized and the following year this cross-country
route was jointly purchased by the MR and the GNR, who opened
the western extension in 1894. The other new route through
Lincolnshire arose from the desire of the GER for access to the
coalfields of Yorkshire. In the mid 1860s the GNR defeated GER
schemes by obtaining authority for various lines of its own in
Lincolnshire but in 1878 agreement was reached between the GNR
and the GER for a joint line crossing the county from March to
Doncaster. Much of it was on existing track transferred from the
parent companies, and it opened in 1882. [18]

TO THE COAST

Except for the two joint lines, most railway activity in Lincolnshire
after 1867 was related to the east, particularly the Lindsey coast
between Wainfleet and Grimsby. As early as 1863 the MSLR had
built a short branch from Grimsby docks to Cleethorpes but it was
not until the 1870s that visitors started arriving on the Lincolnshire
coast in large numbers. [19]

A branch line to Skegness was opened in 1873 and excursionists
were soon arriving. The MSLR doubled the short Cleethorpes
branch in 1874 and, in the 1880s, spent over £10,000 on improving
the amenities there, but it was the ninth earl of Scarbrough
(1813–84) who developed Skegness. The branch lines in the Marsh
were provided to carry agricultural produce rather than holiday
makers, though some promoters with greater vision hoped to
develop a new dock on the Lincolnshire coast. In the event, three
docks were to be opened in the space of six years though not one
was on the mid Lindsey coast. The LECR from Louth to Mablethorpe, where a convalescent home had been built in 1870, was

---

[18] Wright, *Spalding — An Industrial History*, p. 40; Leleux, *East Midlands Railways*,
pp. 198, 200; L. Elvin, *Lincoln as it Was*, II, Nelson, 1976, p. 5.
[19] Leleux, *East Midlands Railways*, p. 199; White and Tye, *Grimsby and Cleethorpes*,
p. 10.

opened in 1877; contrary to expectations excursion taffic to the seaside proved more profitable than agricultural traffic. Pavilions were erected on the sandhills at Mablethorpe in the 1880s. At nearby Saltfleet part of the foreshore had been reclaimed in 1854 and it failed to develop into a modern resort. A dock with a thirteen-acre basin was built at Sutton Bridge in 1881, but within a month it was to be ruined by the defects of the soil in which it was built. Train loads of limestone were brought to the dock and tipped in to replace silt that was being washed away, but on 11 June about five hundred feet of the concrete facing on its west side was undermined and slid into the basin. From that day the dock was abandoned; in 1937 the basin and adjacent areas became a golf course.[20]

DEVELOPMENTS AT GRIMSBY

From 1866 the original Fish Dock at Grimsby was gradually enlarged to thirteen acres and in 1876–77 a second Fish Dock of eleven acres was built. The new commercial dock authorized in 1869 was slower to materialize; in 1873 the MSLR even looked at a site in Stallingborough further along the coast before purchasing 153 acres in the West Marsh of Grimsby. In 1873–74 a connecting link called Union Dock was made between the Royal Dock and the Old Dock, out of which the new commercial dock was to be built. Even then, the final decision to go ahead was delayed until December 1878 owing to the state of Grimsby's trade. Work started in 1879, and that year the prince of Wales officially opened the Union Dock and named the new scheme Alexandra Dock in honour of his princess; it was reported as complete in July 1880. From the 1880s coal exports increased and so did food imports, particularly protein such as butter, which by 1900 formed a quarter of all Grimsby's imports.[21]

After 1871 the fishing industry grew rapidly as first wet fish shops and then fried fish shops spread inland from Grimsby to Sheffield, Manchester and other northern towns. The number of smacks increased from 219 in 1869 to at least 625 in 1881; they then caught one third of the fish landed in England and Wales. These

[20] Wright, *Railways of Boston*, p. 46; Pearson, 'Railways in relation to Resort Development in East Lincolnshire', p. 284; White and Tye, *Grimsby and Cleethorpes*, p. 33; *Kelly's Directory*, 1913; p. 449; Leleux, *East Midlands Railways*, p. 206; N. R. Wright, *An Industrial History of Long Sutton and Sutton Bridge*, Lincoln, 1970, pp. 23, 24, 28, 29; D. N. Robinson, *The Book of the Lincolnshire Seaside*, Buckingham, 1981, p. 32.
[21] Dow, *Great Central*, II, pp. 162, 164, 165; White and Tye, *Grimsby and Cleethorpes*, pp. 10–12.

new smacks needed more apprentices than the local community could supply, and skippers were driven to recruiting from the workhouses of London. The number of new apprentices indentured rose from 229 in 1868 to 576 in 1877 and in the latter year there were 1,794 apprentices compared with only 1,676 fishermen. In a crew of five three would be apprentices and there were cases where only the skipper was not an apprentice. Young lads of little more than twelve were ill-equipped for the tough life of the smacks, where they were often regarded as merely part of the machinery for catching fish. In the period 1880–95, the annual loss of life among Grimsby fishermen exceeded twelve per thousand; among the inexperienced and unsupervised apprentices perhaps about one in twelve was lost. When on shore, about half the apprentices stayed with their masters; others were paid off and left to look after themselves, some of the older lads frequenting brothels. [22]

The county prison at Lincoln became an essential adjunct to the Grimsby system of apprenticeship. Under the Merchant Shipping Act of 1854, apprentices who deserted their ship could be arrested without warrant, tried by magistrates and imprisoned. In 1872 twenty apprentices were sent to Lincoln prison, 132 in 1873 and 244 in 1877. They were marched through Lincoln streets in chains and when national press reports in 1873 reduced the supply from workhouses, skippers then recruited from reformatories, whose lads were usually healthier and more spirited than workhouse boys. More than half the sentences of imprisonment passed by Grimsby magistrates were on fisher lads and in 1877 it was said that almost a thousand Grimsby apprentices had been in the new Lincoln prison since it opened in 1872. Some boys saw no disgrace in going to 'Lincoln College' as they called it and Home Office inspectors found it understandable that in bad weather a boy with venereal disease should prefer prison to life at sea in a smack. The Merchant Shipping Act of 1880 was intended to end imprisonment for desertion but Grimsby magistrates circumvented this by dealing with cases as breaches of indentures under section 248 of the 1854 act. It was the change from smacks to larger steam trawlers that undermined Grimsby's peculiar institution and led to the employment of more weekly hands. By 1882 there were only eight hundred apprentices still serving in smacks and that year only 380 new apprentices were indentured. [23]

[22] White and Tye, Grimsby and Cleethorpes, p. 11; Gillett, Grimsby, pp. 247, 248, 256, 257, 259, 263.
[23] Gillett, Grimsby, pp. 247–49, 252, 254, 260–63; White, Directory, 1872, p. 97.

The phenomenal growth of the fishing industry led to the need for support services. In 1883 the Grimsby Ice Co. had been importing Norwegian ice for twenty years and it then started to manufacture ice locally. The Coal, Salt and Tanning Co., formed in 1873, became the principal supplier of nets, provisions, ironmongery and steel wire as well as coal and salt, and by 1908 its annual turnover exceeded £1 million. Support companies such as these were backed by the leading boat owners, who thereby grew even more prosperous at the expense of the small owners. During the 1880s steam started to replace sail, iron to replace wood and trawlers to get larger. The industry's character changed as capital flowed in and owners became more remote. Share-fishing declined and most crews became wage employees of large companies.[24]

By the early 1880s over £1 million had been invested in the smacks but the number of vessels rose faster than the total catch and there were signs that their exploitation of the North Sea was near its limits and might soon become unprofitable. Conditions were critical for some of the smaller owners and there was a switch from single-boating to 'fleeting', principally under the Ice Company, which at one time controlled up to a hundred boats. The boom in sailing smacks still continued for a time and they were built for Grimsby owners in Whitby, Burton Stather, Gainsborough and even Altona on the Elbe, but this decade saw the ruin of the little man in Grimsby's fishing industry. Steamers cost at least £5,000 and although some small owners combined to purchase one or two the industry passed into the hands of large companies backed by banks and London money. In the 1890s the building of sailing smacks was abandoned and unhappy owners competed to get rid of them. The industry now needed boats which could go further for fish. In 1881 the Great Grimsby Steam Trawling Co. was formed and introduced the first steam trawlers into the port. By 1894 trawlers 110 feet long were becoming commonplace, and to accommodate the fleet the No. 2 Fish Dock was enlarged by five acres in 1897–1900 and a floating dry dock for repairs was also completed. The two fish docks had twenty-nine acres of water and a third dock was authorized in 1912 but its construction was postponed by the outbreak of the war.[25]

[24] White and Tye, *Grimsby and Cleethorpes*, pp. 12, 29; Dow, *Great Central*, II, pp. 162, 165–67.
[25] White and Tye, *Grimsby and Cleethorpes*, p. 20; Gillett, *Grimsby*, pp. 264, 265, 268, 270; Dow, *Great Central*, II, pp. 168, 171, 264.

FISH LANDED AT GRIMSBY[26]

Year	1850	1860	1870	1880	1890	1900	1910	1912
Tons	nil	4,537*	26,324*	45,000	71,382	133,791	179,792	193,363

* Amount sent out by railway

In 1897 there were 113 steam trawlers based at Grimsby but by 1901 this had risen to 471 and only 67 smacks remained. By 1911 there were 629 steam trawlers totalling 63,485 tons and only 42 smacks totalling 2,714 tons. By then there were two hydraulic coal hoists in No. 2 Fish Dock for fuelling the trawlers. By 1900 the size of trawlers had reached three hundred tons and these large vessels had gone beyond the North Sea and were fishing off Iceland. In the twenty-four years after 1890 fish landings at Grimsby almost tripled as shown in the table above. Ninety per cent of the landings were despatched by rail and in 1911 they brought in £293,030 for the MSLR, which since April 1888 had officially regarded Grimsby as its eastern terminus.[27]

BOSTON DOCK

The GNR and MSLR invested in new docks at Sutton Bridge and Grimsby but the creation of a dock at Boston was undertaken by the local community. John Cabourn Simonds and his son William Turner Simonds were leading merchants in the small port and as private capital seemed unable to provide a dock they turned their attention to Boston corporation and achieved dominant positions, one or other of them being mayor of the town on nine occasions between 1880 and 1904. In 1879 the corporation reached agreement with two bodies of drainage commissioners to share the cost of improving the haven between Boston and the Wash and the necessary act was obtained in 1880. The following year the corporation obtained an act for a dock at the southern end of Boston despite last minute opposition from a rival scheme at Freiston Shore. In June 1882 Mrs Simonds cut the first sod on the site of Boston dock and the first ship entered the seven-acre basin on 15 December 1884 with cottonseed for Simonds's oilcake mill. Between 1880 and 1887 the haven was straightened and deepened to twenty-seven feet for four miles below Boston. The contract for the dock and the railway

[26] White, *Directory*, 1872, p. 200; Leleux, *East Midlands Railways*, p. 216; Dow, *Great Central*, III, p. 264; *Kelly's Directory*, 1913, p. 247.
[27] Dow, *Great Central*, II, p. 168; III, p. 264; *Kelly's Directory*, 1913, pp. 246, 247; Leleux, *East Midlands Railways*, pp. 216, 218.

link to the GNR line was undertaken by Mr W. Rigby for £80,000 and the total cost including purchase of land, hydraulic machinery, warehouses and fish pontoon was about £180,000. The facilities included an hydraulic coal tip (a second one being added in 1910), hydraulic cranes and two grain warehouses. The GNR did not participate in the project, and even though Boston was the company's chief revenue-earning station in the county it was not until 1903 that they increased the size of their goods shed and provided extra sidings. [28]

The number of vessels entering the port of Boston rose from 396 in 1881 (totalling 27,137 registered tons) to 605 in 1894 (124,696 tons) and by 1896 trade was eight times greater than in 1884. The chief imports were grain, fruit, timber and oilseed while oilcake, potatoes, iron and coal were the chief exports. Much of the timber came from the Baltic as sleepers and was treated at the GNR's sleeper depot, which in 1900 had to be moved to a larger site at Hall Hills just north of Boston. Vessels still continued to use the old harbour until after the First World War but then traffic became concentrated around the dock. [29]

Small fishing smacks had operated from Boston since the early nineteenth century and from the 1880s steam trawlers and drifters appeared. The Boston Deep Sea Fishing and Ice Co., formed by local businessmen in 1885 with eight steam trawlers and a number of smacks, came to dominate the industry in the port. It started operations in April 1886 and by 1906 owned thirty-five steam vessels of 90 to 125 feet operating from Iceland to Portugal and employed over five hundred men. The company built an ice factory, various workshops, offices and the fish pontoon. Other steam fishing companies were formed in 1895 and 1900 but both were soon absorbed by the original firm. [30]

BANKING

As industry and commerce expanded in Lincolnshire so banking had to follow suit. The main feature before 1890 was the steady growth of the Stamford, Spalding and Boston Bank but the next twenty-five years saw a spate of amalgamations and by 1914 all the Lincolnshire banks had been absorbed in larger concerns. During Victorian times Garfit's, Ellison's and the Lincoln and Lindsey

[28] Lewis and Wright, *Boston as a Port*, p. 14; *Boston Red Book and Directory for 1913*, Boston, 1912, p. 130; Wright, *Railways of Boston*, pp. 42, 51.
[29] Lewis and Wright, op. cit., p. 14.
[30] Ibid., pp. 20, 48; E. M. Hewitt, 'Deep Sea Fisheries and Fish Docks', in VCH, *Lincs.*, p. 390.

o

Bank also opened branches and agencies throughout the county. The last Ellison partner in the Lincoln bank died in 1859 and for the latter half of the century effective control was exercised by the Honourable Alexander Leslie-Melville (1800–81) and his son A. S. Leslie-Melville representing the Smith family.

Until 1891 most of Lincolnshire's banking needs continued to be met by banks based in the county. The National Provincial had banks in Boston, Spalding and Long Sutton by 1850 but opened no others in Lincolnshire until after 1900. Joint stock banks based in adjacent counties opened a few branches in border towns such as Stamford, Gainsborough and Grimsby but penetrated further only after 1890. Until then the recruiting of new customers among the middle classes was undertaken by Lincolnshire banks who spread to other towns and rebuilt their original premises. By 1889 the Lincoln and Lindsey Bank had fifteen branches and in 1895 even Peacock, Willson and Co., who for a century had restricted themselves to Sleaford, Newark and Bourne, established a branch in Lincoln. The Stamford, Spalding and Boston Bank opened branches in Peterborough, Leicester and Northampton but the only other Lincolnshire bank to venture out of the county was Peacock's. All the Lincolnshire banks were very vulnerable when agriculture went into depression at the close of the century. The long-established Boston bank of Gee, Wise and Gee suspended payments in 1874 following the collapse of a corn merchant who owed £76,000. They went into liquidation and were taken over by the Lincoln and Lindsey, who appointed Thomas Wise, one of the former partners, as their local manager.[31]

In 1889 Garfit, Claypon and Co. became a limited company and its directors were evidently the first to recognize the benefits of amalgamation with large firms outside the county. In 1891 they joined the Capital and Counties Bank, of which William Garfit VI (1840–1920) became a director and eventually, in 1915, chairman.[32]

Until the late 1880s Grimsby was poorly served by Lincolnshire banks; the Hull Banking Co. had almost a monopoly. Even as late as 1885 Smith, Ellison and Co. had only an agency in the town, served by a clerk who rode over from Caistor, but the displacement of smacks by expensive steam trawlers transformed the economy of the fishing industry. By 1889 Smith, Ellison and Co. had established two offices in Grimsby; by the time they opened another

[31] S. N. Davis, *Banking in Boston*, Boston, 1976, pp. 26, 33; Elvin, *Lincoln as it Was*, II, p. 15; P. W. Matthews and A. W. Tuke, *History of Barclays Bank Ltd*, London, 1926, p. 309.
[32] Davis, op. cit., p. 27.

sub-branch on the Fish Dock in 1892, other banks had been opened by the Stamford, Spalding and Boston, the Lincoln and Lindsey, and the York City and County. By 1913 another three banks had joined them in the town. Scunthorpe was similarly short of banks; in 1892 it was only visited by a clerk from Smith, Ellison's Brigg branch for two hours each Tuesday and Friday. Things improved in the twentieth century and by 1913 there were six banks in Scunthorpe High Street.[33]

In the 1890s, banks from other counties opened branches in competition with Smith, Ellison and Co. and Peacock, Willson and Co., who after 1895 were the only remaining private banks in the county. By 1914 they and the county's two joint stock banks had been swept into larger groupings now represented by Barclay's, Lloyd's, Midland and the National Westminster.[34]

SUTTON-ON-SEA

By the final quarter of the nineteenth century there were still a few gaps in the railway network of Lincolnshire but the increasing capital cost of railway branch lines and the reluctance of the major companies to promote them led to the development of rural steam tramways as a cheaper alternative. In response to the opening of the LECR (see p. 188), a steam tramway was built along public roads from Sutton-on-Sea to Alford and opened in 1884. Other rural tramways were authorized from Brigg to Lincoln and from Alford to Skegness, but neither of these lines was completed.[35]

In the early 1880s Trinity House suggested Sutton-on-Sea, then known as Sutton-le-Marsh, as a suitable site for a harbour of refuge on the east coast. In 1884 acts authorized a railway from the ELR at Willoughby to Sutton, where a North Sea Fisheries, Harbour and Dock Co. would establish a fish dock, commercial dock and storm refuge protected by massive breakwaters. The SWR was needed before the dock could be built, and to make the line feasible it was proposed to extend it beyond Sutton to the terminus of the existing line to Mablethorpe, so forming a coastal loop between Louth and Willoughby. After October 1886 the SWR took most of the goods traffic of the Alford and Sutton tramway, leading to its closure in December 1889, but the expensive parliamentary contest had bur-

[33] J. A. S. L. Leighton-Boyce, Smith's the Bankers 1658–1958, London, 1958, p. 290; White, Directory, 1892; Kelly's Directory, 1913.
[34] Leighton-Boyce, op. cit., p. 282; Davis, Banking in Boston, p. 30.
[35] Pearson, 'Railways in relation to Resort Development in East Lincolnshire', pp. 284, 286; P. White, Passenger Transport in Lincoln, London, 1974, p. 3.

dened the railway with considerable debts and its dock scheme did not materialize. The concept of docks at Sutton-on-Sea was taken up as part of the LDECR authorized in 1891. The line between Chesterfield and Lincoln was opened in 1897 but the eastern section was not built and the dream of docks at Sutton finally faded after the LDECR was purchased in 1907 by the GCR, who were building a new dock of their own at Immingham.[36]

RESORTS FOR THE MASSES

It was not until the late nineteenth century that the working classes could follow the nobility and gentry to the seaside and stimulate the development of resorts catering for great masses of trippers. Before the 1870s a few hundred people had visited the Lincolnshire coast each year, staying in cottages or at the few hotels at resorts such as Freiston Shore and Saltfleet. These were as nothing compared with the crowds who started arriving by train in the late 1870s.

The opening of the first Lincolnshire railways in 1848 had not made a great deal of difference to the resorts. The main changes, such as they were, occurred at Cleethorpes, which was only a couple of miles from Grimsby with its railway and the new dock. The Cliff Hotel was built in 1853 and in the ten years before 1856 over a hundred new houses were built there. By the latter date there were also omnibuses to Grimsby several times a day to catch the trains and Humber packet boats. A single-track railway was opened to Cleethorpes on 6 April 1863 and by 1871 the village had a population of 1,768, but the other resorts each had less than five hundred inhabitants at that date. As railways were opened to other resorts and widened to double track so those places grew considerably and overwhelmed the rural villages from which they sprang, though they never reached the same size or importance as Scarborough or Blackpool, whose growth had started earlier. These developments were directly related to the railways, for while Skegness and Cleethorpes became resorts for the industrial workers of the east midlands and south Yorkshire respectively, Freiston Shore and Saltfleet withered for lack of railway connections. Mablethorpe and Sutton-on-Sea also grew but railway access was not so convenient.[37]

The development of Skegness was effectively begun by Lord Scarbrough in the late 1870s, although excursionists had been arriving since the railway opened in 1873. By 1880 a pier 1,843 feet

---

[36] Pearson, op. cit., pp. 287–90; Leleux, *East Midlands Railways*, p. 207.
[37] White, *Directory*, 1856, p. 556; Pearson, op. cit., p. 281.

long (plate VIII), pleasure grounds and a cricket ground had been provided; swimming baths soon followed. A parish church, a network of streets, waterworks, drains and sites for Methodist chapels and a school were provided by Lord Scarbrough, who was also a leading shareholder in companies providing other amenities. The GNR publicized Skegness and benefited from the increasing traffic to the resort, carrying 230,277 excursionists there between April and September 1882, but did not directly develop any of its amenities. [38]

The MSLR not only publicized Cleethorpes and ran excursions but also spent over £100,000 on developing the resort. A pier 1,200 feet long and other improvements were made in the 1860s and 1870s, but the real development of amenities was undertaken by Edward Watkin of the MSLR in the 1880s. Work on the improvements started in 1883 and the following year the railway company also took over the pier: the improvements were officially opened by Prince Albert Victor, eldest son of the prince of Wales, in 1885. In later years the MSLR made other contributions to Cleethorpes and in 1909 enlarged the station. [39]

WOODHALL SPA

As the masses descended on the coast a more select resort was developed inland at Woodhall Spa. The Victoria Hotel had been built in 1838 with baths and a pump room but in 1881 the parish had only 281 inhabitants, a little fewer than in 1841. In the twenty-five years after 1886 more hotels and houses were built and the population increased fivefold to 1,484. In 1886 the Victoria Hotel and Spa with their hundred-acre estate were purchased by a syndicate and improvements carried out in 1887 under the direction of C. E. Davis, architect, of Bath. The new bath house overlooked the sixty acres of wooded Spa grounds, which contained a bandstand and a public recreation ground for tennis, croquet and other activities. The Victoria Hotel could then take about sixty people but by 1913 it had been enlarged to 140 rooms. In 1889 a Robey steam engine was installed to pump up the spa water and in 1890 Countess Brownlow

---

[38] R. Gurnham, 'The Creation of Skegness as a Resort Town by the ninth Earl of Scarbrough', *LHA*, 7 (1972), pp. 71, 73; Pearson, op. cit., p. 287; Ruddock and Pearson, p. 164; Leleux, *East Midlands Railways*, p. 205.
[39] P. J. Aspinall, 'Speculative Builders and the Development of Cleethorpes 1850–1900', *LHA*, 11 (1976), p. 43; Dow, *Great Central*, II, pp. 171, 172; White, *Directory*, 1892, p. 150; White and Tye, *Grimsby and Cleethorpes*, pp. 33, 34; *Kelly's Directory*, 1913, p. 144; Leleux, *East Midlands Railways*, p. 222.

officially opened the Alexandra Hospital, to which a new ward was added in 1894.[40]

By 1892 it was a rapidly rising watering place with five boarding houses and at least twenty other houses where apartments could be taken. A boys' preparatory school and ladies' day and boarding school had been established and Carlton and Sons of Horncastle had opened a photographic studio. The inhabitants now included many joiners, builders and builder's merchants, and a gas and water company had been formed. In 1894 a home for gentlewomen was opened and after 1892 four new churches were built, a larger parish church being followed by new premises for Catholics, Wesleyan Methodists and Presbyterians. By 1896 a rival to the Victoria had appeared in the Eagle Lodge Hotel and four years later the Royal Hydro Hotel had been built in a central situation next to the station and shops. The Royal had not only 120 rooms but its own spa and a winter gardens in which its hotel band played. By 1913 there were four hotels in the town, forty-one houses had apartments to offer and a new golf course had been laid out. From 1898 the GNR ran through carriages from King's Cross direct to Woodhall Spa and Horncastle, and this small spa enjoyed its heyday under Edwardian sunshine.[41]

EDWARDIAN DEVELOPMENTS IN NORTH LINCOLNSHIRE

In the 1900s the GCR spent over £150,000 on developments at the Royal and Alexandra docks in Grimsby, where Peter Dixon and Son established large paper mills in 1906. This was at the zenith of British world trade and in 1911 exports from Grimsby were valued at £20,112,477 and imports at £13,544,125. That year 1,654,112 tons of coal was exported from Grimsby, and a further 90,108 tons was shipped coastwise. Further dock space was needed; rather than expand at Grimsby, the GCR took a scheme for a dock at Immingham and obtained an act in 1904. Immingham was chosen because there the deepwater channel of the Humber swung close to the south bank and almost hit the shore. The entrance to Grimsby is rather shallow but Immingham was a deepwater port for large shipping which could never get near Grimsby. Work started in 1906 and Immingham Dock was officially opened by King George V in 1912. The 45-acre dock basin was the centre of a thousand-acre

---

[40] White, *Directory*, 1872, p. 341; 1892, p. 932; ;1896, p. 932; *Kelly's Directory*, 1913, p. 644; 1937, p. 632.
[41] White, *Directory*, 1892, p. 932; *Kelly's Directory*, 1896, p. 575; 1900, p. 607; 1913, p. 644; N. C. Birch, *Waterways and Railways of Lincoln and the Lower Witham*, Lincoln, 1968, p. 13.

estate and the total development cost £2,600,000. As well as the main basin and dock buildings such as offices, a power house, transit sheds, a huge granary and a passenger station, the scheme also included 170 miles of sidings and dock railways as well as three light railways and one electric railway. The railways ran to Grimsby, Goxhill (for Hull traffic) and Ulceby (for inland traffic).[42]

In the period 1910–14 the GCR also erected a massive new railway and road bridge across the Trent at Keadby to replace the original railway bridge, which was then inadequate for the increased traffic. On the east bank the new bridge included a Scherzer rolling lift span, which could be raised for the passage of Trent river traffic. Sir Sam Fay laid the foundation stone in 1912 and the two fixed bridge spans were completed in 1914; the Scherzer bridge and the deviation railway on each bank were opened in 1916 and the bridge was officially named after King George V. The original bridge had been for railway traffic only but its replacement also had a carriageway for road traffic; it significantly improved road access between north Lincolnshire and England north of the Trent just in time for the real growth of motor traffic.[43]

The powers of the Light Railways Act of 1896 were used not only for lines at Scunthorpe and Immingham but also for two lines which formed the AJR. One was the GMLR from Goole to Fockerby near the Trent and the other was the IALR which was to extend south from the GMLR to a terminus near the GNGEJR station at Haxey. The NER and the LYR both had lines at Goole and in 1902 they cooperated in purchasing these two light railways to form the AJR, which was opened to Haxey in 1905. In 1909 a goods branch was opened to Hatfield Moor with peat as its main traffic.[44]

By 1912 the railway system in Lincolnshire had reached its greatest extent. Each town had its own station and in the country there were few villages or farms that were more than five miles from a railway station. Railway traffic helped the farming community and the amount of coal traffic handled in station yards even in rural areas was quite large.

[42] Dow, *Great Central*, III, pp. 229, 233, 234–36, 239, 242, 259, 260, 263, 275–76; White and Tye, *Grimsby and Cleethorpes*, p. 27; *Kelly's Directory*, 1913, p. 246; R. V. Leafe, 'The Port of Immingham', *East Midland Geographer*, 27 (1967), p. 137; Leleux, *East Midlands Railways*, pp. 219, 220.
[43] Dow, *Great Central*, III, pp. 223, 251.
[44] Leleux, *East Midlands Railways*, pp. 225, 226.

CHAPTER 9

VICTORIAN INDUSTRY

RAILWAYS and ports allowed Lincolnshire to dispatch its products far more easily through Britain, Europe and the world. Railways served more towns and villages than the waterways had done, and their effects were therefore felt more widely. Conversely, they also exposed local craftsmen and traders to the chill wind of competition from outside. The height of Britain's industrial achievement had been demonstrated by the Great Exhibition of 1851 and, although in places there was a growing complacency and reluctance to innovate, in Lincolnshire industrial change was necessary to meet the opportunities and challenges offered by cheap and convenient railway transport. Many industries now tended to concentrate in larger buildings beside railway lines, just as earlier industry had often clustered around canals. Other concerns such as oilseed mills, large steam flour mills and fertilizer plants, which relied on bulk deliveries from abroad, remained faithful to water transport and sprang up at the ports or on the major waterways; but if their raw materials arrived by boat, their finished product departed by rail. Overall, however, the combination of protected imperial markets and an abundance of craft skills meant that there was little incentive to mechanize, and hard physical work remained the mainstay of production. The Lincolnshire brickyards offer a classic example which just survives to this day.

RAILWAY EMPLOYMENT

The opening of the the railways brought many changes to life and work and one of the most direct consequences was the creation of new jobs not only for station staff, drivers, firemen and guards but also in locomotive depots and engineering yards. Lincolnshire was the first part of the GNR to be operational and for a year or two most departments of the company were located in the county, including their traffic department at Louth and audit staff at Lincoln. Even more significant was their locomotive department, located at Boston until 1853. When this moved to Doncaster seven hundred jobs were lost at Boston but the town remained as the headquarters of the GNR lines in the county with a locomotive depot, civil engineer's yard, central sacking store, creosoting works established in 1874 and later a gas-making plant for carriage lighting. The company became Boston's largest employer and several new streets of houses were built alongside the railway. By 1912 the GNR employed nine hundred men in the town, more than half of them in the civil engineer's yard.[1]

The MSLR employed many men on Grimsby docks. They also had a locomotive works and shed at New Holland, which until 1888 was officially regarded as the eastern terminus of their line. In 1850 the company opened a three-acre dock and timber pond at New Holland, together with warehouses, cattle sheds and coal wharves. The *Hull Advertiser* thought that New Holland was 'likely to become an important railway colony, ranking with Crewe . . . Wolverton . . . and some others'. Forty-five houses for railway workers were built in Manchester Square, near the ferry; the population of the new community eventually reached 1,200 to 1,500, but it was only a modest version of Crewe or Wolverton. The company built a school there in 1847 and paid the teacher's salary; church services were held in the waiting room of the town station until a church was opened in 1851. The company had a new Yarborough Arms built by William Kirk of Lincoln, which was completed in April 1851. Almost all the works at New Holland were completed by the beginning of 1851, when there were eighty houses but few other facilities. Many railway companies converged on Lincoln and had small depots and goods yards, but none developed extensive premises there. Grantham was an important stage on the line from London to York with connections to Nottingham, Boston and Lincoln. Later depots were established at other junctions such as Spalding and Sleaford.[2]

CARRIERS AND COACH-MAKERS

Railways made travel much more widely and cheaply available, and their use was encouraged by the Great Exhibition when many people saved through clubs towards the expense of going up to the Crystal Palace. Many more local carriers' services were established

[1] *SM*, 3 November 1848, 23 August 1850; Grinling, *Great Northern*, pp. 104, 137; *Boston Red Book and Directory for 1913*, Boston, 1912, pp. 99, 100.
[2] P. White and A. Tye, *Guide Notes to New Holland and Barton-on-Humber*, Grimsby, 1967, pp. 78, 79; *Hull Advertiser*, 18 October 1850; A. A. D'Orley, *The Humber Ferries*, Knaresborough, 1968, pp. 46, 146–47.

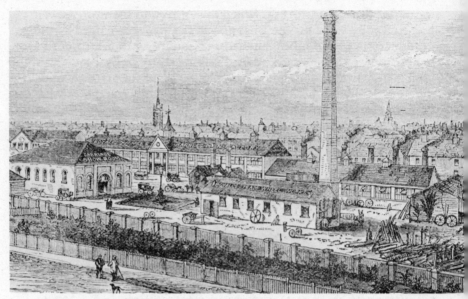

Figure 36   *A view in 1872 of R. J. Boyall's 'Brownlow Carriage and Harness Manufactory and Steam Wheel Works' opposite Grantham railway station in Spittlegate township*

after the arrival of the railways as feeders from villages without a station of their own. Between 1861 and 1891 the number of carters and carriers in Lincolnshire increased from 439 to 1,153 and in consequence of this, and the numbers of business and professional men moving to villas on the edges of towns, the number of coach-makers increased from 247 to 376. Coach-makers like Hayes and Son of Stamford and R. J. Boyall of Grantham (fig. 36) grew into quite large concerns. The Brownlow carriage works in Wharf Road next to Grantham station was started by Richard John Boyall about 1830 and continued until the 1880s. In 1867 the works were modernized for wheel-making by steam, which enabled them to produce wheels in great quantities for the carriage trade and artillery manufacturers. In the 1870s they made horse-drawn tram-cars, two of which still exist in museums. Hayes and Son of the Scotgate works in Stamford were also active coach- and wagon-makers before 1914, and in 1880 claimed that their average production was equal to about three hundred new vehicles a year.[3]

[3] R. J. Olney, *Rural Society and County Government in Nineteenth-Century Lincolnshire*, Lincoln, 1979, p. 171; N. C. Birch, 'The Brownlow Carriage Works, Grantham', *LIA*, 6 no. 4 (1971), p. 65; idem, *Stamford — An Industrial History*, Lincoln, 1972, p. 38.

BOAT BUILDING

Coastal shipping out of Boston and long journeys on the inland waterways were reduced after the opening of the railways but boats were still used for local traffic on the Humber and on the fens of south Lincolnshire. Boston's larger shipyards soon declined but the number of small boatyards increased until about 1880. After that the yards declined, though the Thompson and Keightley families continued into the twentieth century, as did a small yard behind Field Street on the bank of the Maud Foster drain in Boston. Between 1880 and 1900 Dring's yard in Spalding produced less than a dozen boats.[4]

In north Lincolnshire yards flourished as they produced boats for local traffic and smacks for the fishing fleets of Grimsby and Hull. Until about 1850 most boats on the Humber were built beside the waterways of south Yorkshire or at Burton Stather on the Trent. The first fishermen in Grimsby and Hull brought their boats with them, but as families settled they had their boats made at Wray's Burton Stather yard and at other local yards. In 1856 there were only four boat- and ship-builders in Grimsby but the number rose to sixteen in 1872 and twenty-three in 1892. Many were located at Lock Hill just outside the old dock but few grew into substantial firms. In the 1850s Robert Keetley's yard at Grimsby was exceptional in having a dry dock and employing over sixty men. J. Charlton built the first iron ship at Grimsby in 1863 and until 1890 his yard was the only one that could build steam trawlers. In 1890 some eight of the forty-two operating from the port were his, but then the Box and Fish Carrying Co. launched the *Assyrian* from a new yard at Lock Hill.[5]

Demand for boats was generated not only by the rise of the fishing industry but also by the development of Humber-side brickyards, which used the river for nearly all their traffic. By 1851 George Hill had a yard at Barton-on-Humber, employing four shipwrights and an apprentice, and five years later there were also small yards on the Trent at Torksey and Walkerith. In the 1880s and 1890s there were other boat-builders at four Trent-side sites on the Isle of Axholme and others on the Humber bank at New Holland and Winteringham. Many of the builders with premises beside the Trent were blacksmiths and similar craftsmen who could make boats when there was a demand. The change from smacks to trawlers led to the closure of Wray's yard in 1898 and by 1913 the

[4] N. R. Wright, *Spalding — An Industrial History*, Lincoln, 1973, p. 16.
[5] White and Tye, *Grimsby and Cleethorpes*, p. 26.

number of yards in Grimsby had fallen to eight ship-builders. The new boatyards on the Trent and the last yard at Louth also succumbed, but the Clapson family operated the Barton-on-Humber yard until recent times. Most of the yards were small, with just one small shed and a slip, and had more repair work than building, but Wray's Burton Stather yard and some others were larger. Smith and Sons of Gainsborough built *Sheffield* as a Humber ferry for the MSLR in 1849 and in 1864 another Gainsborough firm launched two iron screw steamers for trade between Hull and the Baltic. There were also small yards at Lincoln until 1914, building and repairing keels for the Fossdyke traffic.[6]

BRICK- AND TILE-MAKING

Between 1861 and 1891 there was an increase in the number of people employed in the building trades in Lincolnshire, but railways allowed brick-making to become concentrated in a few places with regional or national markets and the number of brick-makers in Lincolnshire declined.[7] In 1914 most large towns in the county still had one or two local brick-works and on the Humber bank it became a substantial industry, but the building needs of many places were met by London bricks and Welsh slate. The railways also gave brick firms access to stone areas which lacked a suitable clay for local brick-making.

The construction of railways used great numbers of bricks in stations, bridges and other structures and in 1848 the GNR had a brick works at Deeping St James where their line was to cross the river Welland. About the same time the Adamantine Clinker brick works was established at Little Bytham next to the GNR towns line and this yard sold large quantities of fire bricks to the railway company as well as producing clinker bricks remarkable for their strength, hardness and imperviousness to water. In towns with suitable clay it was possible to establish brick works almost anywhere. For the new dock works at Grimsby in 1848–52 large quantities of bricks were made from the Humber silt and in 1870–72 bricks for the new Boston gas works were made by Samuel Sherwin in an adjacent field. But the Lincoln works were along the line of the escarpment on the western edge of the city at Cross O'Cliff Hill, Newland Street West and Long Leys Road, where rows of brick-makers' cottages still remain. A brick works near

[6] Barton-on-Humber Local History Class, *Barton-on-Humber in the 1850s. Part Two. The Town and the People*, Barton-on-Humber, 1978, p. 31; White, *Directory*, 1856; *Kelly's Directory*, 1913, p. 205.

[7] Olney, *Rural Society and County Government*, p. 172.

Stamp End which received its clay by boat from pits east of the city had closed before 1872. In 1889 four brick works in or near Lincoln were united as the Lincoln Brick Works Co. and a few years later they also acquired the Albion brick works of Long Leys Road. In the years after 1850 new brickyards were opened to meet demand but eventually most local yards succumbed to competition from firms outside the county.[8]

During the second half of the nineteenth century the brickyards on the banks of the Humber and adjacent waterways in north Lincolnshire expanded and, particularly after 1860, new ones were established. In the parish of Barton there were five brickyards employing 102 people in 1861 and by 1900, when the industry was at its peak, there were fifteen forming an almost continuous strip along the Humber bank. The clay was of a high quality well suited for tile manufacture. The brick works occupied fields whose boundaries had been laid down in the enclosure award and there was very little consolidation. In 1876 there were also eight brick-yards beside the Ancholme close to its junction with the Humber, but Ferriby sluice was too small for Thames spritsail barges and by 1896 these yards had declined to three. In 1896 there were another ten yards in Barrow-upon-Humber and New Holland and another nine scattered along the north Lincolnshire coast from Burton Stather round to Killingholme. Apparently all these coastal brick works were larger than their inland counterparts though not large by national standards of the time.[9]

Large numbers of bricks were sent to Hull and Grimsby but the main markets for pantiles and high-quality facing bricks were London and the expanding industrial towns of west Yorkshire. The brick works produced a wide range of wares and the expansion of the industry reflected the great growth of commuter suburbs around London and the architectural trends stemming from the arts and crafts movement. The industry was then becoming partly mechanized, engineers in Barton and Louth producing machines which are still used for moulding bricks, tiles and other products in the remaining works.[10]

[8] SM, 7 April 1848, 21 April 1848; E. Dobson, A Rudimentary Treatise on the manufacture of bricks and tiles (1850), reprinted as Journal of Ceramic History, 5 (1971), p. 91; White, Directory, 1872, p. 141; C. Bremner-Smith and C. Page, 'Lincoln — Public Undertakings and Some Industries', Industrial Archaeology Newsletter, 2 no. 3 (1967), p. 7.
[9] S. A. Holm, Brick and Tile Making in South Humberside, Scunthorpe, 1976, pp. 3, 4; Barton-on-Humber in the 1850s. Part Two, p. 51.
[10] Holm, op. cit., p. 4.

The success of the industry was based on water transport, each yard having its buildings close to a wharf on the river bank and digging clay on the inland side. The Barton to New Holland railway line ran past several works but the bulk of the products were carried in Humber sloops and keels to local and inland destinations and in Thames barges to East Anglia and the metropolis. The railways also enabled the Sleaford firm of Kirk and Parry to emerge as public works contractors, predecessors of the many building firms which arose in the closing years of the century. Charles Kirk and Thomas Parry not only erected most prominent mid-Victorian buildings in Sleaford but also undertook contracts with the GNR in Leeds, London and other places as well as in Lincolnshire. They built all the stations on the towns line between Peterborough and Retford in 1848–52 and undertook contracts for the lines between Lincoln and Honington (1864–66) and between Spalding and Ruskington (1880–82). Around Sleaford they had their own brick works, lime kilns and stone quarries as well as a steam flour mill and other enterprises.[11]

POTTERY AND TERRACOTTA

Many brick works had a wide range of products, and between 1841 and 1871 at least there was a pottery in Barton producing coarse earthenware such as sanitary pipes and flower pots. Apart from this firm, Victorian Lincolnshire had no potters on a commercial scale, but for a period Stamford was the home of a firm of national significance. Since 1851 John Marriott Blashfield had been manufacturing terracotta at Millwall, London, using moulds and models from the former Coade factory, and in 1858 he moved his business to Stamford where a suitable clay existed for his purpose. The Stamford terracotta works took over the site of Grant's iron foundry, whose entrance arch still remains, and stayed there until the company failed in 1875. During his years at Stamford, Blashfield did much to develop inlaid encaustic paving tiles, one of the main types of pottery revived in the nineteenth century, but his range of glazed or enamelled architectural enrichments also included statues, vases, medallions, friezes, tracery and window and door heads. His products were particularly suitable for buildings of the Gothic revival, and his greatest success was Dulwich College. His products also embellished Buckingham Palace, Marlborough House and the Royal Mausoleum at Frogmore as well as local

---

[11] Ibid., p. 4; J. Wrottesley, *The Great Northern Railway*, I, London, 1979, pp. 77, 79; II, pp. 75, 94, 95, 136; White, *Directory*, 1856, pp. 439–43.

houses such as Stoke Rochford, where there is a fine Diana after the Borghese original, and a triumphal arch in Bombay, India. [12]

Various Lincolnshire manufacturers also produced pottery containers, partly filled with charcoal or similar material, for filtering impurities out of drinking water. The most successful Lincolnshire manufacturer was George Cheavin, who patented an improvement to his father's design in 1862 when only fifteen years of age. After occupying various premises in Boston, he purchased a site at Bargate End in 1874 and stayed there until 1889, when he moved to London and amalgamated with the Fulham pottery. [13]

CHALK AND LIMESTONE

In north-east Lincolnshire, particularly at Barton-on-Humber and South Ferriby where the Wolds extend close to the Humber bank, chalk was quarried throughout the nineteenth and early twentieth centuries for bank works such as the extension of Alexandra Dock in Hull. In 1856 it was said that about 35,000 tons of chalkstone was sent annually from Barton cliff. Until 1914 at least there were three manufacturers in Barton producing whiting for domestic cleaning from the chalk of the Humber cliffs and from about 1890 there were also manufacturers in Alford, Louth and Barnetby. In many Lincolnshire parishes there were lime kilns during the nineteenth century, and as well as lime for agricultural purposes some also produced building lime, as at Louth where there were nine in 1842. Ancaster stone had been quarried as a building material since the Middle Ages; quarries at Haydor and Wilsford continued until 1939, 1940 and later. In south Kesteven, Woolstone's quarry at Stamford continued until 1915–16 and a quarry for Clipsham stone was opened at Holywell in 1903 by G. A. Medwell and Sons. In the Isle of Axholme, gypsum was still extracted for plaster flooring, as it had been since the sixteenth century; in 1872 James Ryder of Burnham near Haxey called himself a farmer and a gypsum floor manufacturer. The manufacture of artificial cement was developed during the nineteenth century and cement works were established close to natural sources of chalk or limestone and mud or clay. The Tunnel cement works at Kirton-in-Lindsey evidently began as lime

[12] White, *Directory*, 1842, p. 587; 1856, p. 693; Barton-on-Humber Local History Class, *Barton-on-Humber in the 1850s. Part Three. Parish and Government*, Barton-on-Humber, 1979, p. 52; D. L. Franks, 'Llewellyn Jewitt's View of the Stamford Brick and Terra-Cotta Works with Comments', *LIA*, 7 no. 4 (1972) p. 49; Rogers, ed., *Stamford*, p. 88.

[13] N. R. Wright, 'Cheavin's Filters', *LIA*, 6 no. 1 (1971), p. 9.

kilns beside the railway, run in 1882 by H. Parry, but by 1885 they were cement works and remained so until closed in the 1970s. The Barton cement works was under construction in 1889 and apparently opened in 1890 as Skelsey's Adamant Cement Co. Ltd with chamber kilns; it was purchased in 1912 by G. and T. Earle Ltd of Hull, who installed a rotary kiln. It had its own clay pits and chalk quarry. [14]

MILLS

The few water-driven textile mills and paper mills in Lincolnshire in the early nineteenth century had almost all ceased production by 1845. The only remaining paper mill was at Houghton; it had been taken over in 1838 by Richard Hornsby and Sons, who installed the first Fourdrinier machine in Lincolnshire. They disposed of the mill after 1872 but it continued until 1890. Paper-making returned to Lincolnshire thirteen years later when the great West Marsh paper mills were built at Grimsby.

During the middle years of Queen Victoria's reign windmill technology reached its peak and in the ten largest towns of Lincolnshire there were at least eighty-four corn millers. But urban steam roller mills were rising to a dominant position in the flour industry and between 1861 and 1891 the numbers employed in milling in Lincolnshire fell from 1,503 to 1,001; by 1913 the number of corn millers in the ten main towns had been halved. The Sibsey Trader mill erected near Boston by Saunderson's of Louth in 1877 was one of the last tower mills to be built in the county. Steam had been used in mills since the start of the century and several steam mills were built around Lincoln's Brayford, but only in the closing decades of the century did rollers start to replace the old grinding stones. Some steam mills replaced windmills on the same site and Le Tall's Crown mill at Lincoln retained the original tower to support a water tank. [15]

In 1913 there were 280 millers listed in Lincolnshire; only thirty-two of them depended on steam alone, but half of those steam mills were located in towns while most other mills were in villages or the countryside. Flour mills driven by steam were by

[14] White, *Directory*, 1856, pp. 632, 690; 1872, pp. 457, 459, 518; E. M. Hewitt, 'Mines and Quarries', in VCH, *Lincs.*, p. 393; K. Hudson, *Industrial Archaeology — An Introduction*, London, 1963, p. 139; *SM*, 23 August 1889, 1 November 1899; D. Purcell, *Cambridge Stone*, London, 1967, pp. 45, 54–56, 66–68.
[15] Olney, *Rural Society and County Government*, p. 171.

then fairly common in most of the large towns and had superseded windmills, which were disappearing fast and not being replaced.[16]

SEED CRUSHING

The importing of seeds from Europe and the Middle East tended to concentrate the seed crushing industry in eastern England. Hull was the main centre of the industry and by 1845 there were oil mills in several north Lincolnshire towns and ports. Between 1841 and 1856 the tonnage of imported seeds for oil manufacture tripled and more mills opened in Grimsby, Louth and Boston. In the 1860s William and Edward Pearson moved to Gainsborough and took the Ashcroft mill as well as building the Baltic mill and equipping it with machinery from the former Trent Port mill. Larger seed presses were developed in the United States and in 1874 Pearson Brothers of Gainsborough placed an order with a Hull firm for the first Anglo-American mill to be installed in Britain. Their example was followed by other firms including Simonds and Son of Boston. In 1899 Pearson Brothers became part of British Oil and Cake Mills Limited.[17]

J. C. Simonds had built the Britannia oil mill on Packhouse quay, Boston in the late 1850s and moved to the Skirbeck oil mills in 1870, his old premises then being taken by Frederick Frank and Sons. The agricultural depression affected the market for cattle cake, the industry's by-product, and several Lincolnshire oil mills closed after 1880 including Simonds and Son in 1905.

SOAP AND CANDLES

Until late in the nineteenth century there were probably large grocers in many towns and villages who made their own soap and candles. Firms in Louth and Spilsby were soap-boilers on a large scale throughout the second half of the century, the Spilsby works being taken over by Smith and Sons of Louth by 1872. Soap-boilers were occasionally listed at other towns in the years before 1914, and until the 1920s there was also a large candle factory in Barton-on-Humber.[18]

---

[16] *Kelly's Directory*, 1913, pp. 853–55; E. M. Sympson, *Cambridge County Geographies — Lincolnshire*, Cambridge, 1913, p. 77.
[17] H. W. Brace, *History of Seed Crushing in Great Britain*, London, 1960, pp. 48, 53, 54, 60.
[18] White, *Directory*, 1872, pp. 177–78; J. B. Ball, 'Barton Candle Factory', *Lincolnshire Life*, 17 no. 3 (1977), p. 49.

P

FERTILIZERS

Apart from gas works and the few soap-boilers the only significant chemical industry in Lincolnshire was the manufacture of artificial fertilizer. Investigations by chemists in the early nineteenth century had led to the addition of lime to soil and the extended use of natural manures such as Peruvian guano. Following publication of Professor Liebig's paper in 1840, agriculturists also began to use chemical fertilizers to supply other elements that might become depleted in soils. During the second half of the century many chemical manure works were established, including some in Lincolnshire, to treat calcium phosphate with sulphuric acid (vitriol) to produce the more soluble calcium superphosphate. At first the only available phosphate materials were bones, bone ash, spent animal charcoal and poorer grades of guano, and the manufacture of superphosphate did not call for elaborate plant or machinery. While bones were the main raw material, crushing was easy and only when very hard phosphatic rocks were used was it necessary to introduce powerful means of pulverizing the materials, which produced a fine powder and so led to mechanical handling.[19]

All that a chemical manure works needed in the early days was a tank for sulphuric acid, a shed in which to store raw phosphate, another for finished superphosphate, crushing plant and a 'den' for mixing. Many also had plant for producing their own vitriol. They polluted the atmosphere with corrosive vapours and also gave off highly offensive smells. Some works also handled other chemicals such as sulphate of ammonia. At one time there were three separate chemical manure works along the banks of the Fossdyke between Lincoln and Saxilby. By 1856 John Jekyll (1825–1911) and William Gresham had formed a chemical manure business in Carholme Road, Lincoln on a site now occupied by Fisons. Gresham died before 1867 and Jekyll had a succession of partners. In 1897 they produced feeding cake, calf meal and sheep dip as well as vitriol and chemical manure. Before 1864 J. G. Doughty and Sons, who were oil millers in Lincoln, had established a chemical manure works at Burton Lane End on the edge of the city and in 1920 their firm took over Jekyll's Carholme chemical works.[20]

A manure works on the site of the present Lindsey and Kesteven Fertilizers Ltd beside the Fossdyke at Skellingthorpe near Saxilby was first established in the 1860s. In early 1863 the GNR put in a

[19] W. A. Campbell, *The Chemical Industry*, London, 1971, pp. 75, 76, 79.
[20] Ibid., pp. 76, 77, 79; 'Industrial Archaeology Notes, 1976', ed. C. Wilson, in *LHA*, 12 (1977), p. 63; White, *Directory*, 1856, p. 123; *Lincolnshire Chronicle*, 28 July 1911; Hill, *Victorian Lincoln*, p. 118.

siding at Skellingthorpe to serve the manure works set up by George Foottit, who paid £700 towards the cost. A station was opened on 1 January 1865 but closed on 1 June 1868 as Foottit's works closed. The siding, however, remained in use and in 1872 Edward Toynbee of Lincoln was apparently operating the plant. The following year Toynbee and Larkin proposed the formation of the Lindsey and Kesteven Chemical Manure Co., which has operated the premises since 1874. By 1882 at least twenty-five manure manufacturers were listed in the county directory for Lincolnshire, but only Jekyll's and Lindsey and Kesteven were described as sulphuric acid manufacturers, which suggests that the others were smaller concerns. In 1892 the Farmers' Company of the Yarborough oil mills at Brigg were also makers of sulphuric acid. The Farmers' Company had been formed in 1874 to manufacture manure, as successor to a firm launched in 1872.[21]

LEATHER INDUSTRIES

While new industries like the manufacture of chemical manure were appearing old crafts like tanning were in decline. In Horncastle there was only one tan-yard listed in 1856, but later the town's leather industry enjoyed something of a revival through the wholesale manufacture of boots and shoes. There were many traditional boot and shoe makers in Lincolnshire, as elsewhere, but they were slowly being displaced as large manufacturers from Leicester and Leeds opened branch shops selling mass-produced shoes. Few Lincolnshire boot and shoe makers produced them on a factory scale, yet in 1872 there were two such firms in Horncastle.

James Dundas Shera and his partner Thomas Daniel Briggs had the Horncastle tan-yard and were wholesale boot and shoe makers at the Oak Works, 15 St Lawrence Street, Horncastle. At the same time William Chapman and Charles Hall had another large boot and shoe factory at 10 St Lawrence Street. By 1882 Chapman and Hall had been taken over by John Panton, and Shera had been joined by his son, but both firms closed within ten years. When Shera's finished about 1886 they were said to employ hundreds of hands. In 1882 twelve boot and shoe manufacturers were listed in Lincolnshire, but already eight from Leicester and elsewhere had established shops in the county; Freeman, Hardy and Willis had two branches in Lincoln and one in Gainsborough. When lawn tennis

[21] Wrottesley, *Great Northern Railway*, II, p. 167; *Post Office Directory of Lincolnshire*, London, 4th edn 1868, p. 261; White, *Directory*, 1872, p. 381; Hill, *Victorian Lincoln*, p. 119; White, *Directory*, 1892, advertisement 35; *LAOR* 25, p. 47.

became a popular sport Horncastle was for a while a substantial producer of rackets, but this industry evidently ceased before the turn of the century.[22]

CANNON'S GLUE FACTORY

Much of Lincoln's early industry was next to the lower Witham east of High Bridge, but in the second half of the nineteenth century it started to extend along both sides of the upper Witham south from Brayford. One of the first premises here was established by Bernard Cannon, who moved from Dublin to Lincoln in 1863 and established a business in Gaunt Street as a leather dresser and glue manufacturer. In 1874 he leased a site west of the river from Colonel Ellison and put a bridge across. Later Rustons, Fosters and other firms also established industrial premises here. Cannon's glue works was completely destroyed by fire on 5 November 1908 but was rebuilt on the same site, where they stayed until moving to Abingdon in 1959. Another leather and glue works was established in Grantham by John Shaw before 1872 and by 1913 the Forbes Fish Glue Co. Ltd had been established in Grimsby.[23]

MALTING, BREWING AND MINERAL WATER MANUFACTURE

In the middle of the nineteenth century most Lincolnshire towns had maltings to meet the needs of local brewers but Grantham, Stamford, Horncastle and Louth each had over a dozen maltsters and served the needs of more distant places. After the arrival of railways the number of maltings gradually declined and the industry became concentrated in larger buildings often located beside the line near village stations. Those at Barnetby-le-Wold were built in 1875 beside the MSLR main line by the Truswell Brewery Co. of Sheffield and during the 1890s Pidcock and Co. erected others at Ancaster beside the GNR's Boston and Grantham line. The grandest maltings in Lincolnshire were built at Sleaford by Bass, Ratcliff and Gretton Ltd of Burton-upon-Trent between 1899 and 1905 (plate XI). They consist of nine separate buildings, four on each side of a central workshop block and engine house, which provided power for the whole site. The total frontage is nearly a thousand feet long and they are perhaps the largest complex of their kind outside Burton. The number of maltsters in Louth and

---

[22] White, *Directory*, 1872, pp. 357, 358; M. Blakiston, 'Horncastle', *Lincs. Mag.*, 2 (1934–36), p. 179; Sympson, *Lincolnshire*, p. 83.
[23] I. S. Beckwith, 'Brayford East (Lincoln) Survey, Part I', *Industrial Archaeology Newsletter*, 3 no. 2 (1968), p. 8; Hill, *Victorian Lincoln*, p. 119; Lincolnshire Library 'Industry II', p. 89.

Horncastle had declined by 1872 and Stamford followed, but Grantham retained an important malting industry with many kilns in the town and its vicinity. In 1913 there were still maltings in all the Lincolnshire boroughs and some other towns such as Bourne, Gainsborough and Horncastle.[24]

After 1845 the number of small breweries continued to decline. In 1856 over fifty were listed in the ten main towns of the county but by 1913 the number had been halved. Many were taken over by brewers from other Lincolnshire towns or from outside the county in order to extend their markets. Large breweries in the county were Dawber and Co. of Lincoln and Mowbray's Grantham brewery, founded in 1826 and 1828 respectively. By the time of Robert Dawber's death in 1904 the firm had sixty public houses, mainly in the city itself, and he left a considerable fortune to found the Dawber charity.[25]

During the second half of the century there was a steady growth of mineral water manufacturers producing refreshing non-alcoholic drinks, partly in response to the temperance movement. By 1913 forty-six manufacturers were listed, including Bellamy Brothers of Grimsby, J. H. Thomas and Sons of Boston and at least five breweries. In 1864 Robert Mason Mills (d. 1904) established a mineral water business in Bourne and in 1878 was joined by T. M. Baxter. They drew their water from a bore in North Street, sunk in 1861, and sold their Bourne waters throughout the world. By 1913 they were making about a dozen different aerated beverages and were one of the town's largest employers.[26]

LIGHT INDUSTRIES

The main occupation for most women in the nineteenth century was domestic work, a few years as a poorly paid servant usually being followed by marriage and unpaid labour in her own home. In the countryside there was work in the fields for women as well as men, but in the towns there were few jobs for women in the main industries. However as the nineteenth century progressed the scope for female employment in Lincolnshire was widened as new light industries developed.

[24] N. C. Birch, 'Barnetby Maltings', *LIA*, 5 no. 1 (1970), p. 24.
[25] M. Pointer and M. G. Knapp, *Bygone Grantham*, III, Grantham, 1978, p. 37; L. Elvin, *Lincoln as it Was*, I, Nelson, 1974, p. 24; idem., *Lincoln as it Was*, II, Nelson, 1976, p. 12.
[26] *Kelly's Directory*, 1913, pp. 100, 856; J. D. Birkbeck, *A History of Bourne*, Bourne, 2nd edn 1976, p. 87.

One industry established in the first half of the century had been the production of pipe tobacco, but soldiers returning from the Crimean War brought a taste for Turkish cigarettes and, with the introduction of mild Virginia tobacco, cigarettes started to be mass-produced and to displace the pipe. Some of the small Lincolnshire tobacco factories closed, as did most of the humble clay pipe-makers in the county, but a few factories survived by changing to the manufacture of cigars, which continued to be hand-made for a few decades more. Thorns, Son and Co. of Boston was founded by J. F. Smyth in the 1850s and continued until 1928. Between 1890 and 1914 several other cigar factories were established in the ports of Boston and Grimsby, like Peet and Co., which was founded about 1898 and made cigars in Grimsby until 1933. In cigar factories, jam factories and the increasing number of similar premises the bulk of the work force was female, with just a few men to manage, supervise and do heavy tasks such as lifting and carrying.[27]

One minor consequence of the increase in railway travelling was the growth of the market for luggage labels, and in 1855 John Fisher, who had invented an untearable cloth label, established a small factory behind his house in West Street Road, Boston. By 1857 he was employing twenty-two people and as the firm grew it moved to premises in Corn Exchange Yard and Grove Street before finally settling in Norfolk Street in 1903. In 1876 the business was sold to George Clark, whose father had been its first manager, and Fisher, Clark and Co. was managed by this family for the better part of a century.[28]

Many women had taken in washing to supplement their family's income, but the growing demand for this service led to the establishment of steam laundries by limited companies, who gradually displaced the former laundresses. The Grantham Steam Laundry in Belton Lane was built in 1878 by a company with a capital of £8,000 and in 1913 it employed forty to fifty hands. The Boston Steam Laundry Co. formed in 1884 had a capital of only £2,000 and adapted a former cigar factory in Bond Street but the Grimsby Abbey Park Steam Laundry Co. of 1896 had £5,000 and later a second company was formed in that town. At New Holland the MSLR had their own steam laundry, which employed much of the

[27] N. R. Wright, 'Tobacco Manufacturing in Lincolnshire', *Ind. Arch.*, 7 no. 1 (1970), p. 1.
[28] H. Porter, *Boston 1800 to 1835 continued to 1868*, Lincoln, 1943, p. 170; J. Anderson, '130 Years of Label Making', *Lincolnshire Life*, 20 no. 7 (1980), pp. 28–31.

female labour in the village. By 1913 there were perhaps twenty steam laundries in the county and each main town had at least two.[29]

Since about 1830 the Anderson family had been feather merchants and purifiers in Boston and in the final quarter of the century this industry grew considerably in scale. In 1877 Mrs F. S. Anderson erected the factory which still stands in Trinity Street, with an extravagant façade surmounted by a large swan. Within fifteen years there were nine feather bed manufacturers in Lincolnshire, of whom five were located in Boston. By 1903 F. S. Anderson and Co. had moved to the Victoria feather mills in Wide Bargate and their Trinity Street premises were taken by Edward Fogarty and Co., who still use them as a store. The feathers were supplied in enormous sacks by the farmers and poultry dealers and were sorted by cyclone machinery. The fine feathers were then purified by steam in special ovens and the considerable quantities of waste material were sold as manure to fruit growers. The heat was intense in the rooms over the ovens and workers spent only about ten minutes in them at a time, emptying the feathers into the purifiers at intervals of twenty minutes. The industry was centred in Boston but in 1880 Tolly McCann established the Feather Factory of the Fens at Vine Street, Billingborough and soon had over fifty workers. This is now a subsidiary of Fogarty's, the only firm left in the mattress business.[30]

In the late nineteenth century organs were installed in many churches and new firms of organ builders were established. J. R. Cousans formed one such in Lincoln in 1877; in Edwardian times there was another in Lincoln and also one in Boston.[31]

The availability of cheap newspapers for the mass of the population allowed products to be advertised extensively. Producers could now reach mass markets, and as well as packaging branded goods such as tea, coffee, cocoa and chocolate, factories also started to produce jams, ketchup and sauces for urban dwellers. About 1879 T. G. Tickler started making jam in Grimsby; in 1902 the firm acquired a 24-acre site at Laceby to grow its own fruit. By 1892 the Economic Supply Co. of Wragby Street, Grimsby was also making jam in addition to sauces and other products. These jam makers

[29] *Kelly's Directory*, 1913, p. 227; Wright, 'Tobacco Manufacturing in Lincolnshire', p. 9; *Boston Red Book and Directory for 1913*, p. 67; White and Tye, *Grimsby and Cleethorpes*, p. 25.
[30] W. O. Massingberd, 'Industries', in VCH, *Lincs.*, p. 388; R. Hunt, 'Portrait of a Village — Billingborough', *Lincolnshire Life*, 13 no. 3 (1973), p. 43.
[31] Elvin, *Lincoln as it Was*, III, Nelson, 1979, p. 29.

were located in the main centre of population in the county, but other producers of sauces and ketchup were near to the specialized farming area of the fens. By 1872 George Butcher and Co. were making ketchup at Clay Lake, Spalding; twenty years later Charles Lambert was making ketchup in Alford and Joseph Farrow and Co. had established the Carlton works in a large warehouse at Boston. Later there were three separate firms in Brigg, including Spring and Co., who made lemon curd.[32]

Another significant change in Victorian retailing was the development of machines to wrap food and other products before sending them to the shops, with the advantages of economy, convenience and hygiene. The first commodity in England to be mechanically wrapped in packets for sale was tobacco, and the machine that did this was invented by William Rose (c. 1865–1929), a Gainsborough barber, who as a youth had been a rivetter's assistant in a Gainsborough shipyard. As a barber he sold tobacco to his customers and over a period of seven years he designed a satisfactory machine to pack tobacco cylindrically. He patented it in 1885 in the joint names of himself and Henry Wills of Bristol, a tobacco manufacturer who had encouraged his experiments. Rose then began to make his machines in the back room of his barber's shop, and a major development came when Richard Harvey Wright agreed to promote Rose's machines in the United States, modified to produce rectangular packets. As American orders flooded in, Rose's employees increased to fifty and he built a new factory on waste land beside the Trent. By 1895 he had sold machines to the value of over £36,000 and his brother Henry, a working blacksmith, came into the business. In 1906 the firm became Rose Brothers (Gainsborough) Ltd with assets valued at £50,000, but William continued to direct the firm until after the First World War. Tobacco was one of the most difficult substances to wrap, and once his machine had established the basic principles of automatic wrapping they could be applied to other products. He devised machinery for wrapping small chocolate tablets, black lead and a bleaching agent known as blue. Part of his works was set aside for making cardboard cartons for starch produced for Reckitt and Sons of Hull.[33]

About 1902 a Boston firm started to produce packets and sacks of peas for grocers, following a Canadian example, and within two years it was one of the main employers in the town. Some of the

[32] D. Boswell and J. M. Storey, *Grimsby as it Was*, Nelson, 1974, p. 46.
[33] A. Muir, *The History of Baker Perkins*, Cambridge, 1968, pp. 101–4.

work of sorting was done in factories by girls and women described by the Revd W. O. Massingberd in the *Victoria County History* as being of the 'rougher class', and sacks of peas were also supplied to home workers. In 1913 Wilfred B. Beaulah also started canning food at Norfolk Street, Boston.[34]

By the middle of the century Charles Sharpe of Sleaford and W. W. Johnson of Boston had founded seed firms which were to become internationally known, and about the turn of the century they erected large warehouses at Sleaford and Boston stations. In 1868 Charles Sharpe had led a national movement to improve standards in the trade and was largely responsible for the Adulteration of Seeds Bill which W. E. Welby introduced in 1869. In the closing years of the century growers in south Holland started to produce daffodils and narcissus for the cut-flower market, introducing the Darwin tulip in 1905; later the growing of the bulbs became the principal aspect of the industry.[35]

After 1900 some local authorities began to consider the active encouragement of industry in their towns. In 1905 Bourne urban district council set up a committee to consider attracting 'some manufacturing or engineering works, similar to those introduced into neighbouring towns' and by the end of 1908 they had drawn up a list of suitable sites for factories, but no further steps were taken until after the war. There was a similar story in Grantham, where the town council appointed a sub-committee in 1908 to attract new lighter industry to the town.[36]

SHOPPING

As the railways made mass-produced goods readily and cheaply available, so many shops in towns became retail outlets and ceased to make their goods in workshops at the back. Shops increased in number and size; department stores were founded by such men as John Oldrid (1805–79) of Boston and George Bainbridge (1812–78) of Lincoln. New premises like Small's (fig. 37) were erected with windows filling the whole front of the ground floor. As the number of shops increased they spread outward into adjacent streets and houses were converted or demolished. There was an increase in the number of assistants employed in shops, and from the 1840s there

[34] Massingberd, 'Industries', p. 388.
[35] R. J. Olney, *Lincolnshire Politics 1832–1885*, London, 1973, p. 197; White, *Directory*, 1856, p. 441; 'Johnsons', *Lincolnshire Life*, 20 no. 4 (1980), p. 26; Wright, *Spalding — An Industrial History*, p. 26.
[36] Honeybone, *Grantham*, p. 115; Birkbeck, *History of Bourne*, p. xiv.

was pressure to close earlier and give them some time for self-improvement. In 1841 Boston drapers agreed to close at 8 p.m. during the winter months and the grocers followed in 1844. In 1862 the first step towards half-day closing in Boston was taken when shops agreed to close at 6 p.m. on Thursdays. Mawer and Collingham introduced half-day closing in Lincoln in April 1871. Boots Cash Chemists of Nottingham developed a chain of shops, opening a branch in Lincoln in 1884; firms of shoemakers and grocers followed suit. Increases in the demand for postal services led the Post Office to erect buildings of their own in Boston (1885, replaced 1907), Lincoln (1906) and other towns.[37]

The gathering together of large numbers of working men in towns led to the growth of co-operative movements. Their first manifestation in Lincolnshire was in the provision of flour mills. The example of a co-operative corn mill in Hull led artisans and labourers in Lincoln to establish a similar society in that city in 1847 and their steam mill started to produce flour in 1848. Similar mills followed in Louth, Grantham and Stamford but were of limited success. The Lincoln one was wound up in 1857. More successful were the co-operative retail societies. One was started in Lincoln in 1861 and moved to a new large Gothic building on the corner of Silver Street and Free School Lane in 1873. Branches were opened at Bracebridge and other parts of the city, six by 1890, and its activities included a building department, which in 1903 won the contract to erect the present Post Office in Guildhall Street.[38]

In the 1870s co-operative societies were established in several small towns by the new agricultural workers unions: in 1878 the registrar of friendly societies listed fifteen in the county, including the Scunthorpe society formed in 1874. Small rural societies managed by farm labourers with no relevant experience did not last long, and societies opened at Boston, Spalding and Stamford in the 1870s also closed within the decade, but from 1878 the Lincoln society adopted a policy of opening rural branches and in 1887 reached Horncastle and Sleaford. By 1900 the Lincoln society had ten branches outside the city. Successful societies had been formed in most towns by 1905 and each devoted part of their profits to educational purposes. The Lincoln society had a reading room and library which was opened on 30 September 1876 by Dr E. W.

[37] Porter, *Boston 1800 to 1835 continued to 1868*, p. 163; Elvin, *Lincoln as it Was*, III, p. 36; White, *Directory*, 1892, p. 179; Elvin, *Lincoln as it Was*, I, p. 24.
[38] F. Bruckshaw and D. McNab, *A Century of Achievement: The Story of Lincoln Co-operative Society*, Manchester, 1961, pp. 13, 14, 17, 18, 23, 36, 46; *SM*, 5 February 1847, 19 April 1847, 9 June 1848, 7 July 1848, 26 April 1850.

Figure 37   *The tall façade of J. H. Small and Son's draper's shop
in Boston market-place in 1896, with the large windows and grand
architectural style adopted by some successful late Victorian
shop-keepers*

Benson, chancellor of the cathedral and later archbishop of Canterbury.[39]

BICYCLE AND MOTOR MANUFACTURERS

The growing popularity of cycling in the late nineteenth century, due to improvements in both cycles and tyres, led people to set up as dealers and producers of bicycles. The famous 'penny-farthing' or ordinary was introduced in 1871, and in 1874 the chain-driven safety bicycle was designed, but it did not become fully established

[39] Bruckshaw and McNab, op. cit., pp. 76, 77, 80, 88, 89, 99.

until the advent of the 'Rover Safety' in 1885. In 1888 J. B. Dunlop, a Dublin vet, invented the pneumatic tyre and these inventions of 1885–88 led to a boom during the 1890s followed by a slump and then the production of some standard bicycles.

William Gilbert (1838–1922) had moved to Lincoln in the 1860s and after working at Robey's for a while he set up on his own in 1876 to repair sewing machines and similar items at 28 Melville Street. By 1885 he was also repairing bicycles and putting together his own 'Lindum' and 'Royal Lincoln' bikes from parts made in Coventry and elsewhere. His premises became the Lindum cycle works and in 1895 he took the shop next door as an office. Not far away, on the site now covered by the Lincoln telephone exchange in Broadgate, James Kirby started making bicycles in 1891 and later produced motor cycles. In the autumn of 1902 the first 'Lincoln Elk' motor cycle was introduced to the public and was an immediate success. Everything except the tyres, magneto and carburettor was made at 4–5 Broadgate. William Garfoot was making bicycles at 68 London Road, Grantham in 1885 and about five years later Fred Hopper started to make them in Barton-on-Humber. In 1913 Kelly's directory listed fifty-eight cycle manufacturers in Lincolnshire, including W. I. Binks and Co. of Lincoln and several firms which nowadays function as motor car dealers.[40]

Britain had pioneered the development of the steam locomotive but she lagged behind Germany, France and the United States in the development of automobiles. The first British-built car was not made until 1895, and when the following year Henry Chaplin, as president of the local government board, introduced a bill which effectively raised the speed limit from four miles per hour to fourteen miles per hour for vehicles up to three tons the house of commons greeted with laughter his assurance that it was 'even possible that these motor cars might become a rival to light railways'. During the next twenty years 'automobilism' was largely a sport for rich men.[41]

William Gilbert's cycle business became a limited company to deal in cars as well as bicycles in 1897 and two years later they purchased the first car in Lincoln, a Benz, which arrived on 19 July 1899. On Christmas Day they provided the Lincoln postmaster

---

[40] *Lincolnshire Echo*, 6 October 1976; *Kelly's Directory*, 1885, p. 755; Elvin, *Lincoln as it Was*, III, p. 32; F. Jones, 'Some County Engineers', *Lincolnshire Life*, 8 no. 4 (1968), p. 21.
[41] P. S. Bagwell, *The Transport Revolution from 1770*, London, 1974, p. 199; *Local Government Chronicle*, 7 April 1978, p. 370.

with a Daimler Rougemonte wagonette to deliver mail for Wood-hall and Boston. This was reported in the national papers as probably the first time that the Royal Mail was carried by motor transport. The Lincolnshire Automobile Club was formed in 1900 and within two years it had 91 members. By 1914 this had risen to 322, of whom one in six were doctors.[42]

Until the First World War, automobile manufacturers were craftsmen producing cars for the customers' particular specifications rather than standardized cheap models for business or a mass market. Many small firms entered this industry, 393 by 1914, but three-quarters of them failed after only a few years. Between 1901 and 1905 alone 221 new firms started to produce cars but only twenty-two of them were still in business in 1914.[43]

The first car maker in Lincolnshire was John Henry Pick, whose premises were at 5 Blackfriars Street, Stamford between St George's Square and Wharf Street. In 1898 he designed and made a vehicle with a body of a type generally known as a dog cart, which he sold to Dr Henry Thomas Benson of Market Deeping for £85. A second car was then made and this went to the marquess of Exeter. After 1900 the Pick car was advertised as being capable of carrying two people at twenty miles per hour and the price was £95. It was driven by a 2¾ horse power engine mounted at the rear, with power transmitted to the rear axle by the use of toothed belts and friction clutches, one for each of the two gears. The frame, following the bicycle practice of the time, was made of tubular steel with cycle-type forks, one pair to each front wheel. The steering was achieved by a tiller arm, which controlled the front forks through a series of interconnecting links. On 19 March 1901 the Pick Motor Co. Ltd was registered with a capital of £10,000 to carry on the business of bicycle and motor car manufacturers and repairers previously carried on by J. H. Pick and C. Gray. The directors were listed as the fifth marquess of Exeter and his wife's cousin Sir George Whichcote, ninth baronet, W. Bean and Charles Gray. Gray was an ironfounder and iron merchant. In November 1904 Jack Pick moved from Blackfriars Street to premises on the Great North Road which are now the St Martin's garage. He made regular improvements to his design and by 1910 was offering for sale the New Pick at prices ranging from 144 guineas for the chassis to 195 guineas for the open four-seater version; all-weather protection was available for an extra £22. In 1910 the New Pick semi-racer was

---

[42] *Lincolnshire Echo*, 6 October 1976; Birkbeck, *History of Bourne*, p. 96.
[43] Bagwell, *The Transport Revolution*, pp. 199, 207.

offered at 175 guineas, claimed to be 'well-capable of fifty m.p.h.', and in 1912 the firm offered five models ranging in price from £179 to £383 for a five-seater landaulette. These were all powered by the 22.4 h.p. engine, but in 1913 Pick's introduced a slightly smaller vehicle with an engine rated at 20.1 h.p. This firm continued to produce cars for several years after the First World War.[44]

The other main car maker in Lincolnshire was Rose Brothers, the Gainsborough wrapping-machine firm. The Rose-National was designed by Baines Brothers, local motor engineers, and marketed by Lamb Brothers and Garnet. About one hundred and fifty were produced at Rose's Albion works between 1904 and 1912, although the first car had perhaps been produced there in 1900. In 1905 the cost of the chassis, for which the purchaser would have a body made elsewhere, was £450 including tools, lamps, horn, jack and other items. Early models had three-cylinder engines but they also developed a four-cylinder version, and one of these still remained in 1971. In June 1905 an 18 h.p. model with four passengers climbed Steep Hill in Lincoln using only top and second gear. In September 1906 William Rose formed the Northern Manufacturing Co. Ltd in Gainsborough to make gears for his wrapping machines and cars, and also for general sale to engineering firms. In 1908 a Rose-National raced at Brooklands: this vehicle was later converted into a fire engine and used on Rose's works until the Second World War, but in face of growing competition Rose Brothers ceased making cars in 1912.[45]

Some other Lincolnshire firms made brief forays into the manufacture of automobiles and plate XIII shows a Richardson as well as a Rose-National. J. R. Richardson started making cars at Saxilby early in 1903, but his firm closed about 1907 when he is thought to have joined the Daimler company. Hopper's the Barton-on-Humber bicycle makers went into car manufacture on a modest scale in 1908, building bodies for the Torpedo on chassis produced by the Star Motor Co. of Wolverhampton. The first car based on the 6 h.p. Starling was not very successful and was later replaced by a twin-cylinder car from the same source. In 1901 R. M. Wright and Co. of Lincoln marketed a car called 'Stonebow', but it is now generally thought that the whole vehicle was made for them by Payne and Bates of Coventry.[46]

[44] G. Brooks, 'The Motor-Car Manufacturers of Lincolnshire', *LIA*, 5 no. 2 (1970), pp. 18–20; *Kelly's Directory*, 1896, pp. 503, 504.
[45] G. Brooks, 'The Motor-Car Manufacturers of Lincolnshire', *LIA*, 6 no. 2–3 (1971), pp. 44, 45; Muir, *History of Baker Perkins*, pp. 104, 105.
[46] Brooks, loc. cit.

CHAPTER 10

VICTORIAN TOWNS

THE final changes of the Railway Age were in the towns themselves. Some of these changes can be attributed indirectly to the railways, but mostly they continued the processes already begun. The larger towns tended to expand dramatically; some smaller one actually shrank; a few resorts — and Scunthorpe — blossomed out of virtually nothing. The problems of urban growth, though considerable, were different from those of the height of the Industrial Revolution, and the general result was a distinction between commercial centre and residential suburbs. Electricity began to light the scene. Progress towards higher standards of public health, hospitals, education, policing and the like continued under the aegis of an increasingly chaotic pattern of responsible bodies, which were reduced to order by a sweeping reorganization of local government in the last decades of the century. The end product was the relatively complacent society of Edwardian England; far from everything in the garden was lovely, but at last, for a brief spell, social conditions seemed largely to have caught up with the advance of technology.

POPULATION

After the arrival of the railways there were striking changes in the distribution of Lincolnshire's population, as figures 15 and 16 indicate. In 1851 only about a third lived in the towns, but by the end of the century over half were urban dwellers. The total population had increased more in the first half of the century than in the second but that growth had occurred evenly over towns and villages of all sizes. As figures 16 and 18 show, Grimsby, Lincoln and Cleethorpes grew more extensively after 1851 than any other places and by 1901 they had almost half the townspeople of Lincolnshire. Some other towns had grown slowly since 1851 but many had declined in relative or even in absolute terms. Some villages in the ironstone district and on the coast had grown into urban districts, but in contrast the agricultural depression had led to the decline of the small market towns.

In Lincolnshire towns, as in England and Wales as a whole, the largest decennial increase in the second half of the century was in 1871–81 but the rural population, after remaining static for twenty years, then started to decline.

Relations between town and country changed as the countryman looked to the towns to meet more of his needs and the majority of townspeople became remote from their rural contemporaries. The poor law and other branches of village government became organized in districts centred on towns, and as the franchise was extended and constituency boundaries were redrawn so the voters of Gainsborough, Louth and Spalding became a very substantial element in nominally rural divisions. The Brigg division, which included Scunthorpe, returned a Liberal at every general election between 1885 and 1906, though a tory won a by-election in 1894.[1]

	1801	1851	1911
Towns with over 5,000 inhabitants	3	10	12
Towns with between 2,000 and 5,000 inhabitants	8	19	23

The table above indicates that population growth up to 1851 had affected many Lincolnshire towns but after that it was concentrated in a few. Most small towns had a declining number of inhabitants in the closing years of the century and some of the first to experience this trend were Caistor, Swineshead, Market Deeping and other places without a railway station. In other cases the decline did not start until the 1860s or 1870s.

Lincolnshire towns did not reach the size of Hull, Sheffield or Nottingham but some experienced the same problems on a smaller scale. Lincoln reasserted its supremacy over Boston but was then surpassed by the new urban area spreading out from Grimsby into the adjoining parish of Clee. Figure 18 shows clearly the concentration of population in these two urban areas in contrast to Boston, Louth and other towns. Gainsborough started to decline before the prosperity of Marshall's gave the population a steady upward movement which lasted until the First World War. Apart from Lincoln and Grimsby–Clee, the main area of population growth was the ironstone district of north-west Lindsey, whose combined

[1] R. J. Olney, *Rural Society and County Government in Nineteenth-Century Lincolnshire*, Lincoln, 1979, p. 156.

population overtook Stamford and Louth during the 1890s. Between 1851 and 1911 the population of the small and former towns shown in figure 1 declined by 17 per cent as a consequence of agricultural depression, while the combined population of the new urban districts increased fourteen-fold.

TOPOGRAPHY

In the towns which experienced growth the new streets of houses were mainly located near sources of employment such as the docks in Grimsby, the railways in Boston and engineering works in Lincoln, Gainsborough and Grantham. But development was also influenced by the willingness or otherwise of landowners such as the Fydells at Boston or the Sheffields at Crosby to release land for development. Where blocks of land were released the simple grid was usually the basic street pattern, but it was adjusted to follow existing roads and parish and field boundaries. Where large tracts were in a single ownership development could be planned comprehensively, as at greater Grimsby where the Heneage and Grant-Thorold families and Sidney Sussex College, Cambridge owned most of the land concerned, but elsewhere the outward growth of towns was carried out piecemeal as plots came on to the market.

In 1845 there were still many people living in the centres of towns — tradesmen and shopkeepers living over their premises and working people in courtyards and lanes behind them. Towards the end of the century many professional and commercial families moved from such old areas to new houses on the suburban edges of the towns, either terraced houses with front and back gardens or detached or semi-detached villas in their own grounds. This meant that new houses were built even on the edge of Louth, Stamford and other towns where the population was decreasing. Spilsby Road became the select area of Boston as turnpike toll-bars at the Black Sluice and the Carlton Road junction prevented development of London Road or Sleaford Road until the last quarter of the century. In most other towns the bars were too far out to be an impediment to development.

One result of the outward growth of Victorian towns was that different urban functions began to be segregated in their location. As people moved out of their houses in market-places, so the central area became more a commercial zone with large shops, banks and other offices. New housing and industrial premises tended to be located in specialized areas, though there were still many exceptions. One prevailing tendency was for industrial premises to be located beside railway lines and to have their own private sidings.

Building development often led to the establishment of new churches and in several cases ground landlords donated sites and even contributed to the cost of construction. The earl of Scarbrough gave sites at Skegness, the Grant-Thorolds at New Clee and Lord St Oswald at Scunthorpe. Owners of the leading Lincoln engineering firms also contributed to new churches in the city. In several cases pre-fabricated iron chapels were used until permanent structures could be erected. At the same time many older churches were extensively restored, but commendable zeal and enthusiasm often resulted in misguided destruction of medieval remains. The main architect concerned in Lincolnshire was James Fowler of Louth (1828–92), though several churches were the work of Charles Kirk of Sleaford or national figures such as Sir G. G. Scott, who said that his first church was St Nicholas at Lincoln.

Victorian architecture came to show great diversity as numerous ancient styles were revived and adapted, and the quick and cheap transport offered by the railways made Welsh slate, all types of building stone, terracotta and numerous varieties of brick nationally available. Traditional styles and materials might continue in remote areas but in general Victorian houses were built of brick and slate.

Distinctive Victorian and Edwardian additions to Lincolnshire's townscapes were statues and fountains in the streets. The building of Handley's memorial in Sleaford in 1851 was followed by the erection of statues of four other distinguished Lincolnshire men during the next ten years: Dr Charlesworth at Lincoln, Sir Isaac Newton at Grantham, Sir John Franklin at Spilsby and Herbert Ingram at Boston. Public drinking fountains were provided at Boston and Bourne in 1860, but until the time of Queen Victoria's jubilee nearly forty years later the only new statue was one to Prince Albert at the entrance to the MSLR's Grimsby docks. Fountains and clock towers were built to mark the jubilee of 1897 and about the same time statues were erected to F. J. Tollemache at Grantham, Edward Stanhope at Horncastle and Lord Tennyson at Lincoln.

LINCOLN

The reconstruction of Stamp End lock in 1826, the lowering of the water level in Sincil dyke and the construction of a road between the foot of Canwick hill and the end of Broadgate in 1843 enabled land in the south-east quarter of the city to be reclaimed for engineering works and housing in the second half of the century, as shown in figure 20. Much of the residential development of this area was on land purchased in 1852 by the Revd Francis Swan (1787–1878). In 1884 this became St Andrew's parish with a population of three thousand, which by 1911 had risen to 7,500. New streets of houses were also built on the hillside between Monks Road and the Witham, opposite the Stamp End and Sheaf engineering works, and southwards across the fields on both sides of High Street. This latter development eventually spread into part of the adjacent parish of Bracebridge, which had started to grow in the 1860s and became a separate urban district in 1898. Lincoln tried to absorb Bracebridge in 1899, since the city's gas works and tramway depot were within the district, but it remained independent until 1920. After 1880 streets were also built in part of Boultham parish adjoining the Spike Island industrial premises, and there a school was erected in 1897, a Primitive Methodist chapel after 1900 and an iron church in 1912.[2]

Houses also extended west of the city, adjoining Brayford, and north over the hill-top plateau. St Swithin's and St Martin's parishes extended east and west of the city centre and were the first to develop, the population of St Swithin's rising from 2,961 in 1851 to 9,134 in 1901.

GRIMSBY AND CLEETHORPES

The MSLR, whose first chairman was Lord Yarborough, became a potent force in Grimsby and spent over a million pounds on dock and railway facilities there. A new town started to develop near the dock entrance and within twenty years had covered the East Marsh and was extending into Clee and Weelsby townships. The company was virtually responsible for the creation of the town but they did not develop it themselves or control others in that task. Responsibility for the manner in which the town grew fell on the corporation, which for long was to prove inadequate to the job. Even by 1848 it was said that of the 1,554 houses then standing six hundred had been built since 1844, and by 1851 people born in Grimsby were a minority of its population. In 1858 the MSLR and GNR encouraged fishermen to settle by sharing the cost of building fifty houses for them.[3]

[2] Lincolnshire Library, 'Industry II', p. 22; Hill, *Victorian Lincoln*, pp. 127–29; *SM*, 26 August 1842, 16 June 1843; *LAOR* 19, pp. 55, 56; White, *Directory*, 1872, p. 605; *Lincolnshire Chronicle*, 26 July 1974, 18 December 1975; *Kelly's Directory*, 1913, p. 99.

[3] Gillett, *Grimsby*, p. 229; G. Jackson, *Grimsby and the Haven Company*, Grimsby, 1971, p. 53; White and Tye, *Grimsby and Cleethorpes*, pp. 8, 9; Dow, *Great Central*, I, p. 176.

As figure 21 shows, the railway to the dock formed a physical barrier between old and new Grimsby with contact confined to level crossings at Cleethorpe Road and Pasture Street. By 1869 development of the East Marsh was virtually complete and extended over the borough boundary on to the estates of Alexander W. T. Grant-Thorold and Edward Heneage of Hainton. In 1873 Grimsby corporation opened a bridge across the Old Dock and development started in the West Marsh, where the Alexandra Dock was opened in 1879, and extended south to the Gainsborough railway line and a little beyond.[4]

The development of New Clee and Weelsby was even more rapid and extensive, and in 1878 it was said that much of Grimby's criminal population had moved across the boundary. A mission room was opened in 1872, a railway station in 1873 and by 1878 the problems of rapid growth were so extensive that a Clee-with-Weelsby local board of health was formed; ten years later it combined with Grimsby to form a county borough. At the same time a Grimsby poor law union was formed and a large workhouse erected on the Scartho boundary in 1892. In the 1850s there was a social and topographical gap between the fishermen and those who were running the town, but as fishermen grew richer and more numerous so their influence increased and by 1873 four out of sixteen councillors were smack owners. New Clee and Weelsby remained the main areas of development but Edward Heneage, now Liberal MP for Grimsby, developed his Wellow Abbey estate with detached villas in spacious grounds and donated the large People's Park (fig. 39).[5]

Since the 1850s Sidney Sussex College, one of the poorest of Cambridge colleges but the largest landowner in Cleethorpes, had been granting 99-year leases of plots around the original thorpes or hamlets of Hoole and Itterby on a piecemeal basis. But about 1887 they started a comprehensive development of their property at the northern end of the township adjoining New Clee. Henry Doughty, a Grimsby builder, had leased five plots in October 1885 and a few other builders followed, but development really started after 1890 when the college started taking lower yearly rents. Between 1881 and 1901 the number of houses in Cleethorpes, including those under construction, increased from 673 to 3,038

[4] White and Tye, *Grimsby and Cleethorpes*, pp. 9–11; Gillett, *Grimsby*, p. 238; P. J. Aspinall, 'Speculative Builders and the Development of Cleethorpes 1850–1900', *LHA*, 11 (1976), p. 46.

[5] Gillett, *Grimsby*, pp. 232, 239, 244, 283; C. E. Watson, *A History of Clee and the Thorpes of Clee*, Grimsby, 1901, p. 89; White, *Directory*, 1882, p. 242.

and two-thirds of the new houses were erected after 1891. The college used several methods to encourage a high class of development and in 1899 donated twelve acres to the urban district council for Sidney Park.[6]

OTHER TOWNS

On a smaller scale there was also some outward growth at Grantham and Gainsborough, as shown in figures 22 and 23. Within Grantham borough there was little building land left and development occurred mainly in Spittlegate near the railway station and the engineering works of Hornsby, Hempstead and others. There was also some residential development in Little Gonerby and in part of Somerby parish adjoining Spittlegate, and by 1900 only about a third of the townspeople lived within the old borough boundary. A cemetery was established in Somerby in 1858 and opening of the new access road allowed large houses for entrepreneurs to be built in the corner of Harrowby near St Catherine's bridge. Most development took place between 1850 and 1880 and in 1879 Grantham corporation obtained a Borough Extension Act, which brought all the urban areas into an enlarged borough. Only the county police station was excluded, and this formed an island of county territory within the borough. The growth of Grantham was halted in the 1880s when demand for Hornsby's products was badly affected by the agricultural depression, but it started to revive after 1900.[7]

Gainsborough started to decline after the opening of the MSLR and Grimsby dock but then the success of the Marshall brothers built it into a typical company town. The growth of Marshall's accelerated after 1870 and while the works was extended alongside the railway, housing filled the remaining space between there and the old town. In 1872 Henry and James Marshall helped launch the Gainsborough Building Society but did not themselves develop the town. Development was mainly in Holy Trinity parish, whose population increased from 2,436 in 1861 to 6,245 in 1881, but so many workers were attracted to Gainsborough that even the enclosed yards of the old town remained in full occupation. In some Gainsborough streets the houses backed on to a narrow lane, serving houses in parallel streets and known as the ten foot; it was used for the collection of night soil. Such lanes were to be found in

[6] Aspinall, 'Speculative Builders and the Development of Cleethorpes', pp. 43, 46, 51.
[7] Honeybone, *Grantham*, p. 88; A. R. Bowen and C. P. Willard, *The Story of Grantham and its Countryside*, Newark, 1949, p. 39.

many industrial towns but Gainsborough had the only examples in
Lincolnshire. As the new town became tightly packed with houses,
the upper echelons of the working class moved north or south to
new residential areas with gardens and more space. The area they
left behind was occupied by poorer people from the yards of the old
town. The southern development as far as the union workhouse
was largely complete by 1900 but on the North Warren it continued
until after 1914.[8]

In other towns, there was not a great deal of outward growth
apart from the movement of more prosperous workers to superior
terraces on their edges, as shown in figures 19, 24 and 25. Much
development was on land conveniently close to a railway station,
such as the Witham bank, Tunnard Street and Carlton Road areas of
Boston. Many of Boston's railway workers lived in the Duke Street
and Locomotive Street area next to the depot or in Skirbeck
Quarter near the goods station and other railway premises. The
opening of Boston dock coincided with the closure of the adjacent
foundries of the Tuxford family and C. T. Stephenson at Mount
Bridge and with the movement of other families to the edge of the
town, so no new streets were erected in the vicinity of the dock.

In both Stamford and Louth the population fell by about nine per
cent between 1851 and 1901. In Stamford the decline was worst in
the 1850s and 1890s, with a significant but temporary revival when
the open fields north of the town were belatedly enclosed in the
1870s. Stamford was not a major railway junction, but the real
impediment to industrial development was Lord Exeter's restrict-
ion on sites for industry.[9]

URBAN PROBLEMS

Engineering firms and railway companies attracted large numbers
of workers to the towns but in general they did not see it as their
business to build houses. Working-class housing was mainly provided by speculators, who maximized profits by building as many
cheap houses as possible onto each plot of land. Some were built
with no foundations or with drains above basement level; water
supply, ventilation and sanitation were often inadequate. Combined with overcrowding these conditions made rich breeding
grounds for disease; as well as cholera, which broke out in England
four times between 1831 and 1866, deaths were also caused by

[8] I. S. Beckwith, 'Religion in a Working Men's Parish 1843–1893', *LHA*, 5
(1970), pp. 31, 33.
[9] Rogers, ed., *Stamford*, p. 100.

smallpox, typhus and tuberculosis. Villages and country hamlets also lacked sanitation and suffered from polluted water supplies, but in towns the concentration of people in a much smaller space made the effects much worse.[10]

Typhus fever was prevalent in Sleaford in 1848, especially in several crowded courts and yards. The water supply came partly from the river Slea, which was also the main receptacle of the untreated sewage of the town. While liquid sewage found its way to the river, night soil and garbage littered the streets and entries. Boston had a body of improvement commissioners, but in 1849 it still had bad slums, no proper drainage, open cesspools and ditches, and filthy streets; that year the town suffered an outbreak of cholera and in August there were twenty-six deaths. The problem of sewage disposal proved intractable until the closing years of the century. Grimsby started to tackle it in 1855, but in 1871 a government inspector found choked drains, full privies, huge accumulations of manure from pigsties and stables, and offal from slaughterhouses. Every town had sewage flowing through open drains such as the Mowbeck at Grantham, the Barditch at Boston and Clee drain at Grimsby. In 1855 the Mowbeck was described as 'black, muddy and stagnant, appalling to the sight and sickening to the smell'. The Barditch where it passed behind Boston grammar school was not covered over until 1878 following the death from diphtheria of one of the boarders at the school.[11]

Piped water was virtually non-existent in Lincolnshire and in both town and country people were dependent on private wells, public pumps and rainwater butts. In Grimsby in 1848 there were seven public pumps in the old town but only two in the new town developed since 1800. A company started supplying water in 1862, but by 1871 only 1,300 out of 4,053 houses had a piped supply and most drew incredibly bad water from private wells contaminated by surface drainage. 'Everywhere, but especially in the most densely populated parts, [an inspector] found pigs kept in back yards, sometimes as many as ten to a single house'.[12]

The corporations of the six boroughs were responsible for policing their towns (though Grimsby did not establish a regular

[10] M. Aston and J. Bond, *The Landscape of Towns*, London, 1976, pp. 192, 195.
[11] *LAOR* 23, p. 25; H. Porter, *Boston 1800 to 1835 continued to 1868*, Lincoln, 1943, pp. 22, 27, 28; Gillett, *Grimsby*, pp. 279, 280; H. H. Quilter, *Mid-Victorian Grantham*, Grantham, 1936.
[12] Gillett, *Grimsby*, pp. 217, 280.

force until 1846), but they had few other statutory responsibilities.[13] By 1845 there were commissioners who looked after
paving and lighting in most boroughs and care for the poor had
been transferred to the unions, but in all towns and villages the
parish vestries were responsible for the highways and other local
government services.

The vestry system depended on amateurs holding unpaid offices
for a year, with no professional officers, and by the 1850s this was
proving unworkable in all towns. Problems with drains and sewers
were understandable when the responsibility rested with a part-
time surveyor who might earn his living as a farmer, grocer, coal
merchant or brewer. The Barton-on-Humber manorial court leet
still met twice a year in the 1860s and appointed coal meters, a
pinder and some other officials, but in general parish vestries had
assumed the power of appointing such officers.[14]

During Victoria's reign there was a utilitarian tendency to establish authorities that were democratic, efficient and scientific to
control new local services. In many ways the poor law unions were
the model of the new sort of public body, being locally elected but
subject to control and inspection by a central authority. Partly due
to a lingering mistrust of municipal corporations, there was a
tendency to create new authorities for each new duty conferred on
local government, but towards the end of the century urban
responsibilities started to be gathered together in the hands of the
corporations.

The growth of industrial towns brought workers together in
large numbers, and as they started to gain political and economic
power the middle class, who held sway for a century after the
Reform Act, had to deal with the problems of concentrations of
people in urban areas. Following Chartist riots in 1839 a permissive
act allowed magistrates to raise and equip a paid county police
force, but, as in many other counties, the Lindsey magistrates
developed a system of superintending constables based in market
towns and responsible for the parish constables in their area. The
first police station was established in Gainsborough in 1843, and the
Kesteven magistrates erected one in Sleaford in 1845; but in 1856
the three parts were obliged to establish forces, which were known
collectively as the Lincolnshire constabulary and had a single chief
constable. The six borough forces for long remained independent,

[13] Ibid., p. 243.
[14] Barton-on-Humber Local History Class, *Barton-on-Humber in the 1850s. Part
Three. Parish and Government*, Barton-on-Humber, 1979, p. 45.

but in 1888 the Stamford force merged with the county and the separate forces for Lincoln and Grimsby ceased in 1967.[15]

VOLUNTARY AND COMMERCIAL SERVICES

Some services were provided by public bodies, particularly as the century progressed, but there was also reliance on voluntary effort and private enterprise to meet public needs. By 1845 there were voluntary fire brigades in most towns, turning out as and when required. Their equipment was stored centrally and its cost was covered by contributions from public funds, private donations, insurance companies and those who made use of its services. As the century advanced there was a gradual tendency to inject more public funds to improve the service by purchasing equipment, erecting new fire stations, employing a full-time superintendent and paying the men when they turned out for a fire. Lincoln corporation purchased their first steam pump in 1882 and a Dennis motor fire engine in 1910. The provision of piped water in the main towns was also a great help to fire-fighting.[16]

The provision of a piped water supply was initially undertaken by private enterprise, though some such concerns later passed into public ownership. By 1826 a steam pump was supplying some of Gainsborough's needs from the Trent and in 1837 a piped supply was laid from Wothorpe to Stamford, but it was the 1840s before the first steps were taken towards providing modern water supplies in most Lincolnshire towns. The first water company in the county was formed in Boston in 1845 and by 1850 companies had also opened water works at Lincoln and Grantham. The Lincoln works, with a 23-acre reservoir at Hartsholme lake, was acquired by Lincoln corporation in 1871. Despite concern about the quality of the water no improvement was made until a typhoid outbreak in 1904–5 caused 131 deaths in the city. A new source was found at Elkesley, twenty-two miles west of Lincoln, and the new supply commenced on 4 October 1911, when a ceremony was held at the Arboretum. J. M. Rendel produced a plan for Grimsby's water supply in 1851 but the supply was not provided until 1862 by a waterworks company; in 1884 they extended the service to Clee-thorpes. Other acts for water supply were obtained by Bourne in

[15] A. Wickstead, *Lincolnshire, Lindsey — The Story of the County Council 1889–1974*, Lincoln, 1978, p. 105; L. Golding, *Local Government*, London, 1959, pp. 99, 100; Rogers, ed., *Stamford*, p. 108.
[16] *SM*, 5 February 1847, 24 August 1849, 15 March 1850; Porter, *Boston 1800 to 1835 continued to 1868*, p. 41; L. Elvin, *Lincoln as it Was*, I, Nelson, 1974, p. 36.

1856, Spalding in 1860 and Gainsborough in 1865; the latter was taken over by the local board of health in 1871.[17]

Street lighting by gas involved public and private enterprise: companies who produced the gas, and lighting authorities who in the early days were the main customers. By 1845 all the principal towns in Lincolnshire had gas to light streets, shops and public buildings, and the houses of the more prosperous inhabitants. During the 1850s and 1860s more gas works were built in the smaller towns and large villages as well as at large country houses such as Brocklesby Hall and Syston Hall. As demand increased the works were enlarged and in 1875 the Lincoln works was rebuilt on a completely different site. As the first electricity generators appeared, so gas companies promoted other uses for gas, particularly heating and cooking, and offered terms more attractive for the working classes. All gas works in Lincolnshire were established by companies but by 1914 those in Spalding, Lincoln, Horncastle, Bourne, Brigg and Gainsborough were owned by local councils.

Street improvements in Victorian towns were sometimes the result of voluntary action rather than public activity. Voluntary contributions paid for the removal of the Middle Row in Market Deeping's market-place in 1847, but leaving the provision of pavements to the initiative of frontagers in most towns gave haphazard results.[18]

HEALTH CARE

The health of the individual was largely dependent on self-help and the charity of the well-to-do. The rich and middle classes were cared for in their own homes and paid their own way, the poor were cared for by the guardians but the working class occupied a middle ground. By 1845 there were hospitals in Lincoln and Stamford and dispensaries in six Lincolnshire towns. The original charitable foundations had been modified to suit the Victorian concept of self-help and the dispensaries received contributions from those concerned to make provision for their own illness or infirmity. An important part was played by friendly societies; in Grantham, Gainsborough and Lincoln they and trade unions established dispensaries of their own. In 1850 there were 5,487 Oddfellows in

[17] Thompson, *Boston*, p. 102; White, *Directory*, 1856, pp. 291, 577; K. Middleton, 'General Living Conditions in Lincoln, 1840–1914', *LIA*, 5 no. 3 (1970), p. 41; *Lincolnshire Chronicle*, 6 December 1979; White and Tye, *Grimsby and Cleethorpes*, p. 24; I. S. Beckwith, *The Industrial Archaeology of Gainsborough*, Gainsborough, 1968, p. 6.
[18] *SM*, 8 January 1847.

Lincolnshire organized by ninety-nine lodges but by 1900 there were 6,209 in Lincoln city alone. Many were middle class or superior working class, for the lower class could not afford the initiation fee or weekly subscription. Several lodges built public halls.[19]

The work of Florence Nightingale during the Crimean War led to a changed view of nurses and hospitals. In 1865 Mrs Bromhead of Lincoln established an institution to provide home nurses in the county and in 1869 started one of the first nursing homes in the kingdom. In the next few years small cottage hospitals were provided in several Lincolnshire towns. One with nine beds opened in Grimsby in 1866 and others with up to six beds each were started in Market Rasen, Louth and Boston in 1869 and 1871. They were soon replaced with slightly larger ones and new hospitals were built at Grantham (twenty-eight beds) in 1874–75 and Spalding (twenty-six beds) in 1881. By this time the county hospital in Lincoln had one hundred beds, but the site had serious problems and the hospital was rebuilt east of the city in 1876–78. A large part of the building cost was met by Mr and Mrs Nathaniel Clayton, whose home adjoined it, and by Mrs Ann Dixon of Holton. Other general hospitals were opened at Woodhall Spa, Bourne, Spilsby and Gainsborough by 1914 and some existing hospitals were enlarged. The new sanitary authorities began to provide isolation hospitals for infectious diseases after 1875.[20]

A rough and ready general medical service for the poor was provided by the guardians, and by a legal fiction it could also serve other people who were only partly destitute.[21] The guardians had established a district medical service in 1834; as well as wards attached to workhouses they also built detached infirmaries. The former workhouses at Bourne, Caistor, Holbeach and Louth are still in use as hospitals. For the mentally ill a large county lunatic asylum, now St John's hospital, was established on Bracebridge Heath near Lincoln in 1850. It was subsequently enlarged several times and in 1899–1902 a separate Kesteven county asylum was erected near Sleaford.

The problem of drink was tackled by voluntary action and self-help through the temperance movement. Temperance halls had been built in most towns by 1850 so that public meetings could

[19] T. H. Storey, 'The Oddfellows Hall, Grimsby, and its Place in the Social Life of the Town', *LHA*, 12 (1977), pp. 49, 50.
[20] *Lincolnshire Echo*, 23 September 1978; K. B. Smellie, *A History of Local Government*, London, 1963, p. 66.
[21] Smellie, op. cit., p. 68.

get away from public houses, and temperance hotels also opened for short periods in some towns.

LOCAL BOARDS OF HEALTH

Under the Public Health Act of 1848, the general board of health could authorize the creation in any locality of a local board of health, either on receipt of a petition signed by a least one tenth of the ratepayers or, if no petition was received, where the death rate was at least twenty-three per thousand. In response to such petitions William Lee and William Ranger visited Holbeach, Sleaford, Grimsby and Gainsborough to hold local enquiries and local boards had been formed there by the end of 1851. The Gainsborough board took over the powers of the lighting, watching and improvement commissioners.[22] In boroughs the corporation could become the local board by adopting the act but in other towns an entirely new authority was elected. The board's activities could include water supply, sewerage, drainage, street repairs and improvements, scavenging, prevention of nuisances and regulation of buildings. They appointed a clerk, surveyor and inspector of nuisances and had power to levy a rate, but in their early years their actual powers fell far short of their responsibilities. The provision of piped water supplies and sewage disposal systems were expensive projects and proved beyond the means of local boards. Public companies tackled the water supply, and solutions to the sewerage problem had to wait until the end of the century, when new authorities had replaced the boards.

Lincoln had a death rate of twenty-four per thousand when in September 1849 George Giles produced plans for a general underground sewerage system, but a town meeting rejected adoption of the act and the scheme. Lincoln corporation did not adopt the act until 1866 and only commenced its sewerage scheme in 1878 under extreme pressure from central government and the High Court.[23]

In 1851 William Ranger held a local enquiry in Spalding, Lincolnshire's largest unincorporated town at the time, but instead of adopting the Public Health Act the local people promoted a private Spalding Improvement Act to create a body of commissioners with more power than a local board would have. Ranger considered that Spalding's main needs were a supply of cheap and abundant water and a general efficient system of sewers and house drainage, but the

---

[22] *SM*, 3 August 1849, 10 August 1849, 9 November 1849, 16 November 1849, 23 November 1849, 28 November 1850; *LAOR* 23, p. 24.

[23] Hill, *Victorian Lincoln*, p. 162; *Lincolnshire Chronicle*, 5 October 1978.

commissioners had different priorities: they opened a cemetery in 1854 and built a Corn Exchange in 1856. In 1851 the general board forced adoption of the act onto Grimsby corporation, but in 1853 the corporation obtained an Improvement Act which gave them wider powers. Under this they undertook a sewerage scheme as well as opening a cemetery and erecting a Corn Exchange and the present town hall.[24]

The effectiveness of the Public Health Act of 1848 was restricted because its adoption depended on local initiative which would lead to considerable expense, and was further reduced in 1858 when the general board was dissolved. Grantham corporation adopted the act about 1854 but their local board powers were restricted to the borough and excluded Little Gonerby and Spittlegate. Boston corporation became a local board on 16 May 1859 and thereby took over the powers and duties of the lighting and paving com-missioners; in 1860 they decided to build a drain to serve the western side of the town. Separate local boards were established in Sutton Bridge and Long Sutton in 1859 and 1860, and in 1863 and 1864 villages like Ruskington and Broughton formed local boards of health to avoid the operation of the Highways Act of 1862 and so retain the management of their roads.

After 1868 new local boards in Lincolnshire were created only for Market Rasen and rising places such as Cleethorpes and Scun-thorpe. The Public Health Act of 1872 made borough councils, local boards of health and improvement commissioners into urban sanitary authorities and for other places the boards of guardians became rural sanitary authorities. The Public Health Act of 1875 made standards of adequate construction, ventilation, sanitation and access enforceable for all new houses. This led to 'bye-law terrace housing': long, straight, parallel streets of red brick and slate houses which met the statutory standards at minimum cost. They had a narrow frontage but greater depth and some had a small front garden. They could have the scullery and kitchen to the rear, with a lavatory and coal shed entered from the yard. The public health legislation of the 1870s enabled local authorities, if they were willing, to control future housing developments, but only slowly were authorities given power to deal with the slums that had already been created. Neither did Lincolnshire authorities do much to provide working class housing before the First World War.[25]

[24] N. R. Wright, *Spalding — An Industrial History*, Lincoln, 1973, p. 70; Gillett, *Grimsby*, p. 217; White, *Directory*, 1856, p. 577.
[25] *LAOR* 9, p. 60; Porter, *Boston 1800 to 1835 continued to 1868*, pp. 21, 26; Aston and Bond, *Landscape of Towns*, pp. 196, 197.

CEMETERIES

The dead were usually buried in ground adjoining parish churches and other places of worship, but by the middle of the nineteenth century the overcrowding of urban churchyards was becoming a serious health risk and a cause of concern. Even before the Burial Act of 1853 allowed the creation of burial boards to provide cemeteries and close the old churchyards as places of sepulture, some towns had already devised their own solutions. In 1846 Gainsborough dissenters formed a company to provide a cemetery north of the town, and in 1847–48 the Horncastle churchwardens erected a nominal chapel of ease on the edge of the town with a large burial ground attached. Spalding and Grimsby included burial grounds in their own private acts of 1853, and Louth, Boston and Stamford quickly opened cemeteries under the general act. Nine Lincoln parishes opened a joint cemetery on Canwick Road in 1856, next to which St Swithin's established its own parish cemetery. Later another one was opened in Newport for the north of the city.[26]

EDUCATION

In education, as in so many other spheres, Victoria's reign saw a gradual change of emphasis from voluntary to state provision. The formation of the Lincoln diocesan board of education in 1839 had stimulated activity among supporters of the established church and many new National schools were founded in Lincolnshire towns in the 1840s and 1850s. Some existing schools were rebuilt or enlarged; by 1870 Boston had about twelve schools and Stamford eight as well as the old grammar schools and numerous private-venture schools.[27]

By 1851 there were 705 Methodist chapels of all connections in Lincolnshire compared with 657 Anglican churches. Of those who attended a place of worship on 30 March 1851, 46 per cent prayed and sang in Methodist chapels, while 43 per cent worshipped in the established church. Similarly there were more children in Methodist Sunday schools than Anglican Sunday schools, but only in the towns did Methodists establish day schools as well. Most Methodist educational impact was made through its Sunday schools, adult class meetings and other chapel activities. In 1844 there were only six Wesleyan day schools in the whole of Lincolnshire, but Sir

[26] White, *Directory*, 1856, pp. 171, 760.
[27] S. de Winton, 'The Coming of the School Board', in *The First Stone and other papers*, Boston, 1970, p. 13.

James Graham's factory bill of 1843 stimulated all nonconformists into action. By 1860 at least fifteen more Wesleyan schools had been opened in Gainsborough, Grimsby, Louth and other places. Support for the Primitive Methodists was strongest among the labouring class; only where they had a large congregation in a large town such as Grimsby could they afford to establish a school. Very few other denominations set up day schools in Lincolnshire; even joining together, sometimes with Methodists, they did not establish many British schools. Small Catholic schools were set up in Grantham and Boston about 1860. After that date there was little further progress in the creation of nonconformist day schools in the county. The passing of the 1870 Elementary Education Act led to the establishment of twelve more Methodist schools but others collapsed and overall there was a gradual decline.[28]

The diocesan training college for masters had not been a success but it was reopened in 1862 as a training school for females and eventually became the Bishop Grosseteste College. It was enlarged in 1901 to take 104 students (eighty-three resident and twenty-one day) compared with the previous fifty-six. By the middle of the nineteenth century the old grammar schools had declined to a very bad state and those at Bourne and Holbeach closed completely. Grimsby grammar school had the support of the corporation; new buildings were erected on either side of the town hall, for the girls' school and the boys' school, in 1863 and 1866–67 respectively; until 1940 it admitted only the sons and daughters of freemen of Grimsby, and educated them at the expense of the ratepayers. But others were in a poorer situation; for a time Boston had no pupils and in 1870 Stamford had thirty pupils and no headmaster, but by then the charity commissioners were starting to tackle the problem and divert the funds of ancient charities. By this means the De Aston grammar school was created at Market Rasen in 1862 and Stamford was revived in 1873. The grammar schools were reorganized to meet modern needs; after 1900 science laboratories and gymnasia were added. In 1892 the funds of Christ's Hospital Bluecoat school in Lincoln were diverted to support a new High school for girls; other grammar schools for girls were opened at Louth in 1904 and Grantham in 1910. Until the revival of the grammar schools many of the sons and daughters of the middle class had been educated in private-venture schools, whose quality varied from excellent to abysmal.

[28] R. C. Russell, *A History of Schools and Education in Lindsey, Lincolnshire 1800–1902*, IV, Lincoln, 1967, pp. 7, 44; Russell, *Schools and Education in Lindsey*, I, Lincoln, 1965, p. 64.

The stimulus to the improvement of education facilities was the Eduction Act of 1870, which provided for the election of school boards in boroughs or parishes which lacked satisfactory provision for poor children. In many places the church of England managed to make its school provision 'sufficient, efficient and suitable' and so delay the need for boards. In January 1871 the Lincoln diocesan board were told that of 737 places in the county nearly half had adequate provision, in a quarter efforts were being made to provide it, and in the remaining quarter there was a deficiency and no local means of supplying it. Attendance was compulsory after 1870 and in the expanding towns of Lincoln, Grimsby and the ironstone district there was tremendous pressure on the voluntary provision of school places. In Lincoln the church of England made a great effort and opened or enlarged a school nearly every year until 1907. The population of Scunthorpe was still small enough for the munificence of Lord St Oswald and the ironmasters to meet their needs until the turn of the century.[29]

At Grimsby a school board was formed before 1874 and one followed at Boston in 1894, but most Lincolnshire towns avoided them. The population of Louth was declining; though the town had some 2,400 school places available in the 1880s average attendance before 1900 seldom exceeded 1,500. Lincoln avoided a board, but they were formed in the growing suburbs of Bracebridge and New Boultham in 1878 and 1894 respectively. Anglicans, Wesleyans and Primitive Methodists all built schools in Grimsby but only the board with its power to levy rates could meet the need; by 1900 it had provided about eight thousand places. Boards were formed in Boston and Skirbeck when a government inspector condemned five schools. The old charity schools tended to disappear during the nineteenth century, particularly after 1870, and several had their endowments transferred to National schools.[30]

From the 1850s evening classes for adults were held in several towns and were encouraged by the science and art department of the Privy Council formed in 1852. Some were held in National schools and others in mechanics' institutes. Boston science and art class started in 1860 and in 1904 was given three rooms in the new municipal buildings. A school of science and art was built in Monks Road, Lincoln in 1886; its façade was later incorporated in new

[29] Winton, 'The Coming of the School Board', p. 17; Russell, *Schools and Education in Lindsey*, IV, p. 43.

[30] Winton, op. cit., pp. 24, 27; Robinson, *Louth*, p. 67; Russell, op. cit., pp. 40–44; Gillett, *Grimsby*, p. 284.

buildings for the Lincoln college of technology. Board schools could provide only elementary education but the growth of night schools indicated a need for higher education, and in 1889 the Technical Instruction Act allowed county councils and county borough councils to provide it. They quickly took over the role played by the mechanics' institutes and other bodies, though they were mainly involved in distributing government grants. In 1902 these authorities replaced the school boards, except in Boston and Grantham, where the municipal borough councils became responsible for elementary education. In Cleethorpes, Gainsborough and

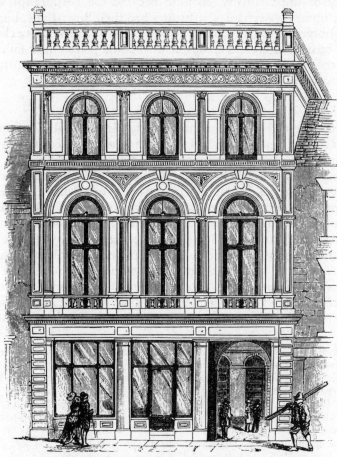

Figure 38 *The market-place façade of the Boston Athenaeum (built 1855–56, demolished c. 1962) incorporated the same classical architectural details as the Athenaeum in Boston, Massachusetts, erected a few years earlier*

R

the Scunthorpe area, the Lindsey County Council opened several new schools after 1902, but in other places few new schools were needed before 1914.[31]

The Boston Mechanics Institution merged in 1851 with the public library to form the Boston Athenaeum (fig. 38), which in its name, concept and architectural details followed an institution built in the capital of Massachusetts in 1849. This cultural similarity perhaps owed much to Pishey Thompson, who had links with both towns. The Athenaeum closed in 1866, and most other mechanics' institutes in the county had ended by 1900. In 1899 the premises and library of the Grimsby institute became the corporation's first public library. Mechanics' institutes had their limitations, but they made libraries available to the working class and provided a club for small businessmen and tradesmen. In some places their failure to meet the need for adult education led to the formation of mutual improvement societies.[32]

RECREATION

By 1845 the old Georgian theatres had closed in all Lincolnshire towns except Lincoln and Stamford, and the latter became a billiard hall in 1871. For performances by travelling actors and local amateurs most corn exchanges and other public halls had stages and proscenium arches even if they lacked boxes or a gallery. The earl of Yarborough laid the foundation stone of Louth town hall on 16 June 1853 and similar meeting rooms were provided at Grimsby in 1863 and Grantham 1868–69, but general purpose public halls were usually provided by private enterprise or by voluntary associations such as friendly societies or the temperance movement.[33]

Towards the end of the century a new type of popular 'music hall' entertainment developed in rooms attached to public houses and led to the erection of large new variety theatres for a mass audience. A

[31] Robinson, Louth, p. 67; J. N. Clarke, Education in a Market Town: Horncastle, Chichester, 1976, p. 129; S. J. Curtis and M. E. A. Boultwood, An Introductory History of English Education since 1800, London, 4th edn 1966, pp. 95, 282; White, Directory, 1872, p. 817; Boston Red Book and Directory for 1897, Boston, 1896, p. 51; Porter, Boston 1800 to 1835 continued to 1868, p. 123; Kelly's Directory, 1913, p. 47; Hill, Victorian Lincoln, p. 278; Wickstead, Lincolnshire, Lindsey, p. 43; Honeybone, Grantham, p. 123.
[32] Thompson, Boston, p. 220; Porter, op. cit., pp. 118, 122; D. S. Tucci, Built in Boston, Boston USA, 1978, p. 24; Hill, Victorian Lincoln, p. 276.
[33] White, Directory, 1872, p. 703; 1856, p. 247; N. Pevsner and J. Harris, The Buildings of England — Lincolnshire, London, 1964, p. 256; M. Pointer and M. G. Knapp, Bygone Grantham, II, Grantham, 1977, p. 2; Quilter, Mid-Victorian Grantham, p. 7.

chairman introduced individual performances by comic and senti-
mental singers, dancers, comedians, jugglers and novelty acts. A
new Theatre Royal was erected in George Street, Grantham in
1875, but it was called the Empire when putting on variety shows.
A masonic hall built in Newland, Lincoln in 1872 could be used for
theatrical performances after 1877 and in 1902 became the Palace
theatre. In 1885 the Kings theatre was opened as a music hall in
Trinity Street, Gainsborough; after 1884 Joseph Henry Curry
opened several large variety theatres in Grimsby including the
Prince of Wales and the Tivoli. [34]

About the turn of the century moving pictures were seen in
Lincolnshire as sideshow novelties in fairground tents and as inter-
ludes in halls of entertainment. In 1909 only one establishment
listed in Kelly's directory of the county had a name that sounded
like that of a cinema, the Picturedrome in Railway Street, Grimsby,
but in 1913 thirteen 'cinematograph halls' were identified including
four in Grimsby and two in Scunthorpe. One pioneer was George
Aspland Howden, who in 1910 was granted a licence to hold film
shows on Bargate Green, Boston. Later that year he took over the
Premier Electric theatre at the Corn Exchange and ran it as the New
theatre (with an entrance through the former Athenaeum — figure
38) until its demolition in 1962; by 1913 he had also established the
Spalding Picture House in Westlode Street. [35]

As streets of bricks and mortar marched over the fields in serried
ranks, concern for the health and social well-being of the working
classes led to the creation of large public parks. The commercially
operated pleasure gardens in Boston and Lincoln closed about the
middle of the century (Vauxhall Gardens in 1857 and Temple
Gardens in 1863), but in 1871 Boston corporation provided the first
People's Park in the county. It covered 33½ acres at the southern
end of the borough next to the riverside walk and the swimming
baths; it had pleasant walks through trees and shrubs and a bandstand. By 1892 there were facilities for cricket, skittles, quoits,
bowls, croquet and football. In 1872 Bishop Wordsworth opened
the thirteen-acre Arboretum on the eastern edge of Lincoln, and in
1883 the duke and duchess of Connaught opened the 27-acre
People's Park at Grimsby (fig. 39). The need for parks was one
result of the increasing leisure as working hours were reduced and
bank holidays were extended to more people. Another result was

[34] Honeybone, *Grantham*, p. 125; Elvin, *Lincoln as it Was*, I, p. 34; D. Boswell and
J. M. Storey, *Grimsby as it Was*, Nelson, 1974, p. 24.
[35] *Lincolnshire Echo*, 30 August 1976; Wright, *Spalding — An Industrial History*,
p. 48.

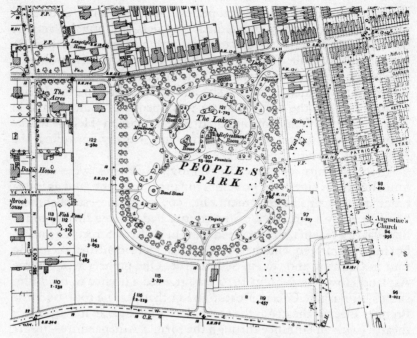

Figure 39   *The Ordnance Survey's plan of the People's Park, Grimsby in 1905 with its lake, lawns, bandstands and refreshment rooms; the Grimsby tramline ends just in front of the park. Notice how the development disregards the parish boundary and falls into distinct zones around the park*

the growth of sports such as bicycling, tennis and football. Horse racing continued in popularity and became more of a spectator sport.[36]

Organized sport was at first a middle-class activity, spreading out from the public schools and universities into ordinary life. In the 1850s the England team of cricketers played various Lincolnshire teams; Boston Rowing Club held its first regatta in 1865; and an athletics match held in Hopkin's Park, Boston in 1867 included seventeen events. Lawn tennis barely existed in 1875 but by 1880 it was the rage. Golf similarly grew in the 1890s and several courses were laid out.[37]

[36] A. J. Strachan and I. R. Bowler, 'The Development of Public Parks and Gardens in the City of Leicester', *East Midland Geographer*, 6 pt 6 (1976), p. 276; Porter, *Boston 1800 to 1835 continued to 1868*, pp. 47, 136; Elvin, *Lincoln as it Was*, II, Nelson, 1976, p. 27; Gillett, *Grimsby*, p. 239.

[37] Porter, op. cit., pp. 129, 130.

There had been sea-water swimming baths at Boston since 1835, but they were unsatisfactory and eventually in 1864 the corporation took over and improved them. One for ladies and a second for gentlemen had a charge of 6*d*. and were filled daily with fresh sea water. Swimming became more popular in the 1870s, following the feats of Matthew Webb; in 1879 Boston corporation built new baths near the General Hospital and People's Park and opened them on 3 May 1880. Skegness, Grantham and other towns also provided swimming baths during the 1880s.[38]

During Victoria's reign football evolved from inter-village mauls and public school kickabouts into two highly sophisticated team games. The Football Association formed in 1863 inaugurated its annual Challenge Cup competition in 1871, but for some time the clubs consisted of gentlemen amateurs and only as popular support increased were they supplemented by paid professional players. The Lincolnshire Senior Cup competition was inaugurated in 1881–82 and was won for the first three seasons by Spilsby. In 1884 the various clubs in Lincoln united to form Lincoln City with the object of taking away the trophy from the presumptuous little east-coast town. In 1888 the twelve top professional clubs in England formed the Football League; in 1892 they enlarged it to sixteen clubs and also formed a second division, whose twelve members included Lincoln City and Grimsby. By 1913 Kelly's directory of the county listed seventy sports clubs, including thirteen cricket, thirteen football and thirteen golf, as well as six lawn tennis, five bowls and three rowing.[39]

Clubs were formed not only for sports but also for other interests. The second Reform Act of 1868 had enfranchised all male householders in the towns and was followed by a growth of political clubs. Working men's clubs were also formed, some of which were of a political character.

By the middle of the nineteenth century there were libraries belonging to mechanics' institutes or churches in most Lincolnshire towns, but in general the quality of the provision was poor. Not until 1892 did Lincoln city council adopt the Libraries and Museums Act; in 1893 a ballot of Grantham ratepayers rejected adoption of the act. Lincoln's library was opened in 1895 on the upper floor of the Butter Market, but few other towns had one until after the turn of the century. After 1893 the establishment of a free public library in a borough no longer needed the approval of a ballot

[38] Ibid., p. 130.
[39] G. H. Grosse, 'Lincoln City Football Club', *Lincs. Mag.*, 1 (1932–34), p. 299.

of the ratepayers and the occasion of Queen Victoria's jubilee stimulated interest in the idea, but the decisive factor was the availability of generous grants by the Scottish-American steel magnate Andrew Carnegie and other private benefactors. Between 1903 and 1906 Carnegie contributed to the construction of libraries at Scunthorpe, Boston, Gainsborough, Stamford and Ashby and later gave £10,000 towards the construction of the present Lincoln central library opened in 1913. However, even with the Carnegie buildings the library service was still restricted to the product of a penny rate, and this was not sufficient to provide an adequate service. Their clients were working class, the surroundings were poor and the hours were restricted.[40]

NEWSPAPERS

An important part of any library was its newsroom, and in the second half of the century there was a great increase in the number of county newspapers. The main one continued to be the *Stamford Mercury*, which about 1870 was reckoned to make £10,000 p.a. for its proprietors, the Newcomb family. In 1852 its circulation averaged 12,060 copies weekly in Lincolnshire, Rutland and adjacent parts compared with 1,540 copies of the *Lincolnshire Chronicle*, 450 of the *Boston Herald*, 400 of the *Lincolnshire, Boston and Spalding Free Press* and 300 of the *Lincolnshire Times*. Until the *Spalding Free Press* was launched as a reform journal by Henry Watkinson in 1847, newspaper production had been confined to Stamford, Boston and Lincoln, but from 1854 there was a great expansion of the cheap weekly press in the county, stimulated by the abolition of stamp duty on newspapers in 1855. Successful papers launched in 1854 included the *Boston Guardian* and the *Grantham Journal*, but Grimsby had a succession of short-lived newspapers.[41]

Before 1854 most papers had tried to serve the whole county, or at least a large part of it, but many of the new penny papers gave more attention to particular towns, where many more people could now afford a weekly paper. After 1854 a new newspaper was launched somewhere in the county almost every year, and some became established parts of the local scene. These penny papers often had too small a circulation to be partisan and adopted a neutral

[40] Report to library sub-committee of Lincolnshire County Council on 6 December 1977; *Kelly's Directory*, 1913, p. 371; *Lincolnshire Echo*, 16 December 1976; Quilter, *Mid-Victorian Grantham*, p. 57.
[41] R. J. Olney, *Lincolnshire Politics 1832–1885*, London, 1973, pp. 85, 87.

political position, though by 1880 several did have pronounced political views. The need for a substantial Conservative paper in the Boston area led to the launching of the *Lincolnshire Standard* in July 1912; in the course of the next seventy years, under the direction of the Robinson family, this absorbed most other Lincolnshire papers to form the dominant group in the county. The growing resort of Skegness could support two newspapers by 1914, but Scunthorpe did not have one of its own until after that date.[42]

THE END OF TURNPIKES

The reformers of the 1830s had made little change to the system of highway maintenance; the main effect of the Highways Act of 1835 had been to reduce the control of justices of the peace over parishes' highway functions. The Public Health Act of 1848 made local boards of health responsible for roads in their areas and the Highways Act of 1862 allowed quarter sessions to form highways districts in rural areas. Some parishes became local boards of health to avoid inclusion in a highway district, but in fact very few such districts were formed in Lincolnshire. By 1865 nearly all of Nottinghamshire and Leicestershire had been formed into highway districts, but there was only one in Lincolnshire.[43]

The opening of railways reduced long distance road traffic and so turnpike trusts and bridge companies had less income to spend on maintenance. This led to the closure of Fosdyke bridge in 1868; only after a new act made the Holland magistrates responsible for the bridge was it repaired at public expense and reopened in 1871; the tolls continued until 1890. In the 1870s the house of commons started to bring the turnpike system to an end by allowing acts to lapse when they came up for renewal. Six of the Lincolnshire trusts had already lapsed by 1866, including those for the Lincoln–Horncastle and Bawtry–Hainton roads and some shorter roads. Toll bars were abolished on the Great North Road, the Lincoln–Barton road and many of the county's other main roads between June 1870 and November 1872. All of the other turnpikes in Lincolnshire ceased by 1878 except for the Bourne section of the Lincoln to Peterborough road, which was finally freed in 1882.[44]

---

[42] Ibid., p. 87; L. Robinson, *Boston's Newspapers*, Boston, 1974, p. 33.
[43] Smellie, *A History of Local Government*, pp. 83, 91; S. and B. Webb, *The Story of the King's Highway*, London, 1913, pp. 208, 209, 234; Golding, *Local Government*, p. 114.
[44] W. H. Wheeler, *A History of the Fens of South Lincolnshire*, Boston, 2nd edn 1896, pp. 449, 450.

Under the Highways and Locomotives Act of 1878, main roads came under the supervision of the county surveyor and most roads so classified were former turnpikes. The end of the turnpikes was followed by a revival of road usage. The well-to-do drove coaches; bicycles gave the less well off the chance to enjoy the countryside; rural tramways were proposed and restrictions on steam road vehicles were relaxed. Finally the motor car appeared and soon led to demands for improved road maintenance and the provision of warning signs at places which had posed no dangers in the quiet days of horse transport.

LOCAL GOVERNMENT REORGANIZATION

By 1885 local authorities had been created to deal with health, highways, burials, education, poor law and the police. Their boundaries often overlapped and local government presented a chaos of areas, functions, authorities and rates. Acts of 1888 and 1894 started to bring order out of this chaos by establishing organs of local government which survived until 1974. In most places powers were divided between county councils and district councils, but in very large towns such as Lincoln powers were combined in county borough councils. District councils were of three types: municipal boroughs, urban district councils and rural district councils. Urban district councils replaced the former local boards of health and improvement commissioners in towns such as Gainsborough and Spalding. By 1894 most unincorporated Lincolnshire towns had a local board and so became urban districts, but there were a few surprising exceptions: Alford, Bourne and substantial suburbs such as Skirbeck and Bracebridge contined to be governed by parish authorities. Mablethorpe, Woodhall Spa, Bracebridge and Frodingham as well as Alford and Bourne were created urban districts after 1894, but Caistor and other small towns remained parishes within rural districts.

Rural districts replaced the rural sanitary districts, which embraced all areas outside the boroughs and urban districts. The new rural districts, unlike the unions on which they were based, could not cross county boundaries and in several cases this created very small districts. Crowland was the only Lincolnshire parish in Peterborough union and became a rural district on its own. Three small rural districts around Stamford had their headquarters in the town and shared the same clerk and offices. Separate county councils for Holland, Lindsey and Kesteven were elected by the ratepayers, except in Lincoln and Grimsby, which became county boroughs. Grimsby was not in the original list of county boroughs, but by absorbing Clee-with-Weelsby it achieved the necessary size and became one in 1891.[45]

Grimsby corporation had adopted the Public Health Act and appointed a medical officer of health in 1874, but only after 1891 did the corporation start to take seriously its responsibility for public health. On 25 March 1893 it opened a sewage and salt water pumping station, and a further eleven miles of new drains were completed in 1895. The salt water was to flush the sewers, water the streets and extinguish fires. Lincoln had been similarly reluctant and had only accepted a tender for its underground sewerage scheme in September 1876 following a High Court order; even then the system did not extend into Bracebridge. The parish made sewerage arrangements with the city in 1881, but only in 1912 were the mains of the parish connected with Lincoln's sewerage system.[46]

TRAMS AND ELECTRICITY

As Victorian towns grew, some workers lived far from their place of work and horse-drawn buses appeared on regular routes at regular times. Poor road surfaces led to vehicles being put on rails and such tramways gained popularity after 1870. A Tramways Act made it easier to establish such systems though it allowed compulsory purchase by a local authority after twenty-one years. Tramways were also proposed as cheap substitutes for railways in some rural areas, and the first tramway scheme in Lincolnshire appeared in 1871 as part of efforts to revive the port of Boston. A line was to run to Freiston Shore and along a pier to deep water in the Wash. Efforts to raise support by modifying the scheme to include lines through other Boston streets were ineffective and it was abandoned. Other rural tramways were proposed during the 1880s from Brigg to Lincoln and south-eastwards from Alford but were ineffective; the Alford and Sutton tramway, opened in 1884, was forced to close in 1889 when faced with competition from a standard gauge railway.[47]

Horse-operated urban tramways in Lincoln and Grimsby were more successful and were established in the early 1880s, replacing

[45] Wickstead, *Lincolnshire, Lindsey*, pp. 70, 147.

[46] Gillett, *Grimsby*, pp. 280, 281, 283; White and Tye, *Grimsby and Cleethorpes*, p. 24; *Kelly's Directory*, 1913, p. 245; *Lincolnshire Chronicle*, 27 November 1975, 23 September 1976; *Lincolnshire Echo*, 11 November 1978.

[47] R. E. Pearson and R. O. Knibbs, *Towns and Transport*, Derby, 1974, p. 19; N. R. Wright, *The Railways of Boston*, Boston, 1971, p. 39; W. H. Bett and J. C. Gillham, *The Tramways of the East Midlands*, London, 1979, p. 10.

earlier horse omnibuses. The Great Grimsby Street Tramways Co. was a subsidiary of the Provincial Tramways Co. Ltd and its services started on 4 June 1881. The main line ran from Bargate to their depot on the eastern boundary of New Clee, with a branch extending down Freeman Street as far as Hainton Square. A horse bus extended the service to Cleethorpes and the tramway itself gradually crept along that road to reach Albert Street in 1898. In the year 1898–99 they carried over 1.7 million passengers. Lincoln's horse trams started in 1883 on a single track running between St Benedict's Square and their depot in Bracebridge. Proposed extensions to the north, east and west were never built. By 1902 the company had ten cars and twenty-four horses and the following year, for the first time, they carried over a million passengers. About the turn of the century the Lincoln and Grimsby tramways like others throughout the kingdom were the subject of proposals for electrification, related to the introduction of a public electricity supply into those two towns. [48]

Cleethorpes had briefly experimented with electric street lighting in 1882, but for many years electricity generation in Lincolnshire was restricted to small dynamos or large generators belonging to individual concerns such as the Frodingham Iron and Steel Co. and Boston docks. Robey and Co. provided portable generators for the electrical illumination of Lincoln cathedral on the occasion of Queen Victoria's jubilees of 1887 and 1897. For many years the advocates of public electricity supplies were a minority on most town councils. Lincoln, Grimsby, Sleaford, Stamford and Grantham were each provided with a public supply between 1898 and 1903, but other towns had to wait another ten years at least. Lincoln corporation started to supply power on 20 December 1898 from their works, whose shell still stands on Brayford North. In 1909 they reached an agreement with Clayton and Shuttleworth, who had a large generating plant. Grimsby started to provide a public supply in February 1901. Sleaford urban district council opened its own generating station on 1 September 1901, and by 1903 the Urban Electric Supply Co. had opened power stations at Grantham and Stamford. Barton-on-Humber had a public supply from 1 August 1913, but most towns still had to wait, though in

---

[48] P. White, *Passenger Transport in Lincoln*, London, 1974, p. 4; White and Tye, *Grimsby and Cleethorpes*, pp. 14, 15; Boswell and Storey, *Grimsby as it Was*, p. 25; Bett and Gillham, op. cit., p. 9; Hill, *Victorian Lincoln*, p. 227; *Lincolnshire Echo*, 8 February 1979.

Cleethorpes and Frodingham street lighting was provided by excess power purchased from a local private generator.[49]

After electricity became available in Lincoln and Grimsby, horse trams were soon replaced by electrically-powered vehicles. In Grimsby, this involved the extension and doubling of their main line as well as electrification; for the Cleethorpes section the tram company built their own power station. The system was working by 1902 and the number of passengers rose from two million in the last full year of horse operation to five million by 1903 and ten million by 1913.[50]

In Lincoln the initiative for electrification of the trams came from the corporation as early as 1899 but efforts to buy out the old company were resisted until 1904; the corporation took over with effect from 1 July that year. The horse trams ceased on 22 July 1905 and wagonettes provided a service until the electric trams started running on 23 November. The delay arose because the corporation had decided to install the Griffith-Bedell surface contact system rather than the more usual overhead wires. Under this system the power was supplied from metal studs, between the tracks, which became live when energized by a magnetic skate carried under the tram. It soon gave problems and was replaced by overhead wires in 1919. Lincoln's tramline was small in comparison with other cities and as late as 1915 it was carrying only one and three-quarter million passengers a year.[51]

Electric tramways were the main form of public street transport during the first quarter of the twentieth century, but the internal combustion engine, better suspension and improved road surfaces allowed experiments to revive buses. In June 1900 a bus company started services in Lincoln with two vehicles running between the Arboretum and West Parade but it ceased on 6 July 1901. Another bus service was proposed in 1913 but protracted negotiations were brought to an end by the outbreak of war.[52]

---

[49] White and Tye, *Grimsby and Cleethorpes*, pp. 18, 21; *Lincolnshire Echo*, 21 February 1975, 5 July 1977; Middleton, 'General Living Conditions in Lincoln, 1840–1914', p. 44; Boswell and Storey, op. cit., p. 18; *Kelly's Directory*, 1913, pp. 201, 325; N. C. Birch, *Stamford — An Industrial History*, Lincoln, 1972, p. 14; J. B. Ball, 'Barton Candle Factory', *Lincolnshire Life*, 17 no. 3 (1977), p. 49.
[50] White and Tye, *Grimsby and Cleethorpes*, pp. 15–18.
[51] White, *Passenger Transport in Lincoln*, p. 4; Bett and Gillham, *Tramways of the East Midlands*, pp. 10, 50, 58; Hill, *Victorian Lincoln*, p. 227.
[52] White, op. cit., p. 4; *Lincolnshire Chronicle*, 14 March 1975, 15 May 1975, 2 July 1976.

The electric telegraph had been in use since the early days of railways and in 1891 a public telephone service became available in Lincoln when the National Telephone Company opened an exchange. When the Post Office took over in 1912, the Lincoln exchange had 250 subscribers.[53] By then another door had been opened into the future when Guglielmo Marconi had used equipment powered by a Hornsby generator to make the first experimental wireless signals.

Since 1845 the railways had contributed to great changes in the towns and industry of Lincolnshire, and the county's great engineering firms had developed world markets for their agricultural machinery and other equipment. More than half of the county's inhabitants lived in its towns and this drift from the country was to continue during the twentieth century. Lincolnshire's small towns had suffered from and with the agricultural depression, but in the years before 1914 the main towns and the county's small resorts basked in the comfort of Edwardian sunshine.

Lincolnshire towns today in their location, their relative size and their physical appearance are much as they were when the First World War broke out. They may have a fringe of new housing added to their outer margins; they may have been adapted to the motor car by means of car parks and ring roads, but they remain at heart creations of Georgian and Victorian enterprise. The twentieth century has elaborated or modified the historic structure and accomplished enormous social changes. Individual entrepreneurs — the Rustons, Marshalls, Hornsbys and their like — have vanished and industrial power resides with anonymous boards of directors who play no part in local life. Those who still go to the seaside instead of taking a package holiday in the Mediterranean go by car, perhaps towing a caravan, rather than by train. The complex of services required to support both towns and villages — power, health, education, media of communications — were tentatively started in Victorian times but have been developed far beyond the comprehension of Victorian imagination.

[53] *Lincolnshire Echo*, 10 March 1976.

APPENDIX I

LIST OF THE TOWNS IN LINCOLNSHIRE

NOTES

1 Columns 1 and 2 are based on information in White's 1856 *Directory* and list those places which had a market at that date, plus a few marked * where the market had ceased before 1856.

2 Column 3 shows the other urban districts which developed after 1856. Urban district councils were set up in those places which had got a local board by 1894 (except Clee with Weelsby, which had already merged with Grimsby) and any other towns or parishes which were predominantly urban, even where they did not have a market.

3 Columns 4 and 5 show the haphazard use of the word town in 1982. The Local Government Act of 1972 ended the former urban districts and municipal boroughs and some of them became parishes. The only old boroughs which became new district councils were Lincoln, Scunthorpe and Grimsby; the others became parts of larger districts, which in the cases of Boston, Cleethorpes and Glanford (Brigg) took their name from a former borough or urban district. The 1972 act allowed any parish council to call its parish a town by a simple vote of the council, irrespective of whether it had a market, and column 4 shows parishes which have done so. The letters NA indicate those places which do not have parish councils and so cannot vote to become towns.

4 Planners have their own criteria, and column 5 shows places classified as towns in the Structure Plan prepared by the Lincolnshire County Council. Several of the towns in their list include suburbs in adjoining parishes; 'the Deepings' combines Market Deeping with Deeping St James. The letter (H) indicates those places which are now in the new county of Humberside created on 1 April 1974.

5 Places which were municipal boroughs are shown in capitals and marked †; each of them, except Louth, sent two members to parliament until 1832. Those places which were urban districts under the Local

253

Government Act of 1894 are marked (UD). Crowland was made into a rural district containing only one parish and had virtually the same powers as an urban district.

6 Brumby and Frodingham UDC and Scunthorpe UDC were amalgamated with adjacent areas to form the urban district of Scunthorpe and Frodingham in 1919. This became a borough in 1930.

7 Clee with Weelsby local board amalgamated with Grimsby borough in 1888.

8 Partney market was moved to Spilsby in 1613 or 1616 because of plague; it did not move back.

Towns (and former towns*) shown in White's 1856 Directory		3. Other places which became urban	Towns in 1982	
1. Over 2000 inhabitants in 1851	2. Less than 2000 inhabitants in 1851	districts by 1914	4. Parishes which have voted to be towns	5. Towns listed in LCC Structure Plan
Alford (UD)			Alford	Alford
Barton-upon-Humber (UD)			Barton-upon-Humber	(H)
	Binbrook*			
	Bolingbroke*			
BOSTON†			NA	Boston
			Bottesford	(H)
Bourne (UD)			Bourne	Bourne
		Bracebridge (UD)		
Brigg (UD)			Brigg	(H)
		Broughton (UD)	Broughton	(H)
		Brumby and Frodingham (UD) (see note 6)	NA	(H)
	Burgh-le-Marsh			
	Burton Stather*			(H)
Caistor			Caistor	Caistor
		Cleethorpes with Thrunscoe (UD)	NA	(H)
		Clee with Weelsby local board (see note 7)		(H)
	Corby*			
Crowland (RD) (see note 5)				
Crowle (UD)				(H)
	Donington*			
	Epworth			(H)

Towns (and former towns*) shown in White's 1856 Directory		3. Other places which became urban districts by 1914	Towns in 1982	
1. Over 2000 inhabitants in 1851	2. Less than 2000 inhabitants in 1851		4. Parishes which have voted to be towns	5. Towns listed in LCC Structure Plan
	Folkingham			
Gainsborough (UD)			NA	Gainsborough
GRANTHAM†			NA	Grantham
GRIMSBY†			(Grimsby borough)	(H)
Holbeach (UD)				Holbeach
Horncastle (UD)			Horncastle	Horncastle
			Immingham	(H)
Kirton-in-Holland*				
	Kirton-in-Lindsey		Kirton-in-Lindsey	(H)
LINCOLN†			(Lincoln City)	Lincoln
Long Sutton (UD)				Long Sutton
LOUTH†			Louth	Louth
		Mablethorpe (UD)	Mablethorpe and Sutton	Mablethorpe
	Market Deeping*			The Deepings
Market Rasen (UD)			Market Rasen	Market Rasen
	Market Stainton*			
			North Hykeham	
	Partney* (see note 8)			
		Roxby-cum-Risby (UD)		(H)
		Ruskington (UD)		
	Saltfleet*			

Towns (and former towns*) shown in White's 1856 Directory		3. Other places which became urban districts by 1914	Towns in 1982	
1. Over 2000 inhabitants in 1851	2. Less than 2000 inhabitants in 1851		4. Parishes which have voted to be towns	5. Towns listed in LCC Structure Plan
		Scunthorpe (UD) (see note 6)	(Scunthorpe borough)	(H)
		Skegness (UD)	Skegness	Skegness
Sleaford (UD)			Sleaford	Sleaford
Spalding (UD)			NA	Spalding
	Spilsby (see note 8)		Spilsby	Spilsby
STAMFORD†			Stamford	Stamford
		Sutton Bridge (UD)		
Swineshead				
	Tattershall			
	Wainfleet			
	Winterton (UD)		Winterton	(H)
		Woodhall Spa (UD)		
	Wragby			
22	18	12	19	19

S

TURNPIKE TRUSTS IN LINCOLNSHIRE IN CHRONOLOGICAL ORDER OF FORMATION

Year formed	Trust and roads	Approx. mileage	Date freed from tolls	Notes
1726	Great North Road (part) Spitlegate (Grantham) to Little Drayton, Notts.	29 (10 in Lincs.)	WC–FB 1.11.1870 FB–LD 1.11.1872	Great North Road between Stamford (S) and Little Drayton (LD) subsequently reorganized as three trusts; Stamford to South Witham (SW), Witham Common (WC) to Foston Bridge (FB), Foston Bridge to Little Drayton
1739	Great North Road (part) Stamford to Grantham	20 (10 in Lincs.)	WC–FB 1.11.1870 S–SW 31.12.1873	
1739	Lincoln–Wragby–Baumber 1759 extension to Horncastle and further into Lincoln	18 3		At Hainton and Elkington joined Bawtry–Hainton trust
	Wragby to Hainton	6		
	1780 Hainton to Elkington	8	1.11.1865	
1749	Great North Road (part) Wansford to Stamford	6 (0 in Lincs.)		Wansford to Stamford was in Northamptonshire
	1756 Stamford to Bourne	10	1.11.1871	
	1776 extensions at Stamford and Bourne	2		1776 trust rebuilt Stamford town hall
1756	Lincoln Roads Lincoln to Dunham and Littleborough (Saxilby Road)	17	1.11.1875	

	Road	Miles	Date	Notes
	Road at foot of South Common (Branston Road)	1		
	Lincoln to Bracebridge (Newark Road)	1		
	Lincoln to Graby with branch to Waddington (Sleaford Road)	13	1.11.1872	At Graby joined Lincoln Heath trust
	1777 extension Bracebridge to Potter Hill (Newark Road) and up Canwick Hill (Branston Road)	2		Potter Hill on county boundary
		8		
	1841 Canwick Road etc. in Lincoln	1		
1756	*Lincoln Heath to Peterborough trust* Graby (north of Sleaford) to Peterborough			At Graby joined Lincoln Roads trust Partly in Northants.
	1. North: Graby–Sleaford?	6	1.11.1875	1860 the districts of the trust reorganized as follows: 1 & 2 Sleaford; 3 & 4 Bourne; 5 Billingborough
	2. North-east: Great Hale–Sleaford	9		
	3. Middle: Sleaford?–Market Deeping	25	1.11.1882	
	4. West: Bourne–Colsterworth	13	1.11.1875	
	5. South-east: Donington–Hacconby	12		
	6. South: Market Deeping–Peterborough	8 (0 in Lincs.)	1860	
	1822 Bourne–Spalding	12		
1757	*Spalding–Deeping–Maxey*	12 (11 in Lincs.)		At Maxey (Northants.) joined Lincoln Heath trust Partly in Northants.
	1843 new road at Deeping St James	1	1.11.1878	
1758	*Donington trust* Donington (Bridge End) to Boston via Swineshead	10		At Great Hale and Donington joined Lincoln Heath trust
	Swineshead to Great Hale	6	7.7.1877	
	Kirton End to Langrick Ferry	2		
	Boston to Bicker haven	8		
1759	*Grantham to Nottingham*	25 (6 in Lincs.)	1.11.1876	Eastern district — Lincs. Western district — Notts.

Year formed	Trust and roads	Approx. mileage	Date freed from tolls	Notes
1759	*Leadenham–Newark–Mansfield* Eastern district Newark to top of Leadenham hill	11 (6 in Lincs.)	30.6.1870	Most roads of this trust were in Notts.; western district freed from tolls 1.11.1867
1762	*Deeping to Morcott (Rutland)*	16 (9 in Lincs.)	1.11.1872	At east end joined Spalding–Maxey trust; at west end joined Peterborough–Leicester trust of 1754; passed through Stamford
1764	*Spalding to Tydd St Mary* High road via Holbeach, with branch Long Sutton to Sutton Wash 1827 low road across South Holland fen	16 3 ?	1.11.1866	At Tydd joined turnpike of 1765 to Wisbech (Cambs.) 1765 new turnpike in Norfolk from Sutton Wash to King's Lynn
1764	*Spalding to Donington* Branch Gosberton to Bicker haven	10 2	1.11.1865	At Donington and Bicker haven joined Donington trust
1765	*Great Grimsby haven to Wold Newton church* Branch from Nuns Farm to Irby	9 4	1856	Branch to Irby actually established later
1765	*Bawtry to Hainton trust* First district Bawtry to Louth Branch to Hainton	47 (34 in Lincs.) 3	1.11.1857	Part of first district in Notts. 1765 act included other roads not improved. At Bawtry joined Great North Road. At Hainton and Elkington joined Lincoln–Wragby–Baumber trust. At Louth joined other trusts
	Second district or *Dexthorpe trust*, Louth to Ulceby Cross	12	1.11.1876	Second district joined Spilsby trust (1765) at Ulceby Cross
1765	*Barton to Riseholme (Lincoln)* Branch to Melton Ross Branch to Caistor 1786 roads in Brigg and Caistor	35 5 9 1	1.11.1872	

Year	Trust / route	Gates	Ended	Notes
1765	*Spilsby trust*			
	Alford to Boston, and branch to Cowbridge	27	1.11.1878	At Ulceby Cross joined Dexthorpe trust
1770	*Louth trust*			
	Saltfleet to Louth	12	1.11.1878	
	Louth to Horncastle	14		
1772	*Spalding barrier bank*			Flood relief bank. Barrier bank (5 miles) liable to tolls since 1665. Part of turnpike near Glinton was in Northants. 1772 Act lapsed, but tolls still collected. 1838 part declared to be a turnpike for official purposes
	Spalding via Welland bank to Glinton on Lincoln Heath trust (avoiding Crowland)	17 (13 in Lincs.)	(Act lapsed 1793)	
	1838 Spalding high bridge to Brotherhouse bar declared a turnpike again	5	1.11.1871	
1773	*Oakham trust*			Mainly in Rutland. At Stamford joined Great North Road and other trusts
	Stamford to Oakham	11 (2 in Lincs.)	1.11.1871	
	1795 Oakham to Greetham	8 (0 in Lincs.)		At Greetham joined Great North Road
1780	Melton Mowbray to Grantham	15 (6 in Lincs.)	1.11.1875	Part in Leics.
1793	Sleaford to Tattershall	13	1.11.1875	Included bridge at Tattershall
1803	Scartho to Louth	15	1.11.1877	At Scartho joined Grimsby to Wold Newton turnpike
1804	*Bridge End trust*			At Bridge End joined Lincoln Heath trust. At Grantham joined Great North Road and other trusts
	Spittlegate (Grantham) to Bridge End (near Donington)	16	1.11.1872	
1817	Crowland to Eye	5 (1 in Lincs.)	1.11.1878	Mostly in Northants. At Eye joined Peterborough to Thorney turnpike (1792); Wisbech to Thorney road turnpiked 1810
1826	Swineshead to Fosdyke	7	1.11.1877	At Swineshead joined Donington trust; crossed it again at Sutterton

RAILWAYS BUILT IN LINCOLNSHIRE

NOTES

1 Dates are not given for parts of GNR, MSLR and others which lay outside Lincolnshire.

2 The position of most towns and junctions referred to are shown on figure 27 on page 130.

KEY TO RAILWAYS REFERRED TO IN THE TEXT AND IN THIS APPENDIX

AJR	Axholme Joint Railway
ANBEJR	Ambergate, Nottingham, Boston and Eastern Junction Railway
AST	Alford and Sutton Tramway
BDJR	Birmingham and Derby Junction Railway
BER	Bourne and Essendine Railway
BILR	Barton and Immingham Light Railway
BMCR	Boston and Midland Counties Railway
ECR	Eastern Counties Railway (later GER)
ELBR	Edenham and Little Bytham Railway
ELR	East Lincolnshire Railway
EMR	Eastern and Midland Railway (later MGNJR)
FWR	Firsby and Wainfleet Railway
GCR	Great Central Railway (formerly MSLR)
GDLR	Grimsby District Light Railway
GER	Great Eastern Railway (formerly ECR)
GGSJR	Great Grimsby and Sheffield Junction Railway (later MSLR)
GIER	Grimsby and Immingham Electric Railway
GMLR	Goole and Marshland Light Railway
GNR	Great Northern Railway
GNGEJR	Great Northern and Great Eastern Joint Railway
GWR	Great Western Railway
HCR	Humber Commercial Railway
HKJR	Horncastle and Kirkstead Junction Railway
HSR	Hull and Selby Railway

IALR	Isle of Axholme Light Railway
LBR	London and Birmingham Railway (later LNWR)
LDECR	Lancashire, Derbyshire and East Coast Railway
LDR	Lynn and Dereham Railway
LECR	Louth and East Coast Railway
LER	Lynn and Ely Railway
LLR	Lincoln and Louth Railway
LNWR	London and North Western Railway
LSBR	Lynn and Sutton Bridge Railway
LSR	Leicester and Swannington Railway
Leeds SR	Leeds and Selby Railway
LYR	Lancashire and Yorkshire Railway
MCR	Midland Counties Railway (later MR)
MER	Midland and Eastern Railway (later EMR)
MGNJR	Midland and Great Northern Joint Railway (formerly EMR)
MR	Midland Railway
MR(SP)	Midland Railway (Syston and Peterborough branch)
MSLR	Manchester, Sheffield and Lincolnshire Railway (later GCR)
NBR	Norwich and Brandon Railway
NER	North Eastern Railway
NLLR	North Lindsey Light Railway
NMR	North Midland Railway (later MR)
NSR	Norwich and Spalding Railway
PWSR	Peterborough, Wisbech and Sutton Railway
SAMR	Sheffield, Ashton-under-Lyne and Manchester Railway (later MSLR)
SBR	Spalding and Bourne Railway
SER	Skegness Extension Railway
SER	Stamford and Essendine Railway
SFR	Spilsby and Firsby Railway
SLER	Sheffield and Lincolnshire Extension Railway (later MSLR)
SLJR	Sheffield and Lincolnshire Junction Railway (later MSLR)
SWR	Sutton and Willoughby Railway
SYR	South Yorkshire Railway
TAGR	Trent, Ancholme and Grimsby Railway (later MSLR)
WPGR	Wakefield, Pontefract and Goole Railway
YNMR	York and North Midland Railway

Date of opening	Name	Between	Operating company	Approx. mileage	Notes
3.8.1846	MR Nottingham to Lincoln line	MR at Nottingham to Lincoln	MR	31 (9 in Lincs.)	
2.10.1846	MR(SP) east part	Stamford to GER at Peterborough	MR	12 (0 in Lincs.)	Operated by GER until 1.5.1848
1.3.1848	ELR (northern part)	MSLR at Grimsby to Louth	GNR	14	Joint services operated at first by GNR and MSLR
1.3.1848	MSLR (eastern part)	ELR at Grimsby to New Holland	MSLR	16	Joint services operated at first by GNR and MSLR
Goods 20.3.1848 Passengers 1.5.1848	MR(SP) (final part)	MR at Stamford to MR at Melton Mowbray	MR	26 (0 in Lincs.)	
3.9.1848	ELR (middle part)	ELR at Louth to Firsby	GNR	18	
1.10.1848	ELR (final part)	ELR at Firsby to Boston	GNR	15	
17.10.1848	GNR Lincs. loop line (part)	MR at Werrington to Lincoln	GNR	58	
1.11.1848	MSLR (part of main line)	MSLR at Ulceby to Brigg	MSLR	10	
1.11.1848	MSLR (Lincoln branch — part)	MSLR at Barnetby to Market Rasen	MSLR	13	
18.12.1848	MSLR (Lincoln branch — final part)	MSLR at Market Rasen to MR at Lincoln	MSLR	16	
1.3.1849	MSLR (Barton-on-Humber branch)	MSLR at New Holland to Barton-on-Humber	MSLR	3	
2.4.1849	MSLR (main line — part)	MSLR at Brigg to Gainsborough	MSLR	18	Final Lincs. section of original MSLR
9.4.1849	GNR Lincs. loop line (part)	GNR at Lincoln to MSLR at Gainsborough	GNR	16	

Date	Line	Route	Operator	Mileage	Notes
15.7.1850	ANBEJR (part)	Grantham to MR at Colwick (near Nottingham)	GNR	20 (6 in Lincs.)	Operated by ANBEJR until 1852
7.8.1850	MSLR (Leverton Branch)	GNR at Sykes Jn to MSLR at Clarborough Jn	MSLR and GNR	8 (3 in Lincs.)	Used by GNR until 1867
Goods 15.7.1852 Passenger 1.8.1852	GNR towns line (final part)	GNR at Werrington to GNR at Retford	GNR	60 (31 in Lincs.)	
1.8.1853	MSLR (dock extn)	MSLR at Grimsby Town to Royal Dock	MSLR	1	
11.8.1855	HKJR	GNR at Kirkstead to Horncastle	GNR	7½	
1.11.1856	SER	Stamford to GNR at Essendine	GNR	4 (1 in Lincs.)	
16.6.1857	BMCR (part)	GNR at Barkston (near Grantham) to Sleaford	GNR	11	
8.12.1857	ELBR	Edenham to GNR at Little Bytham	Lord Willoughby d'Eresby	4	See pages 193, 250, 253
3.5.1858	NSR (part)	GNR at Spalding to Holbeach	GNR	8	
12.4.1859	BMCR (final part)	BMCR at Sleaford to GNR at Boston	GNR	17	
9.1859	SYR (part)	SYR at Thorne to Keadby	SYR	10 (5 in Lincs.)	
16.5.1860	BER	Bourne to GNR and SER at Essendine	GNR	8	
1.7.1862	NSR (part)	NSR at Holbeach to Sutton Bridge	GNR	9	
6.4.1863	MSLR (Cleethorpes branch)	MSLR at Grimsby to Cleethorpes	MSLR	2	Doubled 1874

Date of opening	Name	Between	Operating company	Approx. mileage	Notes
1.11.1864	LSBR	NSR at Sutton Bridge to Kings Lynn	GNR	13 (1½ in Lincs.)	
14.4.1866	SYR (Keadby extn) and TAGR (part)	SYR at Keadby to Scunthorpe	SYR	4	
1.8.1866	PWSR	NSR at Sutton Bridge to MR at Peterborough	MR	26	
1.8.1866	SBR	GNR at Spalding to BER at Bourne	GNR	9	
1.10.1866	TAGR (part)	TAGR at Scunthorpe to MSLR at Barnetby	MSLR	10	
1.4.1867	GNR (March line)	GNR at Spalding to GER at March	GNR	19 (11 in Lincs.)	Later part of GNGEJR
15.4.1867	GNR (Honington line)	GNR at Lincoln to BMCR at Honington (near Grantham)	GNR	18	
15.7.1867	GNR loop line (final part)	GNR at Gainsborough to GNR at Doncaster	GNR	17 (3 in Lincs.)	Later part of GNGEJR
1.5.1868	SFR	Spilsby to GNR at Firsby	GNR	4½	
Goods 11.9.1871 Passengers 24.10.1871	FWR	GNR at Firsby to Wainfleet	GNR	5	
2.1.1872	GNR (Bourne to Sleaford line)	BER and MER at Bourne to BMCR at Sleaford	GNR	16	
28.7.1873	SER	FWR at Wainfleet to Skegness	GNR	6	
27.9.1875	LLR (part)	GNR at Bardney to Donington-on-Bain	GNR	12	

Date	Line	Description	Owner	Miles	Notes
29.10.1875	GNR (Barkston to Sedgebrook line)	End of BMCR to Sedgebrook on ANBEJR	GNR	4	
Goods 26.6.1876 Passengers 1.12.1876	LLR (part)	LLR at Donington-on-Bain to ELR at Louth	GNR	8	
17.10.1877	LECR	GNR at Louth to Mablethorpe	GNR	10	
6.3.1882	GNGEJR (part)	GNR at Spalding to Ruskington (near Sleaford)	GNR until 1.8.1882	21	
1.8.1882	GNGEJR (final part)	GNGEJR at Ruskington to GNR at Lincoln	GNGEJR	16	
2.4.1884	AST	Alford to Sutton-on-Sea	AST	8	Closed 1889
4.10.1886	SWR	Sutton-on-Sea to GNR at Willoughby	GNR	8	
14.7.1888	SWR (Mablethorpe extn)	SWR at Sutton-on-Sea to LECR at Mablethorpe	GNR	3	
15.5.1893	Saxby extn (part)	EMR at Bourne to Little Bytham	GNR and MR	6	1.7.1893 became part of MGNJR
1.5.1894	Saxby extn (part)	MGNJR at Little Bytham to MR at Saxby	MR	13 (8 in Lincs.)	
8.3.1897	LDECR	Chesterfield to GNR at Lincoln	LDECR	38 (4 in Lincs.)	
8.1.1900	GMLR (part)	NER at Goole to Reedness	GMLR	6	1902 became part of AJR
10.8.1902	AJR (part)	AJR at Reedness to Fockerby	AJR	6	
10.8.1902	AJR (part)	AJR at Reedness to Crowle	AJR	4	
2.1.1905	AJR (final part)	AJR at Crowle to Haxey (near GNR station)	AJR	8	
9.1906	NLLR (part)	GCR at Scunthorpe to West Halton	GCR	6	

Date of opening	Name	Between	Operating company	Approx. mileage	Notes
15.7.1907	NLLR (part)	NLLR at West Halton to Winteringham Branch to Winteringham haven	GCR	2½ ½	
1909	AJR (Hatfield branch)	AJR at Epworth to Hatfield (Yorks.)	AJR	6 (3 in Lincs.)	
3.1.1910	GDLR	Grimsby to Immingham dock	GCR	6	Used by contractors since May 1906: passenger service ended 15.5.1912
Goods 29.6.1910 Passenger 15.5.1912	HCR	GCR at Ulceby to Immingham dock	GCR	6	
1.12.1910	NLLR (Whitton branch)	NLLR at Winteringham to Whitton	GCR	2½	
1.12.1910	BILR (part)	Immingham dock to Killingholme	GCR	3	
1.5.1911	BILR (part)	BILR at Killingholme to GCR at Goxhill	GCR	3	
15.5.1912	GIER	Grimsby to Immingham dock	GCR	6	Parallel to GDLR
1.7.1913	GNR new line	GNR loop line at Coningsby to ELR at Bellwater Jn	GNR	15	
17.11.1913	GIER	Extended onto dock estate	GCR	1	

BIBLIOGRAPHY

NEWSPAPERS, PERIODICALS AND JOURNALS EXTENSIVELY CONSULTED

East Midland Geographer
Economic History Review
Illustrated London News
Industrial Archaeology
Industrial Archaeology Newsletter of the Lincolnshire Local History Society
Industrial Archaeology Review
Journal of the Railway and Canal Historical Society
Lincolnshire Archives Office *Archivists' Reports*
Lincolnshire Chronicle
Lincolnshire Echo
Lincolnshire History and Archaeology
Lincolnshire Industrial Archaeology
Lincolnshire Life
Lincolnshire Magazine
Lincolnshire, Rutland and Stamford Mercury
Local Government Chronicle
Local Historian formerly *Amateur Historian*
Transactions of the Newcomen Society

BOOKS

Albert, W., *The Turnpike Road System in England 1663–1840*, Cambridge, 1972
Allen, C. J., *The Great Eastern Railway*, London, 4th edn 1967
Ambler, R. W., ed., *Workers and Community: The People of Scunthorpe in the 1870s*, Scunthorpe, 1980
Armstrong, R. E., ed., *An Industrial Island: A History of Scunthorpe*, Scunthorpe, 1981
Aston, M., and Bond, J., *The Landscape of Towns*, London, 1976
Audin, E., and others, *Aspects of Life and Work in Nettleton in the Nineteenth Century*, Nettleton, 1980
Bagwell, P. S., *The Transport Revolution from 1770*, London, 1974
Barley, M. W., *The English Farmhouse and Cottage*, London, 1961
——, *The House and Home*, London, 1963
——, *Lincolnshire and the Fens*, Wakefield, 2nd edn 1972

Barnes, E. G., *The Rise of the Midland Railway 1844–74*, London, 1966

Barton-on-Humber Local History Class, *Barton-on-Humber in the 1850s. Part Two. The Town and the People.* Barton-on-Humber, 1978

——, *Barton-on-Humber in the 1850s. Part Three. Parish and Government.* Barton-on-Humber, 1979

Beastall, T. W., *Agricultural Revolution in Lincolnshire*, History of Lincolnshire, vol. 8, Lincoln, 1979

Beckwith, I. S., *The Industrial Archaeology of Gainsborough*, Gainsborough, 1968

——, *The History of Transport and Travel in Gainsborough*, Gainsborough, 1971

——, ed., *The Louth Riverhead*, Louth, 1976

Bett, W. H., and Gillham, J. C., *The Tramways of the East Midlands*, London, 1979

Bidwell, W. H., *Annals of an East Anglian Bank*, Norwich, 1900

Birch, N. C., *Waterways and Railways of Lincoln and the Lower Witham*, Lincoln, 1968

——, *Stamford — An Industrial History*, Lincoln, 1972

Birkbeck, J. D., *A History of Bourne*. Bourne, 2nd edn 1976

Bonnett, H., *Saga of the Steam Plough*, London, 1965

——, *History in Camera — Farming with Steam*, Princes Risborough, 1974

Boston Red Book and Directory for 1897, Boston, 1896

Boston Red Book and Directory for 1913, Boston, 1912

Boswell, D., and Storey, J. M., *Grimsby as it Was*, Nelson, 1974

Bowen, A. R., and Willard, C. P., *The Story of Grantham and its Countryside*, Newark, 1949

Boyes, J., and Russell, R., *The Canals of Eastern England*, Newton Abbot, 1977

Brace, H. W., *History of Seed Crushing in Great Britain*, London, 1960

——, *Gainsborough, some Notes on its History*, Gainsborough, 1965

Brears, C., *Lincolnshire in the Seventeenth and Eighteenth Centuries*, London, 1940

Brears, P. C. D., *The English Country Pottery. Its History and Techniques*, Newton Abbot, 1971

Bruckshaw, F., and McNab, D., *A Century of Achievement: The Story of Lincoln Co-operative Society*, Manchester, 1961

Campbell, W. A., *The Chemical Industry*, London, 1971

Christiansen, R., *The West Midlands*, A Regional History of the Railways of Great Britain: 7, Newton Abbot, 1973

Clarke, R. H., *Steam Engine Builders of Lincolnshire*, Norwich, 1955

Clarke, J. N., *Education in a Market Town: Horncastle*, Chichester, 1976

Cook, A. M., *Boston (Botolph's Town)*, Boston, 2nd edn 1948

Cove-Smith, C., *The Grantham Canal Today*, Long Eaton, 1974

Crick, W. F., and Wadsworth, J. E., *A Hundred Years of Joint Stock Banking*, London, 1936

Curtis, S. J., and Boultwood, M. E. A., *An Introductory History of English Education since 1800*, London, 4th edn 1966

Darby, H. C., *The Draining of the Fens*, Cambridge, 2nd edn 1956

Davis, S. N., *Banking in Boston*, History of Boston, vol. 14, Boston, 1976

Defoe, D., *A Tour through the whole Island of Great Britain*, London, 1724–26 republished 1971

Derry, T. K., and Williams, T. I., *A Short History of Technology*, Oxford, 1960

Dobson, E., *A Rudimentary Treatise on the manufacture of bricks and tiles* (1850) reprinted as *Journal of Ceramic History*, 5 (1971)

D'Orley, A. A., *The Humber Ferries*, Knaresborough, 1968

Dow, G., *Great Central*, London, 1959

Dudley, H. E., *The History and Antiquities of the Scunthorpe and Frodingham District*, Scunthorpe, 1931

Elvin, L., *Lincoln as it Was*, I, Nelson, 1974

——, *Lincoln as it Was*, II, Nelson, 1976

——, *Lincoln as it Was*, III, Nelson, 1979

Exley, C. L., *A History of the Torksey and Mansfield China Factories*, Lincoln, 1970

Franks, D. L., *South Yorkshire Railway*, Leeds, 1971

Gillett, E., *A History of Grimsby*, London, 1970

Golding, L., *Local Government*, London, 1959

Gordon, D. I., *The Eastern Counties*, A Regional History of the Railways of Great Britain: 5, Newton Abbot, 1968

Gregg, P., *A Social and Economic History of Britain*, London, 5th edn 1965

Grigg, D., *The Agricultural Revolution in South Lincolnshire*, Cambridge, 1966

Grinling, C. H., *The History of the Great Northern Railway*, London, new edn 1966

Hadfield, C., *The Canals of the East Midlands*, Newton Abbot, 2nd edn 1970

——, and Skempton, A. W., *William Jessop, Engineer*, Newton Abbot, 1979

Haining, J., and Tyler, C., *Ploughing by Steam*, Hemel Hempstead, 1970

Hance, F., *Stamford Theatre and Stamford Racecourse*, History of Stamford, vol. 3, Stamford, *c.* 1975

Hemingway, G. Y., *Newark: Its Railways and Navigation*, Nottingham, 1976

Henthorn, F., ed., *Letters and Papers concerning the establishment of the Trent, Ancholme and Grimsby Railway, 1860–62*, LRS, vol. 70, Lincoln, 1975

Hewlett, H. B., *The Quarries — Ironstone, Limestone and Sand*, Stanton, 1935, reprinted Market Overton 1979

Hill, J. W. F., ed., *The Letters and Papers of the Banks Family of Revesby Abbey 1704–60*, LRS, vol. 45, Lincoln, 1952

——, *Georgian Lincoln*, Cambridge, 1966

——, *Victorian Lincoln*, Cambridge, 1974

Hills, R. L., *Machines, Mills and Uncountable Costly Necessities*, Norwich, 1967

Hindley, G., *A History of Roads*, London, 1971

Holden's Directory, London, 1805–6–7

Holm, S. A., *The Heavens Reflect Our Labours*, Scunthorpe, 1974

——, *Brick and Tile Making in South Humberside*, Scunthorpe, 1976

Holmes, C., *Seventeenth-Century Lincolnshire*, History of Lincolnshire, vol. 7, Lincoln, 1980

Honeybone, M., *The Book of Grantham*, Buckingham, 1980

Hoskins, W. G., *The Making of the English Landscape*, London, 1955

Hudson, K., *Industrial Archaeology — An Introduction*, London, 1963

Hughes, W. H., *A Century of Traction Engines*, Newton Abbot, 1968

Jackson, G., *Grimsby and the Haven Company*, Grimsby, 1971

——, *The Trade and Shipping of Eighteenth-Century Hull*, York, 1975

Kelly's Directory of Lincolnshire, London, 1st edn 1885, 2nd edn 1889, 3rd edn 1892, 4th edn 1896, 5th edn 1900, 6th edn 1905, 7th edn 1909, 8th edn 1913

Kelly, T., and E., *Books for the People. An Illustrated History of the British Public Library*, London, 1977

Lambert, R. S., *The Railway King — A Study of George Hudson and the Business Morals of his Times*, London, 1934

Leighton-Boyce, J. A. S. L., *Smiths the Bankers 1658–1958*, London, 1958

Leleux, R., *The East Midlands*, A Regional History of the Railways of Great Britain: 9, Newton Abbot, 1976

Lewis, M. J. T., *Dunham Bridge — A Memorial History*, Lincoln, 1978

——, and Wright, N. R., *Boston as a Port*, Lincoln, 1974

Mann, J. E., *Clay Tobacco Pipes from Excavations in Lincoln 1970–74*, Lincoln Archaeological Trust Monograph Series xv–1, London, 1977

Marshall, J., *The Lancashire and Yorkshire Railway*, Newton Abbot, 1969

Mathias, P., *The Brewing Industry in England 1700–1830*, Cambridge, 1959

Matthews, P. W., and Tuke, A. W., *History of Barclays Bank Ltd*, London, 1926

Measom, G., *Official Illustrated Guide to the Great Northern Railway*, London, 2nd edn 1861

Molyneux, F. H., and Wright, N. R., *An Atlas of Boston*, History of Boston, vol. 10, Boston, 1974

Muir, A., *The History of Baker Perkins*, Cambridge, 1968

Newman, B., *One hundred years of good company*, Lincoln, 1957

North, T., *The Church Bells of the County and City of Lincoln*, Leicester, 1882

Olney, R. J., *Lincolnshire Politics 1832–1885*, London, 1973

——, *Rural Society and County Government in Nineteenth-Century Lincoln-shire*, History of Lincolnshire, vol. 10, Lincoln, 1979

Owen, D. M., ed., *The Minute Books of the Spalding Gentlemen's Society 1712–1755*, LRS, vol. 73, Lincoln, 1981

Page, C. J., *History of the Ancholme Navigation*, Lincoln, 1969

——, *Sleaford — An Industrial History*, Lincoln, 1974

Page, W., ed., *The Victoria History of the County of Lincoln*, II, London, 1906

Pearson, R. E., and Knibbs, R. O., *Towns and Transport*, Derby, 1974

Perkins, J. A., *Sheep Farming in Eighteenth- and Nineteenth-Century Lincolnshire*, Lincoln, 1977

Pevsner, N., and Harris, J., *The Buildings of England — Lincolnshire*, London, 1964

Philpotts, R., *The Grantham Canal: early days*, Nottingham, 1978

Pigot and Co., *Directory*, London, *c.* 1830

Plumb, J. H., *England in the Eighteenth Century*, Pelican History of England, vol. 7, London, 1950

Pointer, M., *Hornsby's of Grantham 1815–1918*, Grantham, 1976

——, and Knapp, M. G., *Bygone Grantham*, I, Grantham, 1977

——, ——, *Bygone Grantham*, II, Grantham, 1977

——, ——, *Bygone Grantham*, III, Grantham, 1978

——. ——. *Bygone Grantham*, IV, Grantham, 1979

Porter, H., *Boston 1800 to 1835 continued to 1868*, Lincoln, 1941–43

Post Office Directory of Lincolnshire, London, 1st edn 1849, 2nd edn 1855, 3rd edn 1861, 4th edn 1868, 5th edn 1876

Priestley, J., *Navigable Rivers and Canals*, London, 1831, reprinted Newton Abbot 1969

Purcell, D., *Cambridge Stone*, London, 1967

Quilter, H. H., *Mid-Victorian Grantham*, Grantham, 1936

——, *Central Grantham — An Historical and Descriptive Sketch*, Grantham, 1938

Riden, P., *The Butterley Company 1790–1830*, Chesterfield, 1973

Robbins, M., *The Railway Age*, London, 1962

Robinson, D. N., *The Book of Louth*, Buckingham, 1979

——, *The Book of the Lincolnshire Seaside*, Buckingham, 1981

Robinson, L., *Boston's Newspapers*, History of Boston, vol. 11, Boston, 1974

Robson, N. G., *Some Notes on the Steam Wagons of Clayton and Shuttleworth Ltd, Lincoln*, Newcastle-upon-Tyne, 1948

Rogers, A., ed., *The Making of Stamford*, Leicester, 1965

——, ed., *Stability and Change. Some Aspects of North and South Rauceby in the Nineteenth Century*, Nottingham, 1969

——, *A History of Lincolnshire*, Henley-on-Thames, 1970

——, and Quinlan, J., *A Short History of the Stamford and Rutland Hospital*, Stamford, 1978

Rolt, L. T. C., *Thomas Telford*, London, 1958

——, *Victorian Engineering*, London, 1970

Royal Commission on Historical Monuments, *The Town of Stamford — An Inventory of Historical Monuments*, London, 1977

Ruddock, J. G., and Pearson, R. E., *The Railway History of Lincoln*, Lincoln, 1974

Russell, R., *Lost Canals of England and Wales*, Newton Abbot, 1971

Russell, R. C., *A History of Schools and Education in Lindsey, Lincolnshire 1800–1902*, Lincoln, 1965–67

——, *Friendly Societies in the Caistor, Binbrook and Brigg Area in the Nineteenth Century*, Nettleton, 1975

Searle, M., *Turnpikes and Toll-Bars*, London, 1930

Smellie, K. B., *A History of Local Government*, London, 1963

Smith, D., *Industrial Archaeology of the East Midlands*, Newton Abbot, 1965

Sparkes, I., *Stagecoaches and Carriages*, Bourne End, 1975

Stark, A., *History and Antiquities of Gainsborough*, Gainsborough, 1817, 2nd edn 1843

Steel, D. I. A., *A Lincolnshire Village. The parish of Corby Glen in its historical context*, London, 1979

Street, B., *Historical Notes on Grantham*, Grantham, 1857

Sympson, E. M., *Cambridge County Geographies — Lincolnshire*, Cambridge, 1913

Tebbutt, L., *Stamford Clocks and Watches*, Stamford, 1975

Thompson, P., *History and Antiquities of Boston*, Boston, 1855

Tresidder, T. S., *Nottingham Pubs*, Nottingham, 1980

Tucci, D. S., *Built in Boston*, Boston USA, 1978

Vale, E., *The Mail-Coach Men of the late Eighteenth Century*, Newton Abbot, 1967

Varley, J., *The Parts of Kesteven — Studies in Law and Local Government*, Sleaford, 1974

Wailes, R., *The English Windmill*, London, 1954

Walshaw, G. R., and Behrendt, C. A. J., *The History of Appleby-Frodingham*, Scunthorpe, 1950

Watson, C. E., *A History of Clee and the Thorpes of Clee*, Grimsby, 1901

Watson, R., *The Transport Revolution*, London, 1971

Webb, S., and B., *The Story of the King's Highway*, London, 1913

Wheatcroft, A., *The Tennyson Album*, London, 1980

Wheeler, W. H., *A History of the Fens of South Lincolnshire*, Boston, 2nd edn 1896

White, P., *Passenger Transport in Lincoln*, London, 1974

——, and Tye, A., *Guide Notes to New Holland and Barton-on-Humber*, Grimsby, 1967

——, ——, *An Industrial History of Grimsby and Cleethorpes*, Grimsby, 1970

White, W., *Directory of Lincolnshire*, Sheffield, 1826, 1st edn 1842, 2nd edn 1856, 3rd edn 1872, 4th edn 1882, 5th edn 1892

Wickstead, A., *Lincolnshire, Lindsey — The Story of the County Council 1889–1974*, Lincoln, 1978

Wood, G. B., *The Industrial Archaeology 1880–1980 of Alford*, Alford, 1980

Worsencroft, K., *Bygone Sleaford*, Grantham, 1978

Wright, N. R., *An Industrial History of Long Sutton and Sutton Bridge*, Lincoln, 1970

——, *The Railways of Boston*, History of Boston, vol. 4, Boston, 1971

——, *Spalding — An Industrial History*, Lincoln, 1973

Wright, P. A., *Traction Engines*, London, 1959

Wrottesley, J., *The Great Northern Railway*, London, 1979

Young, A., *General View of the Agriculture of Lincoln*, London, 2nd edn 1813, reprinted Newton Abbot 1970

INDEX

Places are in the ancient county of Lincoln unless otherwise specified. Canals and navigable waterways are not listed individually but appear by name under 'canals and navigations'. Banks, bridges, diseases, docks, ferries, hospitals, housing, newspapers, sports, textile industries and some other categories are similarly grouped together. Engineering firms are listed under 'iron works (engineering)', railway companies under 'railway lines built' or '. . . proposed'.

275

T*